ATLA PUBLICATIONS SERIES
edited by Dr. Jack Ammerman

The Literature of Islam, by Paula Youngman Skreslet and Rebecca Skreslet, 2006.

The Literature of Islam

A Guide to the Primary Sources in English Translation

Paula Youngman Skreslet
Rebecca Skreslet

ATLA Publications Series

THE SCARECROW PRESS, INC.
Lanham, Maryland • Toronto • Oxford
and
American Theological Library Association
2006

SCARECROW PRESS, INC.

Published in the United States of America
by Scarecrow Press, Inc.
A wholly owned subsidary of
The Rowman & Littlefield Publishing Group, Inc.
4501 Forbes Boulevard, Suite 200, Lanham, Maryland 20706
www.scarecrowpress.com

PO Box 317
Oxford
OX2 9RU, UK

Copyright © 2006 by Paula Youngman Skreslet and Rebecca Skreslet

British Library Cataloguing in Publication Information Available

Library of Congress Cataloging-in-Publication Data

Skreslet, Paula Youngman.
  The literature of Islam : a guide to the primary sources in English translation / by Paula
Youngman Skreslet and Rebecca Skreslet ; edited by Jack Ammerman.
     p. cm. — (ATLA publications series)
  Includes bibliographical references and index.
  ISBN-13: 978-0-8108-5408-6 (pbk. : alk. paper)
  ISBN-10: 0-8108-5408-2 (pbk. : alk. paper)
  1. Islam Bibliography. 2. Islamic literature—Translations into English—Bibliography.
I. Skreslet, Rebecca. II. Ammerman, Jack. III. Title. IV. Series.

Z7835.M6S585 2006
[BP161.3]
016.297—dc22   2006014445

For D.

the source of our inspiration
the ground of our achievement
the joy of our life

~

Contents

~

Preface

The book in your hand is not an introduction to Islam; in fact, it assumes that the reader is already acquainted with the basic proclamation of the Islamic faith, the history of the Muslims as a community, and the major cultural expressions of Islam in various nations and societies. This book is an introduction to the literature of Islam—or, as former editor Don Haymes likes to say, the *literatures* of Islam.

The book is not intended for specialists in Islamic religion, who will already be familiar with these texts in their original languages. It is meant to be a resource for scholars in other fields who need to understand the vast and complex literary heritage of this erudite and vigorous faith community, but are unable to devote years of their lives to achieving a reading proficiency in classical Arabic (or Persian, or Turkish). We expect it to be of particular value to faculty members who are called upon to teach introductory or survey courses outside their own disciplines, and to graduate students in theology, medieval studies, world religions, or related fields who need access to these primary sources in English translation. Also, readers who are interested in understanding the modern Arab or Islamic world may grasp something of the currents of thought and belief through the centuries that produced these important works, which continue to exert a powerful influence upon Muslims today.

Selection Criteria for the Works Included

The primary literatures of Islam are normally classified into several areas of study: the canonical literature, the interpretation of scripture and tradition, law, theology, and philosophy; often, distinct genres are recognized for history and mysticism or spirituality. It is a huge task to select the most significant texts from each of these areas, those representative of important trends in the discipline, and then to present them in some kind of intelligible order, tied together by a sense of chronology or development. We have tried to place special emphasis on what might be called "turning-point texts"—those that made an indelible impact upon the literature, certain to be mentioned in any scholarly study of the subject.

We have not included those genres of literature that derive from predominantly artistic rather than religious expression: poetry, folklore, belles lettres, drama, fiction. Culturally, these works may be infused with an Islamic sensibility and concerned with religious issues, but they are not traditionally regarded as among the religious sciences. The possible exception in this volume is the chapter on history and historiography, in which works are included that originated in the context of the court rather than the mosque. A rationale for the inclusion of such material is explained in that chapter.

Because our purpose is to make this cultural patrimony accessible to readers of English, we have chosen from those texts that are available—at least to some extent—in that language. We have tried to seek out authoritative and reliable translations, not untraceable amateur work (which abounds, especially on the Internet).

Our remarks about each work featured in this volume are designed to meet more than one objective. First, there are comments about the original work and its place in the pantheon of the literature. Then, there is a specific assessment of each published edition and translation of that work. This volume contains critical reviews of these publications by a two-member writing team: a professional bibliographer and a scholar of Arab culture and Islamic religion. We have given particular attention to the possible use of these texts in the classroom, indicating which ones successfully provide the kind of editorial assistance that enables students to comprehend these often difficult and unfamiliar works.

An extensive bibliography lists the editions of primary sources analyzed in each chapter. There are also suggestions for secondary reading, which might be helpful to a student seeking additional information about each genre of literature. Other important works are cited in the endnotes of each chapter. In addition, some works are mentioned in the course of argument, and these will be found in the index.

Please note that each chapter contains a few sources that indicate where the literature seems to be headed in the modern era: what issues are currently under discussion, who the principal interlocutors are, and what is at stake in the theoretical and literary discourse of the present time. The enormous legacy of medieval scholarship is not just a thing of the past. These works are assiduously studied by Muslims today, and the degree to which they are still considered authoritative is very much an open question. Indeed, we would assert that it is impossible to understand key debates about ethics and values in today's Islamic world without some knowledge of and appreciation for these classic texts.

Fundamental Reference Works in the Discipline

Those who share a bibliographer's concern for the analysis of a given literature should be aware of a few of the indispensable sources in Islamic studies dealing with this discipline.

One of the great bibliographers of all time lived in the city of Baghdad in the tenth century of the Common Era (all dates in this volume are stated according to the Western calendar). He was Muhammad ibn Ishaq al-Nadim (d.c. 990), son of a prominent bookseller, probably attached to the court or to the libraries of noble citizens as a savant or consultant. Al-Nadim created the first comprehensive bibliography of Arabic literature, meticulously classified according to his own complex system, which was based upon the enumeration of the sciences by the early Islamic philosophers. He called it *Fihrist al-'ulum* or *Index of the Sciences*; it is also known by the title *Kitab al-fihrist al-nadim*, or *Book of the Index of al-Nadim* (an-nah-DEEM). The work is divided into ten major classes by subject area, within which authors are listed chronologically; a bio-bibliographical entry for each author provides as much as was known of his full name and genealogy, information and anecdotes about his life, and a listing of all of his extant works. Al-Nadim emphasizes that he is personally acquainted with the vast majority of these works and reports information received from others with attribution. Although regrettably many of the works al-Nadim mentions have not survived, the *Fihrist* is still an invaluable source for the first three-and-a-half centuries of Islamic learning.[1]

Specialists in Islamic literature must make the effort to become conversant with Carl Brockelmann's classic of Orientalist scholarship, *Geschichte der arabischen Litteratur*.[2] It is partly a narrative history, but chiefly an encyclopedia of entries on individual Arab writers and their work. Vol. 1 is organized chronologically, then by type/genre of literature (or subject matter), then geographically; vol. 2 organizes first by chronology, then geography, then genre or subject. Indexes for authors, titles, and the European editors of texts are found in the third supplemental volume (after the entries on the modern era up to 1939). Even those who read German easily find Brockel-mann's work challenging to use, thanks to his difficult systems of abbrevia-tion and transliteration, the lack of cross-references, the relationship be-tween the supplements and the original volumes, and the proliferation of addenda and corrigenda.

In the early 1960s Fuat Sezgin, a brilliant Turkish scholar resident in Ger-many, began to update and revise Brockelmann's work to incorporate many newly discovered materials and manuscripts. Sezgin ended up writing an enormous and entirely new work, dealing especially with the sciences (math-ematics, astronomy, geography/cartography, medicine, chemistry, etc.) and is considered the leading authority on that literature. His nine-volume work, *Geschichte des arabischen Schrifttums*, was published in 1967–1984, with an in-dex volume in 1995; vols. 10–12 followed in 2000.[3] Of these, vol. 1 is the source for information about the traditional disciplines of Islamic religion: Qur'anic studies, *hadith*, law, theology, and mysticism (vol. 2 is *Poesie*). There is a scholarly précis or introduction to each area, then encyclopedia entries on the individual authors; vol. 1 is organized by genre/subject first, then chronology, then geography or theological/legal school of thought. Sezgin's work is in German, but there are very clear tables of contents and indexes in every volume, and standard editorial conventions are used throughout.

Anyone doing research in Islamic culture and religion must learn to use the somewhat cumbersome but indispensable *Encyclopaedia of Islam*, 2nd ed. (Leiden: Brill, 1960–2004) and its valuable index volumes. For twentieth-century information, the *Oxford Encyclopedia of the Modern Islamic World* is a must (New York: Oxford University Press, 1995). And for literary figures in particular, the two-volume *Encyclopedia of Arabic Literature*, edited by Julie Scott Meisami and Paul Starkey (London: Routledge, 1998), is a very con-venient source for ready reference, providing concise but informative entries on scholars and writers throughout the centuries. These entries include brief biographical accounts, principal works and their significance, original-language text editions, and some secondary reading. There are also topical articles on literary genres, technical terms, historical movements, and devel-opments, produced by an array of respected contributors.

Other useful reference sources are mentioned in the chapter endnotes of this volume and in our bibliography.[4]

Names and Titles

A constant challenge for a student of this literature is the complexity of me-dieval Islamic names. A writer may have a given name, names indicating that he is the father of someone and the son of someone else, names attaching him to a certain tribe, city, or geographical area, an honorific or professional name, even a nickname or symbolic name. A similar system was used for women. An individual became commonly known by one segment of his or her name, and of course, some portion of the name must appear first in a printed index or catalog. In this book, we follow the guidance of the standard reference works in reproducing a writer's names (the *Encyclopaedia of Islam Index of Proper Names* is especially helpful) and adhere to the practice of providing the person's death date as well, since a number of individuals may be known by the same common appellation.

The titles of many of the medieval works considered here also vary a great deal; we prefer the one best attested by reference sources and try to indicate variants and alternatives. A title often begins with the word *kitab* (kih-TABB) or *Book* [*of . . .*]. We have capitalized the first letter of every Arabic title, even when the first word includes the definite article.

Pronunciation and Spelling

For the sake of those lacking experience with the original languages, we have attempted to indicate how some of the most essential names and vocabulary terms might be pronounced. We furnish a simplified or approximate pronunciation of these names or terms in parentheses: for example, the word *hadith* (hah-DEETH). An Arabic speaker will find these indicators very inadequate, but we hope they will enable others to enter into a discussion of this literature with some ability to recognize and reproduce the spoken sounds.

We rely upon a simplified transliteration system as well, without distinguishing between similar consonants or identifying long vowels. We do include the symbol ' for the letter *'ayn* and the ' for the *hamza* or glottal stop. We also show through pronunciation helps when the definite article is elided into the following word, as in the name al-Nadim (an-nah-DEEM, not al-nah-DEEM). Again, this is merely to facilitate discussion of these sources and issues.

Dialogue

Throughout this volume, one will find observations connecting the literature under discussion with the study of Christian theology and religious history. We are assuming that many of the readers of this work will be familiar with the terminology and concepts of the Western medieval world and with the concerns of Christian theological studies, and we are attempting to help those readers coordinate their knowledge with a new set of modes and materials.

The authors' esteem for the extraordinary power and erudition of Islamic scholarship should also be evident in the pages of this book. We consider it a privilege to apply our efforts to the study of this fascinating literature, and we hope that making it more visible and available to English speakers will enable others to experience it as well.

Notes

1. The work is available in a solid one-volume English translation as *The Fihrist: A 10th Century AD Survey of Islamic Culture* by Abu'l-Faraj Muhammad ibn Ishaq al-Nadim, edited and translated by Bayard Dodge (Chicago: Great Books of the Islamic World, 1998). The author's name sometimes appears as Ibn al-Nadim. This critical edition is extensively annotated, with a helpful introduction, glossary, and extremely valuable biographical index. It was originally published by Columbia University Press in 1970.

A most interesting essay about al-Nadim's work by Hans H. Wellisch, *The First Arab Bibliography: Fihrist al-'ulum*, was published in the University of Illinois Graduate School of Library and Information Science *Occasional Papers* 175 (Dec 1986).

2. Carl Brockelmann, *Geschichte der arabischen Litteratur*, 2. den supplementbänden angepasste Auflage (Leiden: Brill, 1943–1949). Note the two t's in *Litteratur*. It was first published in two volumes in Weimar in 1898 and in Berlin in 1902; then, three huge supplementary volumes appeared, 1937–1942. An updated edition including revisions of the two original volumes plus all three supplements was published 1943–1949, and this five-volume set is now the standard edition.

3. Fuat Sezgin, *Geschichte des arabischen Schrifttums* (Leiden: Brill, 1967–). The index volume is *Geschichte des arabischen Schrifttums: Gesamtindices zu Band I–IX* (Frankfurt: Institut für Geschichte der Arabisch-Islamischen Wissenschaften an der Johann Wolfgang Goethe Universität, 1995). The same institute in Frankfurt (founded by Sezgin) published his three new volumes, Band X–XII, *Mathematische Geographie und Karthographie im Islam und ihr Fortleben im Abendland*, in 2000.

4. Though dated, Margaret Anderson's *Arabic Materials in English Translation* (Boston: G.K. Hall, 1980) is still useful, especially for locating specific texts included in older anthologies.

~

Acknowledgments

The authors are indebted to Don Haymes, editor emeritus of the ATLA Monograph Series, for initiating this project and proposing it to us. We also wish to express our appreciation to Jack Ammerman, the final editor of the work, and to the staff of the Scarecrow Press who assisted in bringing it to completion.

We have had the opportunity to draw upon the knowledge of the superb faculty at the Center for Contemporary Arab Studies at Georgetown University, at the College of William and Mary, and the instructors in Arabic language and literature at the American University in Cairo. Other colleagues, mentors, and friends provided much insight and encouragement throughout the research and writing process.

We have undertaken to maintain the highest possible standard of accuracy throughout the work; however, any errors, misstatements, or lapses in judgment should be attributed to the senior member of our writing team.

~

Abbreviations

DMA   *Dictionary of the Middle Ages*, edited by Joseph R. Strayer (New York: Scribner, 1982–1989).

EI2   *Encyclopaedia of Islam*, 2nd ed., edited by H.A.R. Gibb (Leiden: Brill, 1960 [1954]–2004).

EQ   *Encyclopaedia of the Qur'an*, edited by Jane Dammen McAuliffe (Leiden: Brill, 2001–).

ER   *Encyclopedia of Religion*, edited by Mircea Eliade (New York: Macmillan, 1986).

ER2   *Encyclopedia of Religion*, 2nd ed., edited by Lindsay Jones (Detroit: Macmillan, 2005).

ICMR   *Islam and Christian-Muslim Relations* (Selly Oak and Georgetown), serial.

IQ   *Islamic Quarterly* (London), serial.

MW   *Muslim World* (Hartford), serial; vols. 1–37, 1911–1947 were titled *Moslem World*.

MWBR   *Muslim World Book Review* (Leicester), serial.

OEMIW   *Oxford Encyclopedia of the Modern Islamic World*, edited by John L. Esposito (New York: Oxford University Press, 1995).

REP   *Routledge Encyclopedia of Philosophy*, edited by Edward Craig (London, New York: Routledge, 1998).

CHAPTER ONE

~

The Qur'an: Text and Translation

Transforming an ordinary document or literary work from one human language to another is a demanding task, but a text held sacred by a body of believers will present exceptional challenges even to the most fluent and skillful of translators. The Qur'an, for a number of practical and theological reasons, raises this challenge to its highest level.

The foundation of Islamic religion is the belief that the express and verbatim Word of God was revealed in the text we know as the Qur'an. "For Muslims, the divine Word assumed a specific, Arabic form, and that form is as essential as the meaning that the words convey. Hence only the Arabic Koran is the Koran, and translations are merely interpretations."[1] Orthodox teaching regards the Qur'an (koor-AHN) as eternal and uncreated, revealed through the Prophet Muhammad, who accurately relayed God's message but did not in any sense compose it or author it. Muslim legal scholars have debated whether it is permissible even to attempt to reproduce this revelation in another language. Yet from the earliest stages of Islam's expansion, believers whose native language was not Arabic needed to hear and understand in order to receive and respond.

Some of the problems impeding understanding are inherent in the Arabic source language, which is notoriously difficult to learn, highly condensed, and complex. The fact that Arabic can be written without any punctuation, capitalization, or vowel points may create confusion or ambiguity. Particular stylistic conventions govern the use of pronouns and verb tenses. There are many disputed morphological equivalents and syntactical issues with English as a target language; translating even a simple text from Arabic is hard to do without

1

glosses or additions. The Qur'an, however, is not by any means a simple text. Its style is highly distinctive, unlike ordinary poetry or prose, and many Arabic speakers consider it impossible to match. An additional theological challenge is posed by the doctrine of *i'jaz* (eh-JAZZ), the miraculous uniqueness or inimitability of God's self-expression in the Qur'an.[2] The beauty and rhetorical richness of the book is understood as evidence of its supernatural character and thus as indicative of the veracity of the message of Islam.

Certain structural characteristics of the Qur'an have posed difficulties as well. The text contains passages in a variety of formats—some narratives, some didactic prose, some poetic or prophetic pericopes containing vivid and mysterious imagery and lyricism. The contents have been divided into units known as *suras*, which may be only a few lines long or go on for several pages. Each *sura* (SOO-rah; plural, *suwar*) is divided into verses; different numbering schemes for these verses have been used in the past. Also, the whole text is commonly recited aloud in thirty segments of roughly equal length, and Qur'an commentaries are often organized on the basis of these segments. The decidedly nonlinear composition of the text may be discouraging to the inexperienced reader, but it rewards patient study, reflection, and repetition.[3]

English translations of the Qur'an tend to follow either the verse numbering of the Arabic text published by Gustav Flügel as *Corani Textus Arabicus* (Lipsiae [Leipzig]: Typis et sumptibus Caroli Tauchnitii, 1834) or the different system used in the printed Egyptian edition authorized by King Fouad, *Al-qur'an al-karim* or *Al-mushaf al-sharif* (Cairo: Matba'a al-Amiriyya, 1924); the latter is based upon the reading of Hafs ibn Sulayman (d. 796). English versions published in South Asia often use an Indian/Pakistani system of enumeration.[4] The traditional order of the *suras* has also been radically rearranged by some editors and translators who thought they could create a more comprehensible chronological sequence or a critical redaction on the basis of textual or literary principles. So, in some English editions, just looking up a particular passage becomes confusing and frustrating.

The cultural and historical setting in which the revelation originally appeared is now very far from modern life, even in the Arab societies where the faith first became established. A young Muslim growing up in Europe, for example, might find much of the Qur'an more foreign than familiar. These readers have a need for extensive annotation or commentary (into which biases or errors may be introduced). The order in which the *suras* were revealed, and whether they were first heard in Mecca or Medina, is important for interpretation; likewise, the identities of the persons mentioned, and allusions to episodes known from other sources (such as Sura 18, "The Cave") may be significant, but unknown to the reader. Scholarly notes that clarify without imposing a certain conclusion are not always available.

Perhaps the most serious distortions result from translations undertaken out of doctrinal or political motives. The earliest English versions were created by hostile European scholars or clerics openly intending to defame Islam by exposing the supposed faults of its sacred book. Members of Muslim minority traditions or heterodox movements have attempted to ground their particular sectarian viewpoints in the authoritative scripture, by heavily annotating a plausible translation with apologetic commentary or propaganda. Or, within the translation itself, key verses can be rephrased in such a way that they appear to confirm a controversial position.[5] Some translations are frankly undertaken with partisan ends in mind, while others attempt to introduce their views by stealth. It is safe to say that no human being is capable of producing work that is free of all personal or philosophical bias; on the other hand, the aim of the translator should be to convey the contents of the original as accurately and objectively as possible.

Hundreds of full or partial translations of the Qur'an into English now exist, and their number is increasing rapidly. This chapter will introduce some of the more prominent and distinctive editions—ones that are likely to be found in academic library collections—and try to indicate their suitability for study or classroom teaching. A number in a section heading with the translator's name indicates the date of the initial publication of his or her work.

Translations of Historical Interest

As long ago as 1143, European scholars began to produce translations of the Qur'an into Latin, which first appeared in print in 1543. A version in French by André du Ryer was first published in 1647. It is from that French edition that the first translation into English was made, by Alexander Ross, in 1649, without reference to the original text in Arabic.[6]

The very early English versions were created with the express intention of discrediting Islam and "the Turkish vanities" (Ross) and of providing source material to be used by missionaries in an effort to convert Muslims to Christianity. The translators had little interest in providing access to the contents of the Qur'an for its own sake, and their scholarly rigor was decidedly wanting. While the translation of Ross is rarely seen outside of a rare-book collection, some lengthy excerpts from it (and from its introduction "To the Christian Reader") can be found in the preface to Arthur J. Arberry's *The Koran Interpreted* (London: George Allen and Unwin, 1955), 7–10.

SALE, 1734

George Sale. *The Koran: Commonly Called the Alcoran of Mohammed* (Philadelphia: J. W. Moore, 1850).

The widely circulated English edition by George Sale was first published in 1734 and reprinted over one hundred and fifty times, with various prefatory matter. Starting in 1844, this edition began to include an account of Sale's life by R. A. Davenport. Though Sale leaves the reader in no doubt as to his opinion of Islamic religion (while displaying equal contempt toward Catholicism), he did a more creditable job of translation than had been accomplished up to his time, making an effort to study the Arabic text and compare it to Maracci's Latin edition of 1698.

His English product, however, is heavy and prosaic and gave the sophisticated European reader a poor sense of the book's own qualities. The historian Edward Gibbon, on the basis of Sale's translation, dismissed the Qur'an as an "incoherent rhapsody of fable, and precept, and declamation," inferior to Homer or Demosthenes, or the book of Job. Thomas Carlyle found it "toilsome reading . . . a wearisome, confused jumble."[7]

A Syrian Christian, George M. Lamsa, created a simplified digest or anthology of excerpts from Sale's translation, organized thematically, and published it as *The Short Koran Designed for Easy Reading* (Chicago: Ziff-Davis, 1949). It has a helpful subject index.

RODWELL, 1861

J. M. (John Medows) Rodwell. *The Koran: Translated from the Arabic* [*with*] *the Suras Arranged in Chronological Order, with Notes and Index.* With an introduction by G. Margoliouth (London: J. M. Dent and Sons, 1909).

With the advance of nineteenth-century Orientalist scholarship came the desire to employ the techniques of historical and literary criticism to analyze the text of the Qur'an. The Rev. J. M. Rodwell, on the basis of sources such as Theodor Nöldeke's *Geschichte des Qorans*, concluded that "the text . . . as hitherto arranged, necessarily assumes the form of a most unreadable and incongruous patchwork" (p. 2), and proceeded to rearrange the *suras* in what he believed to be their chronological order. A set of tables at the beginning of the volume is used to reconcile his order with the traditional one in finding a specific passage. The preface to his work sets forth in detail his methods and assumptions. While Rodwell is motivated by scholarly aims and displays some tolerance toward Islam, his firm belief in the superiority of Western rationalism and the scientific culture of his day is evident on every page, and he considers himself fully qualified to pass judgment upon the faith, its book, and its Prophet.

Rodwell used Flügel's revised Arabic edition of 1841 as his source and acknowledges a debt to Sale and Maracci. His translation first appeared in 1861 but attained a very wide distribution when it was selected for the Everyman's Library series in 1909. Rodwell attempted to imitate the rhythm, though not the rhyme, of the Qur'an's more lyrical passages, and his version was considered at the time to be accurate, attractive, and readable.

PALMER, 1880

E. H. (Edward Henry) Palmer. *The Qur'an* **(Oxford: Clarendon Press, 1900).**

A fellow in Oriental languages at Cambridge, E. H. Palmer was asked by F. Max Müller, editor of the Sacred Books of the East series published at Oxford, to produce a new translation of the Qur'an. Palmer did so in record time, and his work first appeared as vol. 6 and vol. 9 of that series in 1880. It was again published as vol. 328 of the World's Classics series in 1928, and both series saw numerous reprintings. Despite this extensive circulation, Palmer's work was little used by scholars; it has been criticized for a number of serious errors, perhaps the result of hasty preparation.[8] Some passages (e.g., the beginning of Sura 7, "Al-A'raf") sound like an unpolished first draft. Palmer provides a lengthy but rather tedious introduction, a synopsis of the contents of the *suras*, and a subject index.

BELL, 1937–1939

Richard Bell. *The Qur'an Translated, with a Critical Re-arrangement of the Surahs* **(Edinburgh: T. and T. Clark, 1937–1939).**

Another Orientalist academic, Richard Bell, taught Arabic at the University of Edinburgh, and conceived some novel theories about the composition and redaction of the Qur'an. He believed that Muhammad himself created a full text of the Qur'an in written form, which was then subjected to "alterations, substitutions and other derangements" by later editors (p. vii). Bell has not changed the traditional order of the *suras*, but broken up and reorganized the verses within many of the *suras*, printing them on the page with columns and dotted lines indicating what Bell believed to be their original or proper (or "natural") order. Sura 2, "The Cow," is a sufficient example of Bell's manipulation and is rendered quite unreadable by it. As Alfred Guillaume remarked, "At the best the reader will say: 'This is how Bell thinks the Qur'an originally ran'; at the worst: 'The man has lost all sense of proportion.'"[9]

Bell's verse numbering is taken from Flügel, then reordered and redivided. His phrasing very often echoes Palmer's—probably not a wise choice. But his notes, chapter introductions, headings, and subheadings make this work an interesting example in the history of Qur'an interpretation.

DAWOOD, 1956

N. J. Dawood. *The Koran, with a Parallel Arabic Text* (London: Penguin, 1990).

The tendency of Qur'an translators to choose an archaic English style reminiscent of the King James Bible resulted in a number of ponderous versions that can alienate the modern reader. In 1956, N. J. Dawood attempted to change this and "present the modern reader with an intelligible version of the Koran in contemporary English" (p. x). The project was undertaken for the Penguin Classics series and thus was very widely available in an affordable paperback format; it was revised and reissued four times up to 1974.

The fatal flaw of this version, however, was once again the desire of the translator to tamper with the traditional arrangement of the *suras*. Dawood reorganized the book not along chronological but rather literary lines, placing the shorter and more lyrical passages first (and those with familiar biblical themes), then the longer and more topical chapters. He also chose to scan the text on the page in paragraphs or dialogue form, with a few verse numbers intermittently in the margins (added in 1964) but no indication of where each verse begins or ends, making it "almost prohibitive of a quick reference."[10]

When the translation was reissued in a fifth edition in 1990, the standard sequence of the *suras* had been restored (though the paragraphing and verse numbering still pose a problem). But as a result of the earlier editions, the damage is done, and Dawood has been classed among the impudent rearrangers. This is regrettable, because Dawood's English style is clean, modern, and often elegant. Though still unsuitable as a reference, the 1990 edition is eminently readable and could serve as a good comparison text.

Other Sources

Many versions of the Qur'an in English may be of interest to the bibliographer or historian, but have yet to gain wide acceptance. Among these are Abdur-Rahman Tariq and Zia-ud-Din Ahmad Gilani, *The Holy Qur'an* (Lahore: M. Siraj-ud-Din, 1966); Syed Abdul Latif, *Al-Qur'an* (Hyderabad: Academy of Islamic Studies, 1969); Hashim Amir 'Ali, *The Message of the Qur'an Presented in Perspective* (Rutland, Vt.: C. E. Tuttle, 1974); Rashad Khalifa, *Qur'an: The Final Scripture* or *Final Testament* (Tucson: Islamic Productions, 1981); Q. Arafat, *The Qur'an: The Conclusive Word of God* (Leicester: Arafat Islamic Publications, 1991); 'Ali Özek, *The Holy Qur'an with English Translation* (Istanbul: Ilmî Nesriyat, 1994); and 'Abdul Majid Daryabadi, *The Glorious Qur'an* (Leicester: Islamic Foundation, 2001; originally published in Karachi in 1956). Still others have been subjected to serious criticism and are not considered reliable. For many examples of this kind, see the articles by Kidwai or Khan.

Sectarian Translations

Several important and interesting versions of the Qur'an in English are closely identified with the views and positions of particular sectarian groups within Islam, or with certain interpretive approaches or currents of opinion. While some of these are worthy of study, the reader needs to be aware that Muslims with a different doctrinal orientation may consider these versions to be unacceptable.

Ahmadi Versions

The Ahmadi movement was founded in 1889 by the followers of Mirza Ghulam Ahmad (d. 1908), who is revered by them as a prophet or messianic figure. This belief places them outside the bounds of orthodox Islam, and in Pakistan the Ahmadiyya are officially considered a non-Muslim minority. In 1914, the movement split into two factions: a highly doctrinaire branch based in Ahmad's hometown of Qadian and a more moderate branch based in Lahore. While the Ahmadiyya remain a marginal movement, they have had an impact upon publishing out of all proportion to their numbers, because they have always maintained a vigorous campaign to propagate their views in print. Lahore in particular has been a center of Islamic publishing in English, both by Ahmadis and by others seeking to counter their beliefs.

MUHAMMAD 'ALI, 1917

Muhammad 'Ali. *The Holy Qur'an: Containing the Arabic Text with English Translation and Commentary.* 2nd ed. (Lahore: Ahmadiyya Anjuman-i-ishaat-i-islam, 1920). His name often appears with the honorific Maulvi (or Maulana).

This translation and commentary, the work of a leader of the more accommodating and tolerant Lahore faction of the Ahmadiyya, Muhammad 'Ali, was first published in 1917. It has found its way into so many libraries that it has probably misled countless students into thinking they were using a standard or orthodox version of the Qur'an. Muhammad 'Ali's apologia is presented in a gentle and reasonable tone, and he frankly identifies his doctrinal convictions and allegiances (p. xciv). Apart from its sectarian character, the translation is unexceptional; what distinguishes the work is the abundance of commentary in the general preface, the lengthy introduction to each *sura*, and the copious footnotes.

Also in the Ahmadi or Qadiani tradition are these translations: Sher 'Ali, *The Holy Qur'an: Arabic Text and English Translation* (Rabwah: Oriental and Religious Publishing, 1955); Pir Salahud-din, *The Wonderful Koran* (Eminabad: Raftar-I-Zamana, 1969);[11] and Zafrullah Khan, *The Koran or Qur'an Majid: The Eternal Revelation Vouchsafed to Muhammad, Seal of the Prophets* (New York: Praeger, 1970–1971). Sir Chaudhury Muhammad Zafrullah Khan was a prominent barrister who served as Foreign Minister of Pakistan, and his translation has been widely reprinted (as recently as 2003), but the specifically Ahmadi orientation of the work is not always acknowledged.[12]

Barelwi or Barelvi Versions

Another sectarian movement originating on the subcontinent is based upon the teachings of Ahmad Riza Khan (d. 1921). The movement is known by the name of his hometown (Bareilly, in North India) as Barelwi or Barelvi. A trained jurist, Ahmad Riza was also a Sufi adept of the Qadiri order; his teachings exhibit some of the vocabulary and conceptual tendencies of Islamic mysticism. The most pronounced characteristic of Barelwi scripture translations and commentary is their extreme depiction of Muhammad as The Beloved of God, an intercessor and wonder-working figure of a superhuman kind.[13]

Two Qur'an translations associated with the Barelwi sect are *Translation of the Glorious Holy Qur'an* by 'Ali Ahmad Khan Jullundri (Lahore: World Islamic Mission, 1962; also published under different titles) and *The Holy Qur'an: An English Translation* by Shah Faridul Haque (Karachi: Darululum Amjadia, 1988), a version of Ahmad Riza's *Kanzul Iman*, an Urdu paraphrase of the scripture.

Rationalists or Modernists

The twentieth-century modernist trend in Islam produced works that emphasized the compatibility of the faith with rational thought and scientific knowledge, while setting aside elements of popular piety that dwelt upon the superstitious or miraculous. Certain findings of modern science were projected back into the Qur'an by means of creative interpretation, seeking to show that the medieval text had revealed or anticipated truths later discovered by scientific means. Some of these interpretations also sought to neutralize passages of the scripture endorsing behaviors that are socially undesirable in the modern world, such as the beating of disobedient wives (Q. 4:34).[14]

MUHAMMAD ASAD, 1980

Muhammad Asad. *The Message of the Qur'an* (Gibraltar: Dar al-Andalus, 1980).

Born into an Austrian Jewish family in 1900, Leopold Weiss was a gifted linguist and writer; he became a Muslim in 1926 and took the name Muhammad Asad. He went to Arabia to live among the Bedouin for several years, attaining fluency in the Arabic language. In 1932 he relocated to Lahore and later became a notable cultural figure in the new nation of Pakistan. His political and philosophical development were strongly influenced by the work of Muhammad Iqbal (d. 1938) as well as that of the important Egyptian reformer Muhammad 'Abduh (d. 1905).

Muhammad Asad's rendering of the text itself is marked by an awkward archaism and formality and by many idiosyncratic interpretations that choose a symbolic or abstract meaning over the more obvious physical or literal one. For example, in Q. 113:4, Asad relegates the "women blowing on knots" to a footnote, while placing the more general expression "occult endeavors" into the text itself. The footnote (like most of Asad's commentary) tries to explain away this phenomenon in rationalist terms. Likewise, in Q. 114:6 he renders *jinn* as "invisible forces" and defines these as intangible influences of nature or "erroneous notions and false values" in the human psyche; an appendix on the concept of *jinn* is included. Asad also allegorizes Jesus' miracle of the clay bird in Q. 3:49 (and footnote).[15]

In the original edition of this work, a manufacturing error displaced thirty or forty pages near the end; a later imprint or reissue should be used instead.

AHMED 'ALI, 1984
Ahmed 'Ali. *Al-Qur'an: A Contemporary Translation* (Princeton: Princeton University Press, 2001).

The Pakistani intellectual Ahmed 'Ali brought a writer's sensibility to his translation of this sacred text; he was a professor of literature who published numerous short stories, novels, and translations of classical Urdu poetry. The English phrasing of his Qur'an translation is clean, contemporary, and readable. But a modernist orientation led him to tamper with certain verses, notably Q. 4:34, from which he chooses to exclude the beating of a refractory wife (his highly original reasoning is explained in a footnote). In both verses that mention Jesus breathing life into a clay bird (Q. 3:49 and 5:110), he eliminates the miraculous event from the text and interprets the meaning metaphorically in a footnote.

The verso of this edition's title page gives the reader a sense of the extreme difficulty inherent in Qur'an translation. First published in 1984, this work appeared as a "second revised edition" in 1986, a "revised definitive edition" in 1988, a "final revised edition" in 1994, and an edition "newly comprising revisions last made by the translator" in 2001.

Other Sources

A translation by a husband-and-wife team, Ahmad and Dina Zidan, was published as *Translation of the Glorious Qur'an* (London: Ta-Ha, 1991). This work is considered by Robinson to be in the tradition of scientific rationalism, at least in their choice of vocabulary.[16] But their work has been sharply criticized by numerous reviewers for an excessive reliance upon the published text of Yusuf 'Ali (not Ahmed 'Ali, above).

Sunni Traditionalists

The most basic source for the formulation of Islamic law is of course the Qur'an itself. But for a huge number of Muslims, the *hadith* narratives are also considered normative (see chapter 2) and the classic interpretations of the great Qur'anic exegetes are also regarded as authoritative (see chapter 3). Sunni traditionalists, particularly those of the Wahhabi sect dominant in Saudi Arabia, have designated interpretations of the Qur'an of which they approve, and they have produced a body of literature intended to make these interpretations available to readers in various languages.

HILALI AND KHAN, 1977
Muhammad Taqi-ud-Din al-Hilali and Muhammad Muhsin Khan. *Translation of the Meanings of the Noble Qur'an in the English Language* (Medina: King Fahd Complex for the Printing of the Holy Qur'an, 1977). This work is also known by the title *Explanatory English Translation of the Meaning of the Holy Qur'an.*

This beautifully printed edition seeks to coordinate chosen verses of the text with *hadith* narratives or commentary from authoritative exegetes, stipulating an approved interpretation. Footnotes provide the full content of relevant *hadiths*, identify the original narrators, and supply a citation from the documentary source (usually the *Sahih al-Bukhari*). The commentary is based upon Ibn Kathir, al-Tabari, and other major medieval interpreters of the Qur'an. Important vocabulary is defined (there is an appended glossary), and often the implications of certain verses for the performance of ritual obligations are explained—for example, the prescribed prayers (*salat*) and charitable giving (*zakat*) in Q. 2:3. The beginning of Sura 2, "The Cow," serves as an example of Hilali and Khan's technique. This material could be very useful in the study of the history of traditional orthodox interpretation of the Qur'anic text.

What is less helpful is the persistent interpolation of interpretive material into the translation itself. Almost every verse is heavily amplified with parenthetical expressions, resulting in a translation that resembles an interpretive paraphrase (e.g., Q. 24:31).[17] Fortunately, Hilali and Khan have enclosed these additions in parentheses or brackets, so there is no question of misleading the reader, but the effect is distracting and imposes one reading of the verse to the exclusion of any others. Occasionally, they indulge themselves in inappropriate political commentary (Q. 5:21) and expressions of intolerance (Q 1:7, footnote),[18] though their translation of Q. 9:29–34 stays close to its literal meaning.

There is also a quantity of extraneous polemical material bound in the volume as prefatory matter and appendixes; of greater value is the helpful subject index. Some English readers may be confused by the printing of the volume back to front, in conformity with the Arabic text.

Shi'i Versions

Like the Sunni traditionalists, the Shi'a have sources of Qur'anic interpretation they believe to be authoritative, and certain doctrinal commitments they perceive to be grounded in the scriptural text. They are chiefly concerned with the legitimacy of the Imamate, with 'Ali as the valid successor to the Prophet, and with the unique nature of Muhammad's family as the *ahl al-bayt* or "People of the Household."[19] Specific verses (such as Q. 2:124, 33:33, and 5:55) are understood by them in a distinctive way that is rejected by Sunni Muslims; translations that incorporate these understandings would be acceptable only within Shi'i Islam.

MIR AHMAD 'ALI, 1964

S. V. Mir Ahmad 'Ali. *The Holy Qur'an: Arabic Text, with English Translation and Commentary.* 4th ed. (Elmhurst, N.Y.: Tahrike Tarsile Qur'an, 2004).

This edition of the work of Mir Ahmad 'Ali (not to be confused with Ahmed 'Ali, above) is positively overflowing with Shi'i commentary, primarily derived from the exegesis of the Ayatullah Agha Pooya Yazdi. Anyone researching the special character of Shi'i interpretation will find ample material here. A representative passage is found on p. 88 of this edition, pursuant to Q. 2:124, in which Abraham is designated as "Imam for mankind." The commentary relates the story from Shi'i tradition in which the Prophet designates his young relative 'Ali ibn Abi Talib as his successor and enjoins the rest of the Quraysh to obey him.

While the commentary and accompanying polemical material are interesting, the translation itself is almost unreadable: highly ornate, archaic, and opaque.

M. H. SHAKIR, 1959

Mahomedali Habib Shakir. *Holy Qur'an*. 2nd U.S. ed. (Elmhurst, N.Y.: Tahrike Tarsile Qur'an, 1983).

Shakir's translation was originally published by the Habib Esmail Benevolent Trust in Karachi, and later reprinted by the World Organization for Islamic Services in Tehran; Tahrike Tarsile Qur'an is its American publisher, and they have chosen to produce Shakir's work without any of its original annotations. The specifically Shi'i character of the work may be discerned from the wording of the particular verses mentioned above and from the entries selected for inclusion in the subject index; among these are 'Ali and the *ahl al-bayt*. The English prose of the translation itself is relatively clear and readable, though it has been faulted for too great a similarity to Muhammad 'Ali's translation of 1917.[20]

Other Sources

A recent version in modern English from a Shi'i perspective—not a translation, but an interpretive paraphrase—is Behbudi and Turner's *The Qur'an: A New Interpretation*, discussed below.

Classic Scholarly Translations

Several English translations have been widely used for study and teaching for many years and have gained an established credibility. Though imperfect, they have a high degree of accuracy and are relatively free of hostile or apologetic bias. They are discussed in every history of or article about Qur'an translation, so they are described only very briefly here.

PICKTHALL, 1930

Muhammad Marmaduke William Pickthall. *The Meaning of the Glorious Koran: An Explanatory Translation* (London: George Allen and Unwin, 1957).

The first translation of the Qur'an into English by a native speaker who was a Muslim appeared in 1930, the work of a British novelist and travel writer who converted to Islam. During many years in Lebanon, India, and Egypt, Pickthall studied the Arabic language and prepared his translation with the help of several knowledgeable Islamic scholars. With some exceptions, his translation tends to adhere closely to the literal contents of the text (see Robinson, p. 261). He uses the standard Cairo verse numbering and provides a few brief notes to introduce each *sura* (occasionally a bit more extensive, as in Suras 20, 30, and 66).

Two drawbacks make Pickthall's version less than ideal for today's classrooms: the language is heavily archaic, and the numbered verses are simply printed one after another, with no formatting to signal a transition in subject or style. The effect in the longer and more complex *suras* is both confusing and monotonous.

YUSUF 'ALI, 1934–1937

'Abdullah Yusuf 'Ali. *The Holy Qur-an* [sic]: *Text, Translation and Commentary* (Lahore: Sh. Muhammad Ashraf, 1975).

The most reliable and respected of the translations with ties to the Indian subcontinent is the work of Yusuf 'Ali (d. 1953), a British-trained barrister and civil servant who taught at the School of Oriental Studies (University of London) and the Islamic College, Lahore; it first appeared in separate portions, published between 1934 and 1937. His translation of the text is somewhat old-fashioned, but readable, and is widely accepted by English-speaking Muslims. However, his extensive annotations, commentary, prefatory matter, and appendixes have been faulted for a tendency toward mysticism and unorthodox views. He usually follows the verse numbering of the Cairo edition.

The work of Yusuf 'Ali has been reprinted countless times, distributed gratis by various religious organizations and governments, even appropriated and modified at will by other parties. Two recent editions have abridged, removed, or edited much of his commentary: *The Holy Qur'an: Text, Translation and Commentary* (Brentwood, Md.: Amana Corporation, 1983, 1988) and *The Holy Qur'an: English Translation of the Meanings and Commentary* (Saudi Arabia: Ministry of Hajj and Endowments, 1990; reprinted several times by the King Fahd Holy Qur'an Printing Complex in al-Medina al-Munawarah). The Amana edition indicates with an "R" where revisions have been made to Yusuf 'Ali's work; the latter does not and fails to acknowledge its excessive dependence upon the work of others.[21]

ARBERRY, 1955

Arthur J. Arberry. *The Koran Interpreted* (London: George Allen and Unwin, 1955). 2 vols.

Arberry, a professor of Arabic at Cambridge, took a fresh approach to the task of translation in the 1950s. He sought to convey not just the meaning of the Qur'anic text, but something of its rhythm, cadence, and rhetorical styles. He regarded the text as a literary artifact and challenged himself to (as Kenneth Cragg puts it) "let the Arabic control the English . . . sometimes to the point of oddity or unintelligibility. . . . The claims of modern English did not determine his rendering."[22] He formats the text upon the page like stanzas of poetry, numbering only every fifth verse in the margin; this, plus the fact that he follows Flügel's enumeration, interferes with the use of this edition for reference. His wording suffers from some archaism and formality. Also, this edition has no annotations or basic background information on the *suras*—only a simple subject index in the second volume.

Other Sources

The eminent Orientalist and professor of Near Eastern languages at Columbia University, Arthur Jeffery, was an authority on the text criticism and vocabulary of the Qur'an. He also produced his own translation of selected portions of the text, in a rearranged sequence, as *The Koran: Selected Suras* (New York: Heritage Press, 1958), with annotations.

Kenneth Cragg—outstanding scholar and theologian, professor of Arabic and Islamic studies at Hartford Seminary, and editor of *The Muslim World*—has in a lifetime of interfaith dialogue displayed great sensitivity and respect toward the faith-claims and scriptures of both Islam and Christianity. He published his own translation of excerpts from the Qur'an, organized thematically, as *Readings in the Qur'an* (London: Collins, 1988). The book includes a very substantial introductory essay.

Modern Scholarly Translations

The effort of scholars to produce accurate translations suitable for classroom use continues. Some of these are so recent that it remains to be seen whether they will gain wide acceptance, remain in print, and establish themselves as credible sources for study. These works have the advantage of being able to employ the findings of current linguistic theory and discourse criticism to inform their approaches; some also take advantage of electronic multimedia resources to enrich the student's understanding of the material.

AYOUB, 1983

Mahmoud M. Ayoub. *The Awesome News: Interpretation of Juz' 'Amma, the Last Part of the Qur'an.* 2nd ed. (s.l.: World Islamic Call Society, 1997).

The Qur'an is traditionally divided into thirty segments (*ajzaa'*; singular, *juz'*) of approximately equal length, for purposes of recitation and memorization. The thirtieth segment, known as *juz' 'amma* (jooz AHM-mah) because of its first word, comprises Suras 78–114.

Mahmoud Ayoub, a professor of Islamic studies at Temple University, prepared this translation of the final segment of the Qur'an specifically for use as a classroom text; simplicity is its guiding principle. Ayoub presents a brief précis or summary of each *sura*, then an extremely restrained, literal rendering in English, appearing on facing pages to the very clearly printed Arabic text. Footnotes provide basic and straightforward information about translation issues, while parenthetical material or interpolations are not included in the translation itself (e.g., Q. 78:12). This legitimate and defensible technique sometimes has the unfortunate effect of producing an unreadable passage, as in the first five verses of Sura 79; however, Ayoub's careful annotation of the passage clarifies it for the reader. There is no attempt to re-create the lyricism of these *suras*—the aim is to convey their basic content. In some cases, the effect is aesthetically disappointing (see Sura 101).

In this small, affordable paperback volume, Ayoub has included a compact but informative general introduction, simple table of contents, and a useful glossary. The book would be a great help to a student beginning to cope with the challenge of reading the Qur'an in Arabic.

SELLS, 1999

Michael Sells. *Approaching the Qur'an: The Early Revelations* (Ashland, Ore.: White Cloud Press, 2002).

The distinguished Islamic studies professor and translator Michael Sells has provided the scholarly community with an exceptional work—one that seeks to introduce the English speaker not just to the text of the Qur'an, but to the experience of the Qur'an. Sells has chosen a set of *suras* from the early Meccan period (most of them from the *juz' 'amma*, the final segment), and he has tried to interpret them in a way that captures some of the lyricism, the spiritual and emotional power, of the passages as believers encounter them. These early *suras* tend to be hymnlike in nature and dwell upon fundamental theological and existential issues in a profound and poetic way; they inspire the deepest reflection and, when properly recited by a trained voice, are both moving and meaningful, conveying what Sells calls the "sound vision" of the Qur'an (p. 16) The book incorporates a compact disc recording of the vocal recitation of the call to prayer and six *suras*, information about the reciters, and a detailed study to accompany the recording (called "Hearing the Qur'an"), designed for use in the classroom or for individual study.

Sells's work also includes a most illuminating introduction, an unusual descriptive glossary, a commentary facing each portion of the translated text, valuable bibliographic notes, even several interesting illustrations. There is also an essay, "Sound, Spirit and Gender in the Qur'an," that explores the special problems of grammatical gender in the Arabic language and its impact on the recited text rhetorically and acoustically; this study also reveals what Sells speaks of as "the distinctive Qur'anic combination of awe and intimacy" (p. 204).

However, the reader must recognize that Sells's book contains only a small selection of *suras*—less than 5 percent of the full text of the Qur'an—and they are not by any means a representative sample. The most challenging and controversial material is not even mentioned here.[23] Sells's book is a rewarding but insufficient source and should be studied in conjunction with a complete text of the Qur'an in English.

FAKHRY, 2000

Majid Fakhry. An Interpretation of the Qur'an: English Translation of the Meanings (New York: New York University Press, 2002).

Majid Fakhry, former professor at the American University in Beirut, is a well-known authority on Islamic philosophy and author of a valuable history of the field (see chapter 6). His translation of the Qur'an, however, is disappointing.

Very clearly printed in parallel columns with the Arabic text, this version makes it easy to locate specific verses; a minimum of footnotes keeps the pages clean and attractive. But this layout also deprives the text of any continuity of thought, paragraphing, emphasis, or breaks: the individual numbered verses march along mechanically, as in Pickthall's version. The translation displays the virtues of clarity and simplicity, but the element of lyricism or rhetorical beauty is strangely absent, even in the early Meccan *suras*; their evocative power has somehow drained away. This edition also lacks an extensive scholarly apparatus suited for classroom study—the annotations address a few translation issues and offer a little background information (but not enough: e.g., Surah 105). The *suras* are not introduced, nor is their time or place of origin identified. A brief introduction to the entire volume is provided, and a helpful index.[24]

This edition has been approved by Al-Azhar University in Cairo.

ABDEL HALEEM, 2004

Muhammad A. S. Abdel Haleem. The Qur'an: A New Translation (Oxford: Oxford University Press, 2004).

A professor at the School of Oriental and African Studies at the University of London, Abdel Haleem is writing in a European multicultural context, aware of the dynamics of interfaith dialogue. The very instructive introduction to his work is in keeping with normative Islamic tradition, yet refreshingly open to the many non-Muslim readers who will seek a fuller understanding of Islam within its pages. The work is well suited to the needs of scholars in other fields who need access to the overall content of the Qur'an in English.

Abdel Haleem has chosen to format the text in paragraphs upon the page, like standard prose, dividing the material into meaningful sections; this works very well in long didactic passages like Sura 33, but not as well in the more lyrical or poetic early Meccan *suras* (e.g., Suras 82, 87, 91). Every verse is numbered to allow for quick reference. He provides a concise introduction to each *sura*, summarizing its message, identifying its place and time of origin, and noting any necessary background information. Limited footnotes also indicate translation problems and clarify historical or cultural allusions. He has tried to use gender-neutral language where all human beings are meant, as in Sura 114 (regrettable). Occasionally, he includes an unusual interpretation—for example, understanding Q. 86:7 to refer to a baby emerging from the womb—but these decisions are taken openly and explained in footnotes.

The book includes a detailed analytical index, a chronology of important dates in the history of early Islam and the Qur'an, a handy map of the Arabian Peninsula, and a selective bibliography. Due to some error, pages 415–447 were printed without page numbers.[25]

Modern Popular Translations

Apart from the academic and critical editions created by scholars mainly for other scholars, there is a growing body of Qur'anic material in English and other European languages for which a wider audience is envisioned. Often, these publications are prepared expressly in the service of *da'wa* (DAA-wa) or the call to faith, to enable people with no knowledge of Arabic to hear and accept the message of Islam and become Muslims. Some are created with pedagogical purposes in mind, to be used as teaching aids especially for young Muslims learning about their own faith. Still others represent a pluralistic or multicultural approach to religion, through which Islam can be made more accessible to non-Muslims seeking dialogue or interfaith understanding. Whatever the initial aim, these works often provide interesting examples of the enculturation of Islam where the community exists as a minority in Western societies.

IRVING, 1985

T. B. (Thomas Ballentine) Irving. *The Qur'an: The First American Version* (Brattleboro, Vt.: Amana Books, 1985).

This controversial work is furnished with an oddly combative and opinionated introduction that seems calculated to offend as many people as possible.

But Irving's stated goal is nothing radical: he wishes to make the Qur'an intelligible in a modern North American idiom, especially for young Muslims growing up at a cultural and linguistic distance from the original text. He makes clear that his work is meant as a *tafsir* (toff-SEER) or interpretation of the text, yet his subtitle gave some critics the impression that he was presuming to create a canonical text in a non-Arabic tongue (the subtitle was changed in later editions). As S. Parvez Manzoor observes, such an aim "exceeds the proper limits accepted for works of this kind."[26] Part of the problem is Irving's mention of a "use in divine worship" for his translation (p. xli), which could indeed be, as Manzoor asserts, "a gross violation of the normative Muslim tradition." However, Irving firmly states later in his introduction that young American Muslims must certainly be trained to recite the prayers in their original Arabic form (p. xlii), so it seems likely that the remark about divine worship refers to quotes from the Qur'an used in sermons, preached in the context of a Friday mosque gathering or similar event.

Of greater concern is Irving's statement that "through the original Arabic we learn what Muhammad was striving to express to his followers, but our problem is to catch *how* he might want this expressed for the people of today who speak English . . ." (p. xlii; emphasis in the original). Such a statement raises issues of cultural indigenization and translation theory, causing F. V. Greifenhagen to characterize Irving as an "accomodationist" who is "adapting the original language to the receptor language," to the detriment of the original.[27]

Irving's translation is fairly idiomatic and readable, though his work is not entirely free of pompous, pseudobiblical expressions (see Q. 11:64). There are also some rather dubious vocabulary choices (e.g., "sprites" for *jinn* in Q. 11:120). He uses a paragraph format with a system of asterisks to indicate verse divisions; he also presumes to print in a bold font phrases he personally considers of "special importance" (p. xl). The translation is certainly of interest, though one could argue that it is not the work of a mature scholar.

KHATIB, 1986
Mohammad M. Khatib. *The Bounteous Koran: A Translation of Meaning and Commentary* (London: Macmillan, 1986).

The publication of this version by Macmillan must have seemed like a good idea at the time; it is printed in an attractive, ornate style, with green borders and small medallions for page numbers, giving the English reader a sense of the customary look and feel of the Qur'an as scripture. It bears the endorsement of Al-Azhar University in Cairo, indicating that it contains no objectionable or unorthodox doctrine in its text or annotations. But unfortunately, the work does not succeed in the target language: it is full of impossible, inaccurate, ineffective expressions in English, such as the "dingy chaff" of 87:5.[28] The presence of these errors seems inevitable when one reads the documents prepared by the examination committee and the director general of Al-Azhar's Research Department, who approved this work. Their inability to write in idiomatic English is painfully apparent. What is less clear is why Macmillan's editors failed to intercept this work on its way to the public.

MALIK, 1997

Muhammad Farooq-i-Azam Malik. *English Translation of the Meanings of al-Qur'an: The Guidance for Mankind.* 2nd ed. (Houston: Institute of Islamic Knowledge, 1998).

Using a traditional text-and-commentary format, Malik has produced an adequate but highly conventional rendering of the Qur'an in English. He uses both parentheses and italics to insert interpretive material into the translation—a distracting device (e.g., Sura 90; compare the far smoother version of this *sura* in the Bewley translation below). At times, he violates this policy and includes glosses without identifying them, as in the very difficult Sura 101. He also falls back on transliterated terms ("Aqabah," "Qariah," "Haviah"), without always including them in the glossary or defining them in footnotes; for some reason, he also does not translate the titles of the *suras*. Among the prefatory matter is a convenient outline of the whole book with synopses of the *suras*, including both verse and page numbers.

The volume contains endorsements from the International Islamic University in Islamabad and Al-Azhar University in Cairo.

BEHBUDI AND TURNER, 1997

Muhammad Baqir Behbudi and Colin Turner. *The Quran* [sic]: *A New Interpretation* (Richmond, Surrey, UK: Curzon, 1997).

A Shi'i *tafsir* or commentary in Persian (*Ma'ani al-qur'an* by Muhammad Baqir Behbudi) was the basis for this work by Colin Turner, a prolific writer and lecturer on Persian language and literature at the University of Durham. It offers a heavily amplified and adulterated paraphrase of the scripture, stuffed with unmarked interpolations, presented as if they were part of the actual Qur'anic text; the unwary reader has no way of knowing which bits are present in Arabic and which have been supplied by the interpreters. Only in the last paragraph of the preface does Turner acknowledge that this work is "not a straightforward translation" but rather "a combination of translation and exegesis" or an "exegetically-led reading" of the text (p. xvi).

This approach leads to some bizarre episodes, such as Q. 19:17–22, 4:35, 12:25, or 101:2–5, and to a passage where an entire theology is developed upon a single ambiguous word (*samad* in Q. 112:3). The liberties taken with the text are quite astonishing. This is unfortunate, because Turner's English paraphrase is often very fresh and articulate, as in the Throne Verse (Q. 2:256 in this edition; the verse numbering follows a system of counting the *basmala* or dedication of each *sura* as verse 1). This version could contribute a great deal to discussion and comprehension if read beside a more literal and disciplined translation, but only if it were clearly identified as a highly inter-pretive and paraphrastic rendering. The packaging of this product in its pres-ent form is misleading and does a disservice to the reader.[29]

Behbudi and Turner have refused to number or translate the titles of the *suras* (either an annoying affectation or an oversight) and failed to list them in the table of contents with page numbers; along with the nonstandard verse enumeration, this makes looking up specific passages harder than it should be. The text in Arabic is bound back-to-back into this volume.

HELMINSKI, 1998

Camille Adams Helminski. *The Light of Dawn: Daily Readings from the Holy Qur'an* (Boston: Shambhala, 2000).

This set of selections from the Qur'an is lovingly edited, translated, and interpreted in the Sufi tradition, producing a book whose overriding concern is Islamic spirituality. Helminski and her husband Kabir have published a col-lection of verses from the *Mathnawi* of the great Sufi poet Jalal al-Din Rumi (d. 1273), as *Jewels of Remembrance: A Daybook of Spiritual Guidance* (Putney, Vt.: Threshold, 1996). The Qur'an receives similar treatment in *The Light of Dawn*.

Favorite verses are presented from various *suras*, as independent ex-cerpts, and rendered into a fluid and attractive English. Certain passages are accompanied by a transliterated Arabic version, in order to give the reader some sense of the way the verses sound in their original tongue. An occasional footnote offers an allegorical or spiritualized interpretation of the text (e.g., Sura 105, "The Elephant"). The translator's decision that is most certain to provoke a reaction is her use of the feminine pronoun at times to refer to God, as in "For with God are the keys to the Unseen: the treasures that none knows but He/She. And He/She knows all that is on the land and in the sea; and not a leaf falls but He/She knows it . . . " (Q. 6:59–60). Those interested in gender concerns and the Qur'an might find this work appealing.

Other Sources

Other daily devotional collections of verses from the Qur'an are available, including *The Bounty of Allah* by Aneela Khalid Arshed (New York: Crossroad, 1999). Arshed has selected verses from Pickthall's translation and updated the English style, then matched them with sayings of the Prophet taken from the *hadith* or quotations from Sufi theologians or poets (Rumi, Rabi'a, al-Hujwiri, and so on), conducive to personal reflection or meditation.

Thomas Cleary has produced a number of popular editions of texts from the Buddhist, Taoist, and Confucian traditions; he also published a Sufi-influenced set of excerpts from the Qur'an, as *The Essential Koran: The Heart of Islam* (San Francisco: HarperCollins, 1994). It was first cataloged with a different subtitle in 1993.

ABDALHAQQ AND 'AISHA BEWLEY, 1999
Abdalhaqq and 'Aisha Bewley. *The Noble Qur'an: A New Rendering of Its Meaning in English* (Norwich: Bookwork, 1999).

'Aisha Abdurrahman Bewley (in collaboration with her husband Abdalhaqq) has conducted for many years a valuable ministry of translation for English-speaking Muslims. She has translated key primary texts of *hadith*, law and jurisprudence, biography, history, theology, and mysticism, often published in inexpensive paperback editions, in service to the education of Muslims in the rich resources of their own faith tradition.

This Qur'an translation incorporates some significant editorial decisions. The entire text is printed in a sort of free-verse format, including the more prosaic *suras*. Very few footnotes appear and no brackets or parentheses to indicate text glosses. These decisions—along with the direct and straightforward contemporary English style—create an impression of accessibility and coherence. Less successful is the constant use of transliterated but not translated Arabic vocabulary, though the rationale provided in the preface is convincing: believers who do not speak Arabic tend to know and use these specific technical terms, which have particular connotations within Islam, and this publication is intended expressly for them. Two glossaries are provided, for Arabic terms and names.

The translation is based, for ideological reasons, upon the reading of Imam Warsh ('Uthman ibn Sa'id; d. 813) of Medina rather than the better-known reading of Hafs ibn Sulayman (d. 796). The text variants are subtle, but the enumeration of verses is also slightly different, making it a little harder to look up specific verses.[30] The ideological character of the Bewleys' work is openly expressed and adds a certain texture to their publications.

All discourse is personal, and it may also be fair to say that all discourse is ideological. It is unreasonable to expect that any translator could be entirely free of human individuality or self-interest. Translators reflect the cultures with which they are in contact and the times in which they live. Some of the works discussed in this chapter are worthy of study precisely because they reveal their biases in a significant manner; all of them contribute to the diversity of this important literature.

Notes

1. Sachiko Murata and William C. Chittick, *The Vision of Islam* (New York: Paragon, 1994), xv.

2. See Richard C. Martin, "Inimitability," *EQ*, v. 2: 526–36.

3. On the nonlinear character of the text, see Michael Sells, *Approaching the Qur'an: The Early Revelations* (Ashland, Ore.: White Cloud Press, 1999), 11–12, 15–16.

4. Helmut Gätje, *The Qur'an and Its Exegesis*, translated into English by Alford T. Welch (Berkeley: University of California Press, 1976), 291.

5. Neal Robinson, "Sectarian and Ideological Bias in Muslim Translations of the Qur'an," *ICMR* 8, no. 3 (1997): 261–78.

6. For detailed data on the known editions of the Qur'an since the advent of print, see J. D. Pearson, "Bibliography of Translations of the Qur'an into European Languages," in *Arabic Literature to the End of the Umayyad Period* (Cambridge: Cambridge University Press, 1983), 502–20. Pearson mistakenly identifies Dawood as a Muslim translator and fails to list Muhammad 'Ali as Ahmadi.

7. Arthur J. Arberry, *The Koran Interpreted* (London: George Allen and Unwin, 1955), 11–12.

8. A. R. Kidwai, "English Translations of the Qur'an," *Muslim and Arab Perspectives* 4, no. 1 (1997): 170.

9. The quote is taken from Guillaume's review of Arberry's translation, in *MW* 47, no. 3 (1957): 248. A full review of Bell by John E. Merrill is found in *MW* 37, no. 2 (1947): 134–48.

10. From a review by Eric F. F. Bishop in *MW* 49, no. 1 (1959): 55.

11. Mofakhar Hussain Khan, "English Translations of the Holy Qur'an: A Bio-Bibliographic Study," *IQ* 30 (1986): 167. A review of Sher 'Ali's work by Kenneth Cragg is found in *MW* 47, no. 4 (1957): 341–42.

12. Robinson, 265–66.

13. Robinson, 263–64.

14. Robinson, 274.

15. Khadiga El Tayeb. *Principles and Problems of the Translation of Scriptures: The Case of the Qur'an* (Temple University Ph.D. dissertation, 1985), 351–52.

16. Robinson, 271–73.

17. Robinson, 275.

18. This work and many others mentioned in this chapter are reviewed in an extremely partisan article by Khaleel Mohammed, "Assessing English Translations of the Qur'an," *Middle East Quarterly* 12, no. 2 (Spr 2005): www.meforum.org/article/717.

19. Robinson, 261–63.

20. Kidwai, 164.

21. A. R. Kidwai, MWBR 12, no. 2 (1992): 18–21.

22. Kenneth Cragg, *Readings in the Qur'an* (London: Collins, 1988), 49–51.

23. Sells's book caused an outburst of controversy and press coverage when it was assigned as summer reading for freshmen at the University of North Carolina in 2002; opinions about that incident are easily located online. A review by Muhammed Haron can be found in *Islamic Studies* 40, no. 2 (2001): 324–26.

24. The work is mentioned briefly in a review by David Waines in *ICMR* 13, no. 2 (2002): 229–31; in one by Hasan Gai Eaton in *IQ* 41, no. 3 (1997): 247–50; also in the Rippin review, below.

25. A brief review of this work by the noted Islamic scholar Andrew Rippin is found in *H-Net Reviews* (Humanities and Social Sciences Online). See H-Mideast-Medieval, Dec 2004: www.h-net.org/reviews/showrev.cgi?path=231841109092997.

26. From the review of Irving's work by S. Parvez Manzoor in *MWBR* 7, no. 4 (1987): 72–75. It should be noted that Manzoor can be quite combative and opinionated himself.

27. F. V. Greifenhagen, "Traduttore Traditore: An Analysis of the History of English Translations of the Qur'an," *ICMR* 3, no. 2 (Dec 1992): 282.

28. Many more errors are noted in a review by Hasan Gai Eaton in *IQ* 31 (1987): 57–61.

29. David Waines, *ICMR* 10, no. 1 (Mar 1999): 88–89; see also the irascible Abdur Raheem Kidwai in *MWBR* 19, no. 3 (Spr 1999). 13–15.

30. A review by Scott C. Lucas is found in the *Journal of Near Eastern Studies* 62, no. 2 (Apr 2003): 112–14.

CHAPTER TWO

~

The Traditions: Hadith

The faith of Islam is more than assent to a set of propositions or belief statements: It is an integrated, coherent, enacted way of life, based upon submission to God and obedience to God's commands. The desire to conform one's behavior to God's will involves a knowledge of what is permitted and what is prohibited; the complex edifice of Islamic law is built upon this knowledge.

A study of the Qur'an alone soon reveals that only a fraction of its contents can be readily applied to the formulation of law, and it does not address many aspects of ordinary life at all. The nascent Muslim community had another means by which to learn how to please God: the example of the Prophet Muhammad. His words and deeds, his customary behavior, his responses to a variety of problems and questions, even his tacit approval of others' behavior in his presence, became the standard to emulate. The *sunna* (SOON-nah) of the Prophet was his exemplary behavior or precedent—his own conduct along the straight path of Islam (Q 1:6).

Preserving a record of the Prophet's *sunna* was a challenge the early Muslim community met through the memory and testimony of eyewitnesses, the Companions, who lived intimately with Muhammad and were in a position to observe and recall his words and behavior. They exchanged accounts or narratives conveying these memories; such an account became known as a *hadith* (hah-DEETH), literally a news report. (The plural may appear properly as *ahadith*, or in an Anglicized form as *hadiths*.) But the term *hadith* may also be used to signify the whole corpus of traditions or the literature that was created to encompass these narratives in written form. A scholar who collected, categorized, and analyzed this body of material was known as a *muhaddith* (moo-HAHD-dith); plural, *muhaddithun* (moo-hahd-dith-THOON). In English, the word *hadith* has typically been translated as "tradition," and *muhaddith* as "traditionist."

When the living Companions began to disappear, their knowledge of the Prophet's *sunna* had to be transmitted to the next generation of believers, the Successors and the Followers. Control over this body of knowledge had to be maintained; it was too easy for errors to enter the data stream, for information to be lost or forgotten, or for deceitful or well-intentioned forgeries to be introduced. The custom arose of identifying each individual who reported a *hadith* narrative and the person from whom it was received, and the person who told it to that person, and so on, back to its original witness. This chain of transmission was known as the *sanad* or *isnad* (iss-NAD); it became the essential first component of every *hadith*, and was carefully preserved along with the *matn* (MAT-un) or body of the narrative itself. Every tradition properly comprises its *isnad* and its *matn*: its chain of transmitters and then the content of the statement or incident being reported.

It was soon recognized that one *isnad* could be far more complete and plausible than another, and a system for ranking narratives emerged. A tradition with an impressive chain of transmitters would be regarded as *sahih* (sah-HEEH) or sound; one with some flaws might be ranked as *hasan* (HASS-san) or good/fair; a seriously defective one would be considered *da'if* (dah-EEF) or weak. Many very fine distinctions were created to identify the exact degree to which a certain tradition's *isnad* could be affirmed, and the precise nature of its defects. The work of the *muhaddith* was to acquire the information needed to make these judgments and to determine when and how the *matn* or content of the tradition could be applied in the process of legal reasoning.

It must be noted that the process of *hadith* formation was never as orderly or straightforward as a brief summary makes it appear. The study of *hadith* history is not only intricate, but littered with ideological land mines; some persons seem to have an interest in undermining the alleged authenticity of the traditions, while others dogmatically defend it. This tension becomes comprehensible when one considers what is at stake.

The message of Islam came originally to a people whose habits of thought and behavior were radically transformed by it. Likewise, in the first centuries of the very rapid expansion of Islam, the faith was adopted by scores of peoples for whom the background cultures of the Arabian Peninsula were quite unfamiliar. As G. H. A. Juynboll points out, "The merits of the civilizations of the conquered had to be either acknowledged as such, renounced, or remolded to fit into the regulations of the new religion. It was then that the behavior of the Prophet, as set forth in the *hadith*, acquired its everlasting importance as the one and only basis from which to proceed, that is, if the Qur'an itself did not provide the answers."[1] The *hadith* accounts were the vehicle by which the cargo of the authoritative *sunna* could be delivered to new believers and new contexts.

The authority who is usually considered the key figure in establishing tradition as a recognized source of Islamic law was the great medieval jurist Muhammad ibn Idris al-Shafi'i (d. 820). In his groundbreaking work, *Kitab al-risala fi usul al-fiqh* or *Treatise on the Principles of Jurisprudence*, al-Shafi'i (ash-SHAA-fi-ee) stipulated the duty of obedience to the Prophet as binding upon all believers, and the Qur'an and the *sunna* together as the two inspired and authoritative sources from which laws are derived to guide and direct the Muslim community. Citing passages in the Qur'an that refer to "the Book and the Wisdom," al-Shafi'i states, "The Wisdom is the *sunna* of the Apostle of God," and explains, "For the Apostle has laid down a *sunna* [on matters] for which there is no [specific] text. But whatever he laid down in the *sunna* God has ordered us to obey and He regards our obedience to him as obedience to Him."[2]

The *Risala* came to be regarded as a turning-point text from one of the founding fathers of Islamic jurisprudence (see chapter 4). Every act in the life of an individual believer or a Muslim community should be in accord with the *shari'a* (sha-REE-ah) or divine law. Therefore, the way that one's understanding of *shari'a* is shaped and the sources from which it is derived take on a crucial importance. The concept of law pronounced in the *Risala* ensured for the traditions a status second only to the Qur'an in the literature of Islam.

Two Important Early Collections

The pivotal figure of al-Shafi'i links two key scholars in the history of *hadith* study. Al-Shafi'i is said to have memorized the Qur'an at the age of seven and the *Muwatta'* of Malik ibn Anas at ten. As a young man, he became Malik's pupil in Medina. In his turn, Ahmad ibn Hanbal studied under al-Shafi'i in Baghdad. The impact of these scholars on the development of Islamic law and literature is discussed here and in chapter 4.

MALIK IBN ANAS (d. 795)
Abu 'Abdallah Malik ibn Anas (MA-lik ibbin AN-nas) ibn Malik ibn 'Amr al-Asbahi. *Kitab al-muwatta'* or *Book of the Smoothed Path*.

Malik ibn Anas is now remembered as the "Imam of Medina" and associated with the Maliki school of law. During his lifetime, he was regarded as an authority on the study of jurisprudence, or *fiqh*; he composed the earliest surviving book of Islamic law, his *Kitab al-muwatta'* (al-moo-WUTTA).³ In it, he developed a legal system based upon the consensus of opinion and precedent in Medina as enunciated by recognized authorities and accepted by the community. Therefore, Malik's landmark work was not a *hadith* collection per se, but an attempt "to establish a system of law based on the *sunna* of Medina,"⁴ using about seventeen hundred *hadith* narratives as an important source.

Malik did not collect these traditions exhaustively for their own sake; nor did he apply critical criteria to determine their provenance or assess their soundness, which became the major preoccupations of professional *muhaddithun* a century later. In a way, this makes the work particularly interesting, because it contains many traditions that are not included in later collections compiled by those criteria, thus demonstrating how the methods of employing and evaluating *hadith* evolved. As Joseph Schacht observes, "The *Muwatta'* . . . represents the transition from the simple *fiqh* of the earliest period to the pure science of *hadith* of the later period."⁵

Historical circumstances produced more than a dozen different recensions of the *Muwatta'*. Of these, two are considered most complete and authoritative.

Malik ibn Anas. *Al-Muwatta of Imam Malik ibn Anas: The First Formulation of Islamic Law*. Translated by Aisha Abdurrahman Bewley (London: Kegan Paul International, 1989).

This edition in English of the *Muwatta'* has the virtues of sharp printing, good binding, and paper quality, with well-formatted pages in two columns. Visually effective titles, subtitles, numbering, and spacing make the layout attractive and intelligible. It is one of the few *hadith* sources that is complete in one volume, without annotations or accretions, making it possible for the reader to obtain a quick, clear overview of the entire work's design and concept.

The *Muwatta'* is organized around key topics in law and ritual. The essentials of Muslim observance are prominently placed, especially prayer and the ritual purification necessary to offer prayer, *zakat* (almsgiving), fasting, the pilgrimage to Mecca, and *jihad*; after this, numerous legal and behavioral concerns are addressed: making vows, sacrificing animals, inheritance and wills, divorce and kinship, human slavery, business transactions (loans and debts, buying and selling goods, money-changing), legal proceedings (rules governing testimony, settling civil disputes, imposing criminal punishments), and finally guidelines for general dress and behavior, modesty, and courtesy. A similar pattern of categorization is typically found in a *musannaf* (moo-SUN-nuff; plural, *musannafat*) or "classified" collection, but it is rarely as transparent as in this edition.

Bewley's translation is fresh and free of heavy formality or euphemism. She relies a great deal on transliterated (untranslated) Arabic vocabulary, but a handy glossary is found in the back of the book, along with a fairly helpful index. The book's introduction by a *shari'a* judge is interesting but contains many assertions not supported by other authorities.

Malik ibn Anas. *Muwatta' Imam Malik*. Translation and notes by Muhammad Rahimuddin (Lahore: Sh. Muhammad Ashraf, 1985 reprint of a 1979 edition).

This is an older but still useful translation, with some helpful footnotes, a brief introduction, and an index. The English prose style is quite readable, if somewhat ornate.

AHMAD IBN HANBAL (d. 855)
Abu 'Abdallah Ahmad ibn Muhammad ibn Hanbal (ibbin HAHN-bal). The *Musnad* or The Supported or Attested [Collection].

Trained in language and law, Ahmad ibn Hanbal devoted himself to the traditions and played a distinct role in developing the culture of *hadith*. He grew up in Baghdad and traveled in Iraq, Yemen, Syria, and the Hejaz learning *hadith* and studied *fiqh* for a time with al-Shafi'i. Ibn Hanbal is conventionally known as "the Imam of Baghdad" and did most of his lecturing there, but he spent a good deal of time in Mecca and Medina (completing the pilgrimage five times); the great fourteenth-century theologian Ibn Taymiyya associates Ibn Hanbal's juristic philosophy primarily with the belief and thought of the Hejaz.

Suffering persecution under the Mu'tazili caliphs, Ibn Hanbal responded with patience and courage and became widely known and respected for his virtuous life. The Hanbali school of Islamic law (see chapter 4) is part of his legacy; through Ibn Taymiyya, he is linked as well with Wahhabism and the Salafiyya movement.

Ibn Hanbal was a prolific scholar, and the work for which he is principally known, his *Musnad* (MUSS-nad), is a compilation of nearly thirty thousand *hadiths*. Like other *musnad* works, it is organized not by topic but by source: All of the traditions believed to originate with a certain narrator are grouped together. The narrators are ordered by seniority, starting with the first four "rightly guided" caliphs, members of the Prophet's family, other Companions, and so on.

Ibn Hanbal included in his compilation the traditions generally accepted in his time. Eventually, selection criteria became more stringent, and the *Musnad* contains many traditions not considered *sahih* or "sound" by some later authorities. The work was completed after Ibn Hanbal's death by his son 'Abdullah.

Ahmad ibn Hanbal. *Foundations of the Sunnah*. English translation and notes by Amjad ibn Muhammad Rafiq (Birmingham: Al-Maktabah as-Salafiyyah Publications, 1997).
This book contains a translation of a short treatise by Ibn Hanbal, his *Usul al-sunnah*, along with a quantity of extraneous and polemical material. Within the book are some *hadiths* from Ibn Hanbal's *Musnad*, but they are too scattered to be useful.

Other Sources
Some narratives recorded by Ibn Hanbal are found in Tarif Khalidi's beautifully edited collection *The Muslim Jesus: Sayings and Stories in Islamic Literature* (Cambridge, Mass.: Harvard University Press, 2001). Another work by Ibn Hanbal, the *Masa'il*, exists in a critical edition in English (see chapter 4), but reliable sources for the *Musnad* itself are unavailable. Scholarly studies that concentrate on this literature may provide insight into the text; see, for example, the dissertation by Scott Cameron Lucas, *The Arts of Hadith Compilation and Criticism* (University of Chicago, 2002), which specifically investigates the *Musnad*.

The Six Books: The Canonical Collections

Written *hadith* collections proliferated in the ninth century CE. Of these, six gradually became regarded by the community as authoritative and are now commonly known as the canonical collections. They are often referred to as *al-Sihah al-Sitta*, the Six Authentic [Ones], or simply *al-Kutub al-Sitta*, the Six Books. The terminology overlaps a bit, as these six are divided into two rough categories: the *sahih* works proper (meaning "genuine" or "reliable") and the *sunan* works (*sunan* is the plural of *sunna*).

The two *sahih* (sah-HEEH) works are those of al-Bukhari and Muslim ibn al-Hajjaj. These two were eventually recognized as superior in concept and execution to any other compilations of traditions and ultimately were accepted as second in authority to the Qur'an. The two *sahih* works were created at about the same time and with the same intention: to select among the many thousands of narratives in circulation only those whose authenticity was confirmed.[6] Al-Bukhari and Muslim subjected the traditions in their keeping to a scrutiny meant to find those with an unbroken *isnad* or chain of trustworthy transmitters leading back to a sound source or original narrator.

They arrived independently at two somewhat different collections of material; however, those *hadiths* that appear in both works (numbering about two thousand) are held in the highest regard by the Muslim community.

AL-BUKHARI (d. 870)
Abu 'Abdallah Muhammad ibn Isma'il al-Bukhari (al-boo-KAH-ree). The *Sahih* or *Jami' al-sahih,* The Comprehensive and Authentic [Collection].

Attracted at an early age to the traditions, al-Bukhari was to become the greatest of all *muhaddithun*. Like many others, he memorized, studied, and collected narratives, reportedly from over a thousand teachers (including Ahmad ibn Hanbal) in Basra, Baghdad, Egypt, and the Hejaz. He migrated as far as Nishapur in Persia, where he experienced some ill treatment, then settled near Bukhara. His erudition and virtue are legendary.

One of al-Bukhari's teachers supposedly remarked that some *muhaddith* should put together a tested collection consisting only of authentic traditions. Bukhari accepted the challenge. He designed a work organized around major themes or juridical concerns (a *musannaf* or "classified" collection) and established a set of criteria by which traditions would be assessed for inclusion. He insisted upon an *isnad* or chain of transmitters made up of individuals whose good character and competence were widely attested, and who were known to have been in personal contact with the previous link in the chain.

Bukhari's collection is wide-ranging and varied, as the term *jami'* (JAM-ee) suggests. In addition to the usual topics such as prayer, purification, and worship, he includes Qur'an commentary, *'ilm* or religious knowledge, doctrinal topics such as eschatology and revelation, historical and biographical accounts, material on family and legal issues, creation stories, and interesting miscellany, like the "Book of Tricks" and the interpretation of dreams.

Many English versions of Bukhari's *Sahih* exist, and excerpts are found in almost any anthology of Islamic literature. Their contents and quality are variable, however.

Al-Bukhari. *The Translation of the Meanings of Sahih al-Bukhari, Arabic-English.* Translated by Muhammad Muhsin Khan (Chicago: Kazi, 1979). 4th revised edition; 9 vols.

The most widely distributed translation is the one by M. M. Khan, issued and reissued by assorted publishers. It is not supremely readable to begin with, and the publisher's formatting in this edition is awkward and confusing. Bukhari's own titles and chapter headings are often abbreviated, and some material is edited out—including the parts of book III that deal specifically with the science and study of *hadith*. The publication contains no translator's notes, only a simple glossary; it also includes a lot of extraneous boilerplate material at the beginning of vol. 1. There is no index.

Kazi's publication terminology is inconsistent. A "sixth revised edition" published by Kazi in Lahore was also examined, and its contents appear to be identical to the fourth edition.

Al-Bukhari. *English Translation of Sahih al-Bukhari*. By Maulana Aftab-ud-din Ahmad (Lahore: Ahmadiyya Anjuman Isha'at-i-islam, 1976). 3 vols.

Ahmad's translation is also available in various forms. This edition, despite its poor print quality and manufacture, has some advantages. The English prose is rather romantic in flavor, but readable, and a fully pointed Arabic text is included. Bukhari's own section headings are printed in full, in italics. Also, his remarks in book III about the work of the traditionist are included here.

Footnotes indicate vocabulary problems, identify persons mentioned, provide cross-references to other narratives, and offer some apologetic interpretation of obscure passages. These notes are mainly derived from an Urdu commentary by the Maulana Muhammad 'Ali, leader of the Lahore Ahmadiyya Movement (see chapter 1).

Other Sources
The well-known Qur'an translator Muhammad Asad (Leopold Weiss) produced an English version known as *Sahih al-Bukhari: Being the True Accounts of the Sayings and Doings of the Prophet Muhammad* (Srinagar: Arafat Publications, 1935); the work was reprinted several times by various publishers, under different titles.

A short but useful excerpt from Bukhari's *Sahih* is found in the excellent anthology by Calder, Mojaddedi, and Rippin, *Classical Islam* (London; New York: Routledge, 2003). It consists of a few pages of freshly translated traditions on the subject of almsgiving or *zakat*. A much more substantial and very interesting excerpt on fasting is included in Arthur Jeffery's *Reader on Islam* (The Hague: Mouton, 1962). The English idiom is a little old-fashioned but perfectly sound. There are brief but helpful footnotes. Also, the work is readily available in hundreds of library collections.

Al-Bukhari. *Moral Teachings of Islam: Prophetic Traditions from al-Adab al-mufrad by Imam al-Bukhari*. Selected and translated with an introduction by Abdul Ali Hamid (Walnut Creek, Calif.: AltaMira Press, 2003). Published in cooperation with the International Sacred Literature Trust.

A separate work by Bukhari known as *Al-adab al mufrad* or *Good Behavior Singled Out* exists in several English translations, including this convenient abridged form. This edition comprises 585 rather simplistic *hadiths* dealing mainly with good manners, kindness, patience, and ordinary daily courtesy. They are loosely organized by the editor and printed in an attractive format that invites browsing; there are no translation notes or other scholarly apparatus (except for a small glossary). Only one narrator is named for each tradition, and those individuals are not identified or indexed.

Bukhari's *Al-adab al-mufrad* is also available in a translation by Yusuf Talal DeLorenzo, *Imam Bukhari's Book of Muslim Morals and Manners* (Alexandria, Va.: Al-Saadawi, 1997), and one by Rafiq Abdur Rehman, *Manners in Islam* (Karachi: Darul Ishaat, 2002). Chapters on *adab* are found in most *hadith* collections and are diligently studied by many believers today.

MUSLIM IBN AL-HAJJAJ (d. 875)
Abul Husayn Muslim (MOOS-lim) ibn al-Hajjaj ibn Muslim al-Qushairi (or Kushayri) al-Nisaburi. His name also appears as Muslim ibn al-Hadjdjadj. The *Sahih*, or *Jami' al-sahih*, The Comprehensive and Authentic [Collection].

Born in Nishapur in eastern Persia, Muslim was an Arab of the noted Qushair tribe. He made long journeys to study with acknowledged *muhaddithun* in Iraq, Egypt, Syria, and the Hejaz; among his teachers was Ahmad ibn Hanbal. He returned to Nishapur to take up his own scholarly work and there became acquainted with his contemporary and senior colleague al-Bukhari. Both men achieved a reputation for probity and piety; they are now revered as *al-Shaykhan*, the Two Sheikhs, and their works as *al-Sahihayn*, the Two Reliable [Ones].

Muslim's compendium of traditions includes about four thousand narratives, selected from what was said to be a huge collection of three hundred thousand. This vast sum, of course, comprises far fewer distinct narratives: If the same story was attached to ten different *isnads* or chains of transmitters, the traditionist would consider it to be ten known *hadiths*.[7] At this stage in the development of the discipline, the *isnad* was the primary means of verification. Muslim composed a lengthy introduction to his work in which he set forth his strategy of *hadith* criticism and his criteria for evaluation.

What distinguishes Muslim's work from al-Bukhari's in the minds of scholars is its superior organization. Like other *musannafat* or classified works, it is gathered into large topical categories or books, such as faith, purification, prayer, and so on. Each book is composed of many highly specialized chapters. But Muslim succeeded in pulling together similar traditions with different *isnads* into these discrete chapters, along with parallel versions or statements of the same idea. By contrast, Bukhari uses a more decentralized approach, placing related traditions under different headings when the contents are pertinent to more than one legal topic or issue. Muslim's technique creates "clusters" of thematic material, allowing the reader to see related traditions presented together in such a way that they form a commentary upon a basic idea and furnish the scholar with indications, according to Juynboll, "indispensable for tradition analysis and dating."[8]

Muslim ibn al-Hajjaj. *Sahih Muslim.* Rendered into English by 'Abdul Hamid Siddiqi. Rev. ed. (New Delhi: Kitab Bhavan, 2000).

Siddiqi's is the standard full translation of Muslim's *Sahih* into English; it has been reprinted many times and is fairly accessible in library collections. The printing and formatting of the publication are good; however, the chapters are ordered with roman numerals—an unfortunate choice. It is also unfortunate that Siddiqi's translation does not include Muslim's important introduction (see Juynboll, below).

The coherence of Muslim's technique can be appreciated in this edition. Under each chapter heading, the reader finds a focused set of traditions in which the main idea is evident and the small variations in detail easily perceived. The first *hadith* in the chapter often poses the presenting problem and the following ones develop it; in some cases, one can witness a sort of progression in the narratives that follow. An interesting example is chapter 234 in the *Kitab al-salat* or "Book of Prayer" (book IV). The chapter heading is "Excellence of Prayers in Congregation and Grim Warning for Remaining Away From It." The first narrative reports that the Prophet said, "Prayer said in a congregation is twenty-five degrees more excellent than prayer said by a single person." The succeeding narratives offer additions to and variations on this idea. Some state that one prayer said in a congregation is equivalent to twenty-five prayers; some say twenty-seven prayers, or that the prayer is 27 degrees more excellent, or "some and twenty" degrees; some say that the prayer must be led by an imam to attain this level. Then is added the command that when public prayer is commenced, an appointed imam should lead it, and then that anyone who does not attend the public prayer should have his house burned by fire. The matter escalates further, as young men are instructed to gather bundles of fuel and use them to burn the houses of those who do not attend—with the people in them. Two more *hadiths* repeat the command to burn in their houses the people who absent themselves from public prayer. Collecting and ordering these fourteen traditions together allows for effective comparison; many of these units would provide good material for classroom discussion.

Siddiqi goes somewhat overboard on the footnoting in this edition; a few notes offer useful background information, but the majority impose highly prescriptive interpretations on a given passage and trespass into exhortation and apologetics.

G. H. A. Juynboll. "Muslim's Introduction to His *Sahih*, Translated and Annotated," *Jerusalem Studies in Arabic and Islam* 5 (1984), 263–302.

Juynboll did Islamic studies a service by producing this highly disciplined translation of the introductory chapter of Muslim's *Sahih*. This chapter is the earliest extant example of systematic *hadith* criticism that is readily available in either Arabic or English. Muslim creates a persuasive theory of transmission integrity in the first seven or eight pages of the chapter, offering the reader a concise synopsis of the issues that mattered to the traditionists of his generation. This portion of the chapter would in itself make interesting material for a discussion of *hadith* criticism.

The long middle portion of the chapter sets forth a sequence of 117 traditions, used by Muslim as evidence to support his principles and methods. They create a vivid impression of the kind of issues that preoccupied a skilled *muhaddith* and the means at his disposal to deal with them; in these narratives, the reader can observe the behavior of a self-regulating intellectual community. In the third portion of the chapter, Muslim enters into a detailed argument about a certain type of defective *isnad*, in which he earnestly refutes the position of another (unnamed) scholar. This discussion is highly technical and burdened with many untranslatable terms, making it difficult reading for the nonspecialist.

Juynboll's translation is perhaps excessively scrupulous: Every word needed in English syntax that is not present in the Arabic text is set aside with brackets, and there are many parenthetical explanations. Even so, untranslatable terms pepper the text and sometimes overwhelm the footnotes. Juynboll also uses the notes and an excursus to pursue discussions found elsewhere in the scholarly literature.

Al-Bukhari and Muslim. *The Translation of the Meanings of Al-lu'lu' wal marjan: A Collection of Agreed-Upon Ahadith from al-Bukhari and Muslim.* Compiled by Fuwad Abdul Baqi; rendered into English by Muhammad Muhsin Khan. 2nd rev. ed. (Lahore: Kazi, 1991). 3 vols.

This edition in English of the *muttafaq 'alaihi* or "agreed upon" texts—those traditions present in both Bukhari and Muslim—seems like a good idea, but the execution is disappointing. The compiler has used the superior structure of Muslim's *Sahih*, then added notes to each narrative indicating where it can be found in Bukhari's collection; the previously published M. M. Khan translation of Bukhari is thus abridged (to 1,906 traditions) and re-arranged in a different sequence. No translation notes or cross-references are provided, nor any scholarly information. There is a simple glossary. Almost one hundred pages of the first volume are devoted to extraneous proselytical material.

ABU DAWUD (d. 889)
Sulayman ibn al-Ash'ath Abu Dawud (AH-boo daw-OOD) al-Sijistani. His name also appears as Sulaiman Abu Da'ud. *Kitab al-sunan*.

The *sahih* collections of Bukhari and Muslim were meant to be exclusive in terms of quality—incorporating only those traditions considered fully reliable—but inclusive in subject matter. Their criterion for inclusion was an intact and unimpeachable *isnad* or chain of transmission. The *sunan* (SOON-nan) works, on the other hand, were assembled to serve a specific purpose: to exemplify legal guidelines or precedents. Recall that *sunan* is the plural of *sunna*, meaning in this context the custom, precedent, or exemplary behavior of the Prophet.

Abu Dawud's was the first of the major *sunan* works, compiling only those *hadiths* pertinent to legal judgment. His approach was explicitly juridical; he consciously excluded traditions concerned with Qur'anic commentary or exegesis, history, asceticism, biographical information about the Companions, and so on. Among the forty-eight hundred traditions selected for his *Sunan* are many with recognizable defects, and those with questionable narrators or chains of transmission are identified. But because they are relevant and applicable to various legal problems, Abu Dawud's decision was to include them with detailed comments evaluating their reliability, thus setting a precedent of his own. "Containing all the legal traditions which may serve as foundations for Islamic rituals and law, and furnishing explicit notes on the authority and value of these traditions, Abu Dawud's book has generally been accepted as the most important work of the *sunan* genre."[9]

Abu Dawud was born in Khurasan and followed the path of the serious traditionist, studying with eminent mentors (among them Ahmad ibn Hanbal) and traveling widely in pursuit of *hadith* knowledge, becoming resident at Basra. He was also a contemporary of al-Tirmidhi, who was one of his students.

Abu Dawud. *Sunan Abu Dawud*. English translation with explanatory notes by Ahmad Hasan (Lahore: Sh. Muhammad Ashraf, 1984). 3 vols.

This edition of the *Kitab al-sunan* (iss-SOON-nan) is legibly printed and properly bound, in three volumes. A brief but useful introduction is provided.

The English prose is readable and direct for the most part, though not without errors.

The editors have taken care to format these traditions clearly, with numbered headings, titles, numbered narratives, and separate paragraphs for the comments of Abu Dawud. The translator's footnotes are distinctly arranged on the page; these notes sometimes refer the reader to other sources where a given issue is discussed, or provide attributed remarks from other authorities. These notes represent the fruit of considerable research and could be of value, though many of them refer to Arabic-language sources. The translator's own explanatory remarks on vocabulary issues are often helpful.

The third volume of this edition provides a very simple but extensive name and subject index. It includes some important legal material: for example, the *Kitab al-aqdiyah* (Book of the Office of Judge) or the *Kitab al-hudud* (Book of Prescribed Punishments). It also includes an amazing amount of sheer trivia, such as the Book of Combing the Hair, or the chapters on the killing of lizards, or on yawning and sneezing.

Other Sources

Portions of Ahmad Hasan's translation of the *Sunan Abu Dawud* are available online at cwis.usc.edu/dept/MSA/fundamentals/hadithsunnah/abudawud. Also, Jeffery's *A Reader on Islam* contains an excerpt from Abu Dawud on clothing; Jeffery's translation and notes are nicely done, the headings are simple and clear, and each narrative is presented with a complete *isnad*. The excerpt provides an obvious instance of the *sunna* of the Prophet as the standard to emulate, in matters great and small.

AL-TIRMIDHI (d.c. 892)

Muhammad ibn 'Isa ibn Sawra al-Tirmidhi (at-tir-MITHI). His name also appears as Tirmizi. *Jami' al-sahih* (The Comprehensive and Reliable) or *Kitab al-sunan*. An abridged version is known as *Kitab al-shama'il*.

A student of Abu Dawud, al-Tirmidhi is believed to have had direct contact with the great traditionists al-Bukhari and Muslim as well. Anecdotes attest to Tirmidhi's prodigious and accurate memory. He traveled to collect *hadiths* and to refine and develop his scholarly methods.

Tirmidhi took Abu Dawud's legal-documentary approach a step further: He selected the traditions used by jurists of the four major Islamic schools of law (see chapter 4) and annotated the narratives to reflect their use by those jurists. The collection's strong emphasis on law accounts for its categorization as one of the *sunan* works, even though its title suggests a wide-ranging, inclusive (*jami‘*) collection. In fact, the work also contains traditions not normally found in *sunan* works, such as Qur'an commentary, information about the Companions, and doctrinal or dogmatic theological material. His *Jami‘* contains almost four thousand hadiths, some of which are found only in Tirmidhi's collection.

Tirmidhi's work includes an important appendix or supplementary volume, the *Kitab al-‘ilal* (al-ILL-al) or *Book of Justifications*, in which he attempted to define and explain his classification methods. It represents a significant early contribution to *hadith* criticism.

Al-Tirmidhi. *The Abridged Shamail-e-Tirmizi.* Translated into English from Gujarati by Murtaz Husain F. Quraishi (Lahore: Progressive Books, 1979).

Tirmidhi himself created a special themed abridgement of his own large collection, consisting only of *hadiths* describing the personal characteristics of the Prophet. This subset is known as the *Kitab al-shama'il* (ash-sha-MAA-il), the Book of Virtues or Qualities. It includes narratives recounting minute details of the Prophet Muhammad's appearance and behavior, right down to the socks he wore and his favorite foods, and the number of gray hairs in his beard.[10]

Only this portion of Tirmidhi's important *hadith* corpus can be obtained in English—and unfortunately, this is a very inadequate edition. A Gujarati-language version has been rendered into awkward English, with many annotations and accretions from an Urdu commentary. Further notes were added for this English edition, so that it is difficult to detect any traces of Tirmidhi's actual text. Although the material is interesting, this edition would be difficult to use for classroom study or research.

M. Hidayat Hosain, "Translation of Ash-Shama'il of Tirmizi," *Islamic Culture* 7:3–8:4 (1933 and 1934), 396–409; 561–72; 46–54; 273–89; 364–86; 531–49.

Hosain's translation of the *Kitab al-shama'il* appeared in the quarterly journal *Islamic Culture* in six installments. (This journal was published in Hyderabad beginning in 1927; Marmaduke Pickthall was one of its editors.) The first installment appeared in the July 1933 issue and the last, in October 1934. Page numbers are given above for each of the issues.

One narrator is named for each *hadith*, and these persons are identified in footnotes. The notes also identify persons named within the narrative, define untranslatable terms, and provide background information; the rather strange convention is used of beginning the footnoting on every page with number 1, even when notes run on to the next page. Due to page-numbering aberrations, some of the cross-references are unusable.

Nevertheless, this is a valuable source, suitable for careful study.

AL-NASA'I (d. 915)
Abu 'Abdul Rahman Ahmad ibn 'Ali ibn Shu'ayb al-Nasa'i (an-nas-SAA-ee). *Kitab al-sunan.*

Born in Khurasan province, al-Nasa'i was trained from childhood in the collection and criticism of *hadith*. It seems he traveled extensively in search of traditions and is believed to have lived and studied in Egypt and Damascus; according to some accounts, he was a pupil of Abu Dawud. His willingness to speak out on the merits of 'Ali and in opposition to the Umayyad caliphs led to his persecution and abuse, and he is considered a martyr as a result.

His original compilation contained over five thousand *hadiths*, but among them many were weak or unreliable. An abridged version known as *Al-mujtaba* or *Sunan al-sughra* was meant to eliminate these and is now viewed as canonical (though not by all authorities). Nasa'i concentrated upon legal traditions, especially ritual or ceremonial details.

Al-Nasa'i. *Sunan Nasa'i: English Translation with Arabic Text.* Rendered into English by Muhammad Iqbal Siddiqi (Lahore: Kazi, 1994). 2 vols.

Two volumes of the *Sunan Nasa'i* have been published in English, but very few library collections own the second; vol. 1 is somewhat more accessible. It contains the first ten "books" or themed sections of the *Sunan*. Unfortunately, these are quite limited in content.

The first four books are those obsessively concerned with ritual contamination and cleanliness in an environment where there is little water for washing; physical and sexual impurity are discussed in great detail. The remaining books dwell on the performance of prayer and mosque worship, appointed times, wording and gestures for prayer, rules governing prayer times during illness or travel, how to remedy an error or missed prayer, and so on. This material is found in almost all *hadith* collections, but it stands isolated here in vol. 1.

The edition provides the text of each *hadith* in Arabic, then in English. One source narrator is identified. Some biographical information about major narrators is offered, along with other background information about *hadith* in general; there is, however, no scholarly apparatus that would assist research.

IBN MAJAH (d. 887)
Abu 'Abdullah Muhammad ibn Yazid ibn Majah (ibbin MAH-jah) al-Qazwini. His name also appears as Ibn Madja or Maja. *Kitab al-sunan.*

Born at Qazwin in Persia, Ibn Majah was a trained traditionist who traveled to Iraq, Syria, Egypt, and elsewhere engaged in the collection and study of *hadith*. His *Sunan* contains more than forty-three hundred narratives, including more than a thousand that do not exist in the other canonical collections. These unique narratives, however, are not well attested, and some authorities are highly critical of Ibn Majah's work. It was eventually ranked among the Six Books by most authorities, beginning in the twelfth century.

Ibn Majah. *Sunan ibn-i-Majah.* **English version by Muhammad Tufail Ansari (Lahore: Kazi, 1993–1996). 5 vols.**

This edition of Ibn Majah's *Sunan* incorporates a minimum of prefatory matter. The text of each tradition is printed in Arabic and English, with one named narrator. Often, there is a comment indicating any concerns about the soundness of the narrative, breaks in the chain of transmission, or the presence of a controversial transmitter.

Ansari has added footnotes where a technical term in Arabic has no equivalent in English, or where an idiomatic expression demands a paraphrase or clarification. This is particularly the case in the first section, in which significant theological precepts are put forth, often in highly concentrated sayings using specialized vocabulary. For example, in Hadith 54, footnotes offer definitions of *aya muhkama*, *sunna qa'ima*, and *farida 'adila*, three key components of religious authority. The footnotes may not offer enough explanation for the English reader, but they do serve notice that a translation issue exists.

Anthologies, Selections, and Digests

In addition to the Six Books commonly accepted as authoritative, many other collections of *hadith* are well known and respected by the Sunni Muslim community. Also, a number of digests or anthologies were created in later centuries, after the original books had attained their canonical status; these digests bring together narratives from a variety of prominent collections. Some of these are compiled on a topical basis: for example, traditions from all of the major authorities on issues of family or social behavior, or stories that form an anecdotal biography of the Prophet; a well-known selection of *hadith* narratives on the topic of prayer compiled by Ibn Taymiyya was translated by Ezzedin Ibrahim and Denys Johnson-Davies and published as *The Goodly Word* (Cambridge: Islamic Texts Society, 2000). Some selections or digests cover the full range of topics typically found in *musannafat* or classified works.

AL-NAWAWI (d.c. 1277)

Muhyi al-Din Abu Zakariyya Yahya ibn Sharaf al-Din al-Nawawi (an-NA-wa-wee). *Kitab al-arba'in* (Book of the Forty) or *Matn al-arba'in fi al-ahadith al-sahiha al-nabawiyya.*

Along with the forming of the great canonical collections, another custom arose—selecting a group of forty *hadith* narratives that ordinary believers could learn and memorize. A saying from Muhammad is recorded in which he promises a blessing to anyone who preserves at least forty traditions, inspiring the creation of the *arba'in* (ar-ba-EEN) books or "forties." The most popular of the "forties" was that of al-Nawawi, a prolific Syrian jurist who wrote important legal texts of the Shafi'i school (see chapter 4). He chose his forty traditions intending that each one should "set forth one of the great points of religious belief" and that each should be attested a *sahih*, or genuine tradition.[11] The believer is expected to regard these as points to which obedience is necessary.

Al-Nawawi. An-Nawawi's Forty Hadith: An Anthology of the Sayings of the Prophet Muhammad. Translated by Ezzedin Ibrahim and Denys Johnson-Davies (Cambridge: Islamic Texts Society, 1997).

Nawawi's much treasured selection of *hadith* is suited to the purpose of training believers in faith and obedience. This attractive and convenient edition is also appropriate for classroom use. A clear, concise introduction defines the translators' intentions, methods, and editorial decisions: for example, the transliteration system and vocabulary chosen, the English version of quotes from the Qur'an used, and so on.

Each tradition appears in English with a simplified indicator of its origin (not a full chain of transmission) and with a note of the source from which Nawawi drew it. The six great books are represented, especially Bukhari and Muslim (and including Ibn Majah, although Nawawi did not recognize that book's canonical status), plus Malik's *Muwatta'* and the *Musnad* of Ahmad ibn Hanbal. In some cases, a detailed ranking of the soundness of a certain *hadith* is noted, though all are considered by Nawawi to be genuine. On the facing page, the Arabic text is found. Helpful footnotes identify persons mentioned, explain unusual expressions or idioms, and suggest interpretations of difficult passages.

Nawawi's selection of forty-two traditions includes several sayings and a few stories (among them the famous encounter with the angel Gabriel, who inquires, "O Muhammad, tell me about Islam"). It also provides one *hadith qudsi*, a type of sayings-tradition in which Allah speaks in the words of the Prophet using a first-person form of address. (A *hadith qudsi* does not have the sacred status of the exact words of Allah as recorded in the Qur'an, but is considered edifying and instructive.) The traditions chosen by Nawawi touch upon vital doctrines in Islam, especially upon the indispensable duties of all believers and the minimum expectations required of those who hope to enter Paradise: for example, issues of eschatology, soteriology, ecclesiology, and ethics. As such, they could serve as valuable discussion material for introductory courses in Islam or in comparative religion.

Al-Nawawi. *The Forty Traditions of An-Nawawi*. In Arthur Jeffery, *A Reader on Islam* (The Hague: Mouton, 1962), 142–60.

Another accessible translation of the same text, capably done. The wording and notes are slightly different from the Islamic Texts Society edition above; it might be desirable to have students in a seminar read the different translations and compare them. *A Reader on Islam* is widely held in academic libraries. Jeffery's version is also available in microform as part of *Islamfiche: Readings from Islamic Primary Sources*, series I–II (Zug, Switzerland: IDC, 1987). The microform set is a product of the Islamic Teaching Materials Project, under the auspices of the American Council of Learned Societies, and it has already been approved for reproduction for classroom use on a nonprofit basis.

Al-Nawawi. *Gardens of the Righteous: Riyadh as-Salihin of Imam Nawawi*. Translated by Muhammad Zafrulla Khan; foreword by C. E. Bosworth (London: Curzon Press, 1975).

This is not an edition of Nawawi's "forty," but a full compilation of about nineteen hundred *hadiths* in a fluent but formal English translation. One narrator and the documentary source are given, but there are no footnotes. A subject index is provided, functioning like a simple concordance to vocabulary in the text. The traditions are organized into small chapters, headed by a chosen verse from the Qur'an, which is illustrated or exemplified by the narratives.

AL-KHATIB AL-TIBRIZI (fl. 1337)
Wali al-Din (wally id-DEEN) Muhammad ibn 'Abdullah al-Khatib al-Tibrizi (al-ka-TEEB at-tib-REEZI). *Mishkat al-masabih* or The Niche for Lamps.

The *Mishkat* is a revised and expanded edition of a much earlier work by a traditionist known as al-Baghawi (d.c. 1117) called *Masabih al-sunna*. Baghawi selected narratives from many tradition collections, organizing them into a new *musannaf* work. Traditions from Bukhari or Muslim appear first under each topical heading, then those from the other canonical works, Ibn Hanbal's *Musnad*, or various prominent books; there is sometimes a third section of related but less pertinent traditions. Al-Khatib al-Tibrizi (also referred to as Wali al-Din) refined Baghawi's collection, adding about one thousand narratives, clearly identifying each source, and developing the notes that indicate whether a certain *hadith* is of sound quality, good or weak. The result is a useful digest of about five thousand traditions, a representative sample of many works, convenient for personal study or for instructing pupils; it is frequently mentioned in the secondary literature.

Al-Khatib al-Tibrizi. *Mishkat al-Masabih: English Translation with Explanatory Notes*. Edited and translated by James Robson (Lahore: Sh. Muhammad Ashraf, 1960–1965). 4 vols.

The *Mishkat* exists in numerous English translations; the foremost critical edition is that of Orientalist scholar James Robson, available in many libraries. Robson provides an informative introduction and restrained footnotes that clarify translation problems, supply cross-references to the Qur'an and to other portions of the *Mishkat*, and some helpful identifications and definitions. Each of the four volumes has a detailed table of contents. The fourth also contains some research helps: indexes of Qur'an quotations, geographical terms, tribes and sects, and two separate indexes of personal names—one for persons mentioned in a narrative and another for persons named in an *isnad* or chain of transmission.

Although the printing and paper quality of this particular edition are poor, the formatting is clear. The organizing principles of the *Mishkat* can be perceived in any of the brief, coherent sections: for example, the chapters on washing and shrouding the dead or on visiting graves (bk. V, chs. 4 and 8).

MUHAMMAD 'ALI (d. 1951)

Muhammad 'Ali. A *Manual of Hadith*. Preface by C. E. Bosworth. 2nd ed. (London: Curzon Press, 1978). His name often appears with the honorific Maulana.

Leader of the moderate Lahore branch of the Ahmadiyya movement, Maulana Muhammad 'Ali was a major interpreter and translator of the Qur'an (see chapter 1) and directed a very important publishing program in English and Urdu.[12] This volume is not a manual in the sense of a critical handbook or guide to the *hadith* literature; rather, it is a selection of representative traditions designed to give the modern reader an impression of the *hadith* corpus and its importance for "the daily life of the average Muslim and the performance of his religious duties."[13]

About three-quarters of the traditions included in this compilation are taken from the *Sahih* of Bukhari, but many other sources are sampled and clearly identified (among them the *Musnad*, *Muwatta'*, and *Mishkat*, and all of the other canonical collections). One narrator is named, and the text of each tradition is provided in English and Arabic. Muhammad 'Ali has organized them into intelligible chapters headed by relevant verses from the Qur'an and a brief expository introduction or summation of salient points in the *hadiths* that follow. Footnotes point out translation and vocabulary issues and offer an informative commentary that is not for the most part sectarian or apologetic. The chapters are held to a convenient length; the reader can easily comprehend all at once the chapters on marriage and divorce, food and drink, and so on. The edition would have been improved by a detailed index. In the Curzon edition and many others, it is held in hundreds of libraries.

The Shi'i Collections

The major collections of *hadith*, especially the Six Books, are respected in Shi'i Islam, thoroughly studied and selectively absorbed into the fabric of the faith. But the issue of authority in the community after the death of the Prophet is of critical importance to Shi'i doctrine; the legacy of his words and deeds is, for them, best preserved and transmitted through 'Ali and the Imams, and the Imams themselves are the originators of authoritative words and deeds.

The body of Shi'i *hadith* combines, therefore, the prophetic traditions (*al-hadith al-nabawi*) with those of the Imams (*al-hadith al-walawi*).[14] This additional material often reflects the distinctiveness of Shi'i theology and esoteric knowledge and tends toward the metaphysical rather than the juridical. Also, these traditions often dwell explicitly upon the legitimacy of the succession of 'Ali and the doctrine of the imamate: the necessity of twelve Imams, the doctrine of Occultation, and so on. Sometimes, these sayings become argumentative or polemical. When the Shi'a have experienced resistance or rejection from the Sunni community or controversy with certain sectarian movements, these texts have served to validate their unique perspectives and beliefs.

The primary *hadith* collections of Shi'i Islam, a set of four "canonical" works that roughly compare to the Six Books, took shape in writing during a period of great scholarly productivity under the Buyid dynasty (932–1062 CE). Many others exist, but four are generally regarded as most authoritative. One of these is al-Kulayni's *Kitab al-kafi*, described below. Another is the *Man la yahduruhu al-faqih* or "[Book for] One Who Is Not in the Presence of a Jurist" by Muhammad ibn Babawayhi (or Babuyah) al-Qummi (or Kummi), who died in 991 CE. Two more were written by the same eminent tradition-ist, Abu Ja'far Muhammad ibn Hasan al-Tusi (d.c. 1067). These are the *Tadhib al-ahkam* or "Refinement of the Judgments" and *Al-ibtisar fima ukhtulifa fihi min al-akhbar* or "Reflection upon Disparities among the Traditions." In the last title, one notes that the word *khabar* (plural, *akhbar*) meaning "re-port" or "news," may be used by the Shi'a as a synonym for *hadith*.

An excerpt from the work by Ibn Babawayhi on the subject of religious taxation is found in the anthology *Classical Islam* (London; New York: Rout-ledge, 2003), 50–53.

AL-KULAYNI (d.c. 940)

Abu Ja'far Muhammad ibn Ya'qub al-Kulayni (al-coo-LAY-nee or coo-LIE-nee). His name also appears as ibn Ya'kub al-Kulini or Kalini. *Kitab al-kafi* or *Al-kafi fi 'ilm al-din*, or *What Is Sufficient for Religious Knowl-edge*. The title of the first section of this work, *Usul al-kafi*, is well known and often referenced.

The foremost of the early Imami (also called Ithna 'Ashari or "twelver") Shi'i tradition collections is that of al-Kulayni, to which later collections re-fer. It contains one of the early *usul* or "fundamentals" works, collections of the teachings of the Imams; it is said that there were once as many as four hundred of these *usul* works, of which a few are extant in manuscript form.

Al-Kulayni was born into a family already distinguished as religious schol-ars; his uncle was the primary religious figure in the city of Rayy in Persia, at that time a center of intellectual activity and expression. He had the oppor-tunity to study with the respected transmitters of Shi'i traditions of the time, including some at Nishapur (where both Bukhari and Muslim had once taught). Al-Kulayni lived during the period after the disappearance of the Twelfth Imam in 878 CE, when four successors were representing the Imam among the Shi'i community. This period ended with the Great Occultation in 941 CE. Therefore, Kulayni is regarded as close to these events and in a good position to collect and record the traditions the community needed to guide them in the absence of the Imam.

Kulayni's lifework, the *Kitab al-kafi* (KAA-fee), is meant to establish the legitimacy and necessity of the imamate and to develop it as the authorita-tive basis for theology and law. The traditions compiled in the first portion of the work deal almost entirely with these doctrinal issues and run into hun-dreds of pages in eight "books" or subdivisions. The second portion, in twenty-six books, contains the legal material familiar in all extensive *hadith* collections: rules governing ritual purity and cleanliness, prayer and worship, alms, fasting, pilgrimage, marriage and family relations, death and burial, food and drink, criminal punishment, wills and inheritance, juridical proceedings, and so on. The third portion contains stories from Islamic history, the lives of the Prophet and the Imams, and other inspirational or hortatory material. Kulayni's preface indicates not only that he intended the entire collection to be comprehensive and inclusive, but also that he considered the traditions he compiled to have sound chains of transmission. The compilers of the other three of the four canonical Shi'i collections, Ibn Babawayhi and al-Tusi, rely upon Kulayni as a quotable source.

Al-Kulayni. Al-Kafi. Translated by Sayyid Muhammad Hasan Rizvi; edited by Muhammad Rida al-Ja'fari (Tehran: Group of Muslim Brothers; Karachi: Khurasan Islamic Research Centre, 1978). Vol. 1, pt. I , bks. I–II.

The first major portion of Kulayni's work is the doctrinal collection known as *Al-usul min al-kafi*, or *Usul al-kafi*, or simply *Al-usul* (os-SOOL). This title is sometimes the one under which the work is cataloged in library collections. Some library records are irregular in their volume and part numbering as well. Two of the subsections or "books" in this portion of the work have been translated into English and published; they are to this date the only readily available English-language sources for any of the four canonical Shi'i works.

This edition, produced by the World Organization for Islamic Services, is an interesting one. The first part issued seems to be a sort of rough draft. Some additional work went on between the publishing of book I, "The Book of Reason and Ignorance," and book II, "The Book of Excellence of Knowledge"; the reader finds that the same foreword in English is somewhat easier to read in book II. The indexing is also much improved. However, there is prefatory material about Kulayni and his work in book I that is not reproduced in book II.

The format is parallel, with the unpointed text printed on the top half of each page and the English translation below. A very obscure numbering system seems to do more harm than good; the hyphenation of these numbers in book II is unexplained. An index of narrators is linked with a table of the Prophet and his line of descendants or successors, but the same individual is known by different honorifics, and several of the Imams have very similar names.

Nevertheless, the editor made the wise decision to reproduce each chain of transmission in its entirety, so the reader can see a host of examples of an approved Shi'i *isnad*. The links back to an Imam as the originator of a certain tradition are plainly seen in many cases. The largest number of narratives originated with Ja'far al-Sadiq, the Sixth Imam (d. 765), considered the most important progenitor of Imami law.

Book I is presented as a continuous stream of traditions on a single theme: the excellence of reason (discernment, understanding, comprehension) as the faculty that distinguishes the worthy and obedient from the impious and ignorant. The structure of book II is more evident to the reader and conforms to an intelligible table of contents; it is possible to read and comprehend one chapter at a time (e.g., "On Quoting Books," "On Blind Following," "On Innovations," or "On the Accountability of the Learned").

AL-MAJLISI (d.c. 1699)

Muhammad Baqir al-Majlisi (MADGE-lis-ee). His name also appears as Bakir al-Madjlisi. *Bihar al-anwar* or *Oceans of Lights* (or, *Rivers of Lights*).

During the Safavid era—another great renaissance of scholarly and artistic activity in Persia—a traditionist arose who would become the revered master of Imami or Ithna 'Ashari ("twelver") Shi'i *hadith*. The son of a prominent scholar of the same name, he is sometimes known as Majlisi al-Thani or Majlisi the Second, or as 'Allameh Majlisi. He first became acquainted with Islamic law and jurisprudence, Qur'an commentary, theology, philosophy, and mysticism under his father's tutelage, but decided to specialize in a field that was somewhat neglected at the time, the science of tradition.

He began collecting Shi'i traditions in Arabic and Persian in 1659 and completed his massive compilation in 1694; his *Bihar al-anwar* has been published in over one hundred volumes. William C. Chittick refers to the collection as "the standard reference work for all Shi'ite studies."[15] Etan Kohlberg describes it as "an incomparable mine of valuable information on Shi'i history, doctrine and tradition" derived from a wide range of sources, and observes that Majlisi "scrupulously mentions the source of each report which he quotes, and his quotations are always accurate."[16] The work contributed to a resurgence of interest in the traditions and in Shi'i faith and practice, and is a focus not only of scholarly attention but also of popular devotion among Shi'a today.

It should be noted that Majlisi also served as a senior jurist under two of the Safavid monarchs and in that capacity dealt harshly with unorthodox and sectarian minorities, including the Sufis and Zoroastrians, and was particularly zealous in opposition to Sunni Islam. The contents of the *Bihar* have also been regarded with disapproval by some modern Iranian critics (such as 'Ali Shari'ati) for conveying a distorted image of the imamate and political authority.[17]

Al-Majlisi. *Bihar al-anwar*. In William Chittick, *A Shi'ite Anthology* (Albany: State University of New York Press, 1981). Selected and with a foreword by 'Allamah Sayyid Muhammad Husayn Tabataba'i; translated with explanatory notes by William C. Chittick; under the direction of and with an introduction by Seyyed Hossein Nasr.

The complicated statement of responsibility for this attractive little book is important. The 'Allameh Tabataba'i ranks among the most influential Imami scholars of the twentieth century (see chapter 3); he personally selected the excerpts from significant Shi'i sources incorporated into this publication. His primary interpreter to Western readers, Seyyed Hossein Nasr, supervised the production of this work and provided a very helpful, concise, and erudite introduction. The translation of these difficult texts and the composition of indispensable comments and notes was done by William C. Chittick.

The selections are arranged by theme and by source: A key to their origin is provided on pages 142–43 of the work, headed "Bibliography." Part I is made up of selections from Majlisi's *Bihar al-anwar*. The chosen material is theologically complex and offers a glimpse of the metaphysical or philosophical subtlety of the *tawhid* doctrine, the essential Unity of God. The absolute transcendence of God, the problems of immanence, revelation, epistemology, and divine sovereignty are evident from the first excerpt on. Some of the syntax displays the dense texture, assonance, and alliteration of poetry rather than prose. Chittick indicates these passages carefully with parenthetical terms and extremely valuable endnotes. His notes also identify allusions to the Qur'an, place individual statements in the larger context of Islamic theology, and direct the reader to scholarly sources for further information.

The chosen portions of the *Bihar* also serve to represent the most significant originators of Shi'i *hadith*: the Prophet, then the First, Fifth, Sixth, Seventh, and Eighth Imams. The narratives are presented without complete chains of transmission. A useful appendix explains very briefly the concept of the imamate, the conflict over succession, and the identities of each of the twelve imams. The book's index lists mainly personal names and Arabic vocabulary.

An excerpt from Chittick's anthology is also available in microform as part of the *Islamfiche* collection, along with brief but pertinent introductory remarks. It is taken from an edition published by the Muhammadi Trust of Great Britain and Northern Ireland in 1980.

Hadith Criticism

As we have seen, early Muslim communities began the effort to collect and preserve stories recording the *sunna* (sayings and customary behavior) of the

Prophet. And as soon as this effort began, the need arose to verify the authenticity of these traditions, to assess the validity of their transmission through the *isnad* or chain of witnesses, and to assemble systematically the information needed to accomplish these tasks. The scholarly discipline that emerged is known as *usul al-hadith* or *'ilm al-hadith* (plural, *'ulum*). The word *usul* (os-SOOL) denotes principles or fundamentals; *'ilm* or *'ulum* (ILM or ol-LOOM) refers to knowledge or science.

Generally speaking, the fulcrum on which *hadith* criticism rested was the *isnad*: the exact method of transmission from one authority to another, and the character or veracity of those authorities (the *rijal*) and their vulnerability to error or misconduct. The content or body of the narrative (the *matn*) was for the most part not the focus of *hadith* criticism.

The medieval literature of tradition criticism is vast, and little of it is accessible in English. One of the earliest sources was discussed above: the introductory chapter to Muslim's *Sahih*, translated by G. H. A. Juynboll. Muslim mentions in it some of the issues of concern to him in the compilation of his authoritative and well-organized tradition collection.

Among the first to attempt a comprehensive summary or guide to the critical discipline was Ibn Khallad al-Ramahurmuzi (d. 971). Later, the great al-Khatib al-Baghdadi (d. 1071) created his *Ta'rikh Baghdad* (*History* or *Chronicle of Baghdad*), a classic work compiling the biographies of more than seventy-eight hundred individuals, intended to serve as a reference work for *muhaddithun* (traditionists or *hadith* scholars), enabling them to evaluate the persons involved in transmitting a particular tradition. Many other scholars contributed their efforts to this discipline as well.

AL-HAKIM AL-NAYSABURI (d. 1014)

Muhammad Abu 'Abdallah ibn al-Bayyi' al-Naysaburi (an-ni-sa-BOO-ree). His name also appears as Naisaburi or Nisaburi; he is often referred to by rank as al-Hakim (al-ha-KEEM). *Al-madkhal ilal iklil* or *Al-madkhal ila ma'rifat al-iklil*, or *An Introduction to the Understanding of Tradition* (literally, "The Crown," title of another work).

Born at Nishapur in northeastern Persia in 933, this scholar consequently became known as al-Naysaburi (one should be aware that some other scholars from that city are also known by this appellation); because he served for a time as a religious judge, he acquired the title of al-Hakim, the Wise. He followed the path of the properly trained traditionist, traveling to Baghdad, the Hejaz, and elsewhere, learning *hadith*. However, his forte became not the collecting of narratives but the analysis of the tradition corpus and the principles of *hadith* scholarship.

Al-Hakim wrote several important works of *hadith* criticism, of which the best known, *Kitab ma'rifat 'ulum al-hadith*, is not available in English; a related work is discussed below.

Al-Hakim al-Naisaburi. *An Introduction to the Science of Tradition.* Edited with introduction, translation, and notes by James Robson (London: The Royal Asiatic Society of Great Britain and Ireland, 1953).

This meticulous critical edition of Naysaburi's *Al-madkhal ilal iklil* in its entirety (about thirty-seven pages long) was created by Orientalist scholar James Robson, and it benefits from his extensive knowledge. He has compared several manuscripts of the work and made explicit text-critical decisions; his introduction and footnotes are devoted to the accuracy of the text and its conformity with evidence from other medieval authorities. Robson has also provided an index of persons mentioned by name, and the handwritten, unpointed text of the entire work in Arabic.

The work begins with a set of significant traditions on the analysis of *hadith*, presented with their complete chains of transmission. Al-Hakim then discusses the history of *hadith* collection and the problem of validity or reliability. He then produces five categories of sound traditions about which there is a consensus among scholars; then come five categories of sound but disputed traditions; then ten classes of invalidated traditions, with detailed explanations of their defects, and some concluding remarks. This fascinating material might be too challenging for the beginning student, but could be assigned to more advanced students of medieval religious literature, law, or comparative religion.

A selection of Orientalist editions of primary texts has been reissued as *Theology, Ethics and Metaphysics: Royal Asiatic Society Classics of Islam* (London; New York: Routledge, 2003). Included in vol. 5 is Robson's edition of Naysaburi—a facsimile of the original publication, complete with Robson's handwritten Arabic text. This welcome reissue should make it possible for many more libraries to add these long out-of-print works to their collections.

IBN AL-SALAH AL-SHAHRAZURI (d. 1245)
Taqi al-Din 'Uthman ibn 'Abd al-Rahman ibn al-Salah (ibbin as-sa-LAH) al-Shahrazuri. *Kitab ma'rifat anwa' 'ilm al-hadith* or *Book about Understanding the Categories of the Science of Hadith.*

The son of a Shafi'i jurist, Ibn al-Salah was first trained in the law and served as a respected jurist himself in Damascus. At the same time, he became widely respected as an authority on the critical study of the *hadith* literature; he taught at several of the leading institutions of his time, where students flocked to his classes. He lectured extensively on the work of al-Hakim al-Naysaburi and began to compose a commentary on al-Hakim's *Kitab ma'rifat 'ulum al-hadith*. This commentary apparently turned into Ibn Salah's own treatise setting forth sixty-five "categories" for the evaluation of *hadith* narratives and their transmitters. His work, often known as the *Muqaddima* or *Introduction*, is regarded as a classic manual on this subject. Other authorities (including Ibn Kathir) have built upon his work with commentaries and annotated editions; his writings are still among the fundamental source materials for *hadith* studies today.

Ibn al-Salah al-Shahrazuri. *An Introduction to the Science of the Hadith*. *Kitab ma'rifat anwa' 'ilm al-hadith*. Translated by Eerick Dickinson; edited by Muneer Fareed (Reading, UK: Garnet, 2005).

This edition of Ibn al-Salah's work was created in Qatar as a part of the Centre for Muslim Contribution to Civilization project, publishing new scholarly translations of important but hitherto unavailable historic texts in English. This edition has the advantages of clear page formatting (often in outline form), enumerated lists, and a detailed table of contents, which itself serves as a convenient summary of the issues typically involved in *hadith* criticism. Important vocabulary is translated, then transliterated within parentheses. Abundant footnotes identify the scores of persons mentioned in the text, provide references to other medieval authorities, call attention to translation problems, and supply some helpful clarification and comment. The translator has also created an informative introduction and an index.

AL-SHAHID AL-THANI (d.c. 1558)
Zayn al-Din ibn 'Ali ibn Ahmad al-Shahid al-Thani (ash-sha-HEED ath-THAA-nee). His name also appears as Zainuddin; his customary appellation means "The Second Martyr." *Dirayat al-hadith* or *Knowledge* (or *Study*, or *Intellectual Investigation*) *of Hadith*.

The specific knowledge required to study and analyze Shi'i *hadith* was in the hands of scholars such as al-Shahid al-Thani (who is referenced by Majlisi in his *Bihar al-anwar*). He composed the first systematic Imami or "twelver" Shi'i text on *hadith* criticism; however, he is primarily known for his writings on jurisprudence and the locus of Imami judicial authority. Once honored and appointed to a major teaching post by the Ottoman Sultan, Suleiman the Magnificent, he was later persecuted and killed and is remembered as a martyr.

Al-Shahid al-Thani. *Dirayat al-hadith*. In 'Abd al-Hadi al-Fadli, *Introduction to Hadith*. Translated by Nazmina Virjee (London: Islamic College for Advanced Studies Press, 2002).

This work as published contains two parts: the treatise by al-Shahid outlining the fundamental issues in *hadith* criticism and a much longer introduction to the *hadith* literature generally, written by another Imami scholar from that distinctive confessional viewpoint. Both portions are translated into precise and elegant English by Nazmina Virjee.

The *Dirayat* is a beautifully organized and concise synopsis of the nature of *hadith* reports, their classification and assessment, the extensive and complex specialized vocabulary of *hadith* criticism, and the qualities of acceptable transmitters and their methods. Only about twenty-four pages in length, it is fairly dense with technical terms; nevertheless, the fluent modern English and clear formatting make it readable for the attentive student. Helpful though sparse footnotes clarify translation issues, define terms, and provide some background information.

The *Introduction to Hadith* by 'Abd al-Hadi al-Fadli, found in the same volume, may be of interest to some readers as an example of an understanding of the *hadith* literature that reflects the unique assumptions and doctrinal preoccupations of the Shi'a. It includes some noteworthy reference features, such as a list of recognized and approved narrators, reporters, and transmitters who were women (pp. 199–204). The book is also supplied with a glossary, bibliography, and general index.

Modern Issues

As the *hadith* literature attracted the attention of Western scholars in the modern era, the scholarly debate became more and more complex and politically sensitive. Some Orientalist scholars—notably Aloys Sprenger, Ignacz Goldziher, and Joseph Schacht—rejected the very notion of *hadith* historicity and analyzed the literature as an artifact of the later Muslim community that establishes no credible record of the Prophet's own point in time. These scholars tended to characterize the traditions as the product of later sectarian or factional movements seeking to anchor their ideas and practices in spurious prophetic authority. The views of these scholars have been challenged by others as biased and excessively negative.

A defense of at least some aspects of the *hadith* legacy was undertaken by other scholars, such as Nabia Abbott, Fazlur Rahman, M. M. Azami, and Fuat Sezgin. They have attempted to apply the methods of modern criticism to recapture and reinterpret more affirmatively the *hadith* literature and the history of its formation.

Some Muslim reformers (among them Sayyid Ahmad Khan, Muhammad 'Abduh, Rashid Rida, and Mahmud Abu Rayyah) tried to detach contemporary faith from what they experienced as a limiting or misleading adherence to the ways of the past; they urged modern believers to use their own judgment to reassess the traditions for harmony with the Qur'an and relevance to today's world. The fundamentalist or reactionary movements tend to seize upon the traditions as a tool for conforming their own lives to the prophetic *sunna*, and disallow any modern scholarly criticism of the *hadith* corpus.

A compelling example of the keen interest of today's Muslims in this largely medieval literature is the work of the contemporary Egyptian writer Muhammad al-Ghazzaly (or Ghazali). In his controversial book, *The Prophet's Sunnah between the People of Hadith and the People of Fiqh* (Cairo: Dar al-Shuruq, 1991), he passionately exposes attempts by militant Muslim extremists to justify their behavior through a selective misuse of *hadith*, as well as the efforts of certain Western interests to discredit legitimate Islamic revival or renewal movements.

Ghazzaly claims that extremist leaders and teachers derive their opinions from misconstrued authentic traditions or from unreliable and marginal ones, without understanding or acknowledging their abuse of these sources. The result is a distorted set of proof texts supporting an ideology that is out of conformity to the Qur'an and the actual thrust of the preserved traditions. He denounces these teachers as dangerous, half-educated, self-appointed judges who issue invalid opinions with the apparent weight of an authoritative text behind them.

Ghazzaly endeavors to reestablish the proper relationship of revelation, precedent, interpretation, and law: to place the Qur'an first, then the *sunna* properly studied and understood, then the work of reasoning and application of valid Islamic principles to contemporary life, with the acceptance of a degree of diversity in interpretation and its formulation into social policy and law.[18]

It may be difficult for Western students to appreciate the vital existential significance of the classics of Islamic literature for believers today. This body of knowledge has an immediacy and a personal relevance that is not often associated with medieval texts, the way in which the tradition is appropriated has serious implications and consequences. It is safe to say that no one can comprehend the current shape of Muslim cultures or social and political movements without some familiarity with the import and influence of the *sunna* and *hadith*.

Notes

1. G. H. A. Juynboll, *The Authenticity of the Tradition Literature: Discussions in Modern Egypt* (Leiden: Brill, 1969), 5.

2. Majid Khadduri, trans. and ed., *Islamic Jurisprudence: Shafi'i's Risala* (Baltimore: Johns Hopkins University Press, 1961), 111 and 119.

3. There is some scholarly dispute about the date and authorship of this work. A highly technical discussion of the issue is found in Norman Calder, *Studies in Early Muslim Jurisprudence* (Oxford: Clarendon, 1993), 20–38.

4. Alfred Guillaume, *The Traditions of Islam* (Oxford: Clarendon, 1924), 20.

5. Joseph Schacht, "Malik ibn Anas," *EI2*, v. 6: 264.

6. Bukhari's criteria for evaluating traditions are not spelled out in the *Sahih*; later scholars have derived them from the text. See Mohammed Zubayr Siddiqi, *Hadith Literature* (Cambridge: Islamic Texts Society, 1993), 56.

7. 'Abdul Hamid Siddiqi, *Sahih Muslim* (New Delhi: Kitab Bhavan, 2000), vii. See also James Robson, *Mishkat al-Masabih* (Lahore: Sh. Muhammad Ashraf, 1963), vii.

8. G. H. A. Juynboll, "Muslim b. al-Hadjdjadj," *EI2*, v. 7: 692.

9. Muhammad Zubayr Siddiqi, *Hadith Literature* (Cambridge: Islamic Texts Society, 1993), 63.

10. A fascinating discussion of the *shama'il* literature, including Tirmidhi's, is found in Annemarie Schimmel, *And Muhammad Is His Messenger: The Veneration of the Prophet in Islamic Piety* (Chapel Hill: University of North Carolina Press, 1985), 32–45.

11. Arthur Jeffery, *A Reader on Islam* (The Hague: Mouton, 1962), 144.

12. For an overview of the movement and its issues, see Yohanan Friedmann, "Ahmadiyah," *OEMIW*, v. 1: 54–57.

13. Muhammad Ali, *A Manual of Hadith* (London: Curzon, 1978), viii. From the preface by C. E. Bosworth.

14. William C. Chittick, *A Shi'ite Anthology* (Albany: State University of New York Press, 1981), 6. From the introduction by Seyyed Hossein Nasr.

15. Chittick, *Shi'ite Anthology*, 17.

16. Etan Kohlberg, "Shi'i Hadith," *Arabic Literature to the End of the Umayyad Period* (Cambridge: Cambridge University Press, 1983), 307.

17. For more detail on these issues, see the sources cited by Abdul-Hadi Hairi in "Madjlisi, Mulla Muhammad Bakir," *EI2*, v. 5: 1088.

18. Ghazzaly's work is not yet available in English. For a cogent and concise account of his positions, see Raymond William Baker, *Islam Without Fear: Egypt and the New Islamists* (Cambridge: Harvard University Press, 2003), 90–93.

CHAPTER THREE

~

Exegesis of the Qur'an: Tafsir

The role of the Qur'an as the bedrock of Muslim life and thought can hardly be overstated. But this heavenly scripture had to be understood by finite human beings and applied to their lives in a wide variety of social settings over centuries of time. Hence the need for interpretation and explanation of the text: the exegetical art and science known as *tafsir* (toff-SEER).

A *tafsir* or commentary upon the Qur'an is intended to clarify in a systematic way the meanings of the text. The exegete or commentator is known as a *mufassir* (moo-FASS-ser); plural, *mufassirun* (moo-fasser-OON). Typically, the exegete will work through the Qur'an verse by verse, explaining any unusual vocabulary or grammatical constructions, or any difficulties in determining the semantic content or sense of the text. For example, early manuscripts of the Qur'an were written without vowel points, and in some places it is possible to point the text in more than one way; exegetes have taken care to choose the reading they believe to be accurate and to defend that choice. This process is similar to that used in scholarly commentaries on the Greek or Hebrew text of the Bible.

A second term, *ta'wil* (ta-WEEL), has been used by many scholars as a synonym for *tafsir*. Various distinctions have been proposed to define a difference between these two words as technical terms used in Qur'anic commentary; for instance, *tafsir* was used by some exegetes to refer to the meaning accessible to human understanding, while *ta'wil* indicated a level of meaning known to God alone (see Q. 3:5–6). In Shi'i and Sufi exegesis,

55

these terms take on particular importance, as *ta'wil* was often used for the hidden or esoteric meanings recognized by those communities.[1] Indeed, some mystical and sectarian movements systematically developed a layered understanding of the text: its apparent meanings on a material or literal level, and its symbolic significance on an allegorical or spiritual plane.

Disciplines or standards governing the methods of text interpretation have formed over time. Among the issues to be decided is the relative value or admissibility of extrascriptural sources in understanding the scripture. The chain of transmission of a certain interpretation from the time of the Prophet or later authorities, the function of the individual's reason or intellect in arriving at an understanding of the text, or the use of external documentary information to shed light on the language of the Qur'an (pre-Islamic Arabic poetry, Jewish or Christian sources) may enter into the exegetical process. Legal reasoning also becomes very important in determining how a given commandment in scripture is to be obeyed or observed by the community. The *mufassirun* need to articulate and justify their methods and sources, not just their conclusions.

The degree of emphasis placed upon the opinions of earlier exegetes is often used to group commentaries into two broad categories: *tafsir bil-ma'thur* (bill-ma-THOOR) or tradition-based exegesis, and *tafsir bil-ra'y* (bir-RAH-ee) or interpretation by individual opinion. These are fluid categories, and of course both opinion and tradition (especially in the form of *hadith* narratives from canonical sources) are likely to be involved in any capable work of interpretation. The balance achieved between them serves as an indicator of a given exegete's primary interests and methods.

Many Muslim sources regard the Prophet's cousin Ibn 'Abbas ('Abdallah ibn al-'Abbas, d.c. 688) as the first *mufassir* or exegete of the Qur'an. It is said that the Prophet conveyed much of his own understanding of the revelation to Ibn 'Abbas, although the latter was only about fifteen years old at Muhammad's death. Ibn 'Abbas may have produced a written commentary that no longer exists; in any case, many of his interpretations were preserved by his followers and are now available as quotations in later works, notably the commentary of al-Tabari. A discussion of *tafsir* will often begin by mentioning him.

Ibn 'Abbas set the early standard and precedent, and countless *mufassirun* great and small sought to carry the effort further. This chapter will select only a few of the wide range of Qur'an exegetes: those commentators who are mentioned in every serious discussion of the history of *tafsir* and those whose work is accessible at least to some extent in English.

Two Great Scholars on the Principles of Tafsir:
Al-Ghazali (d. 1111) and Ibn Taymiyya (d. 1328)

The valuable collection of excerpts edited by John Renard, *Windows on the House of Islam*, contains two beautifully translated essays by major Islamic scholars that demonstrate well some of the issues involved in competent classical *tafsir*. Each excerpt is accompanied by a brief note introducing the scholar and placing the reading in the context of his work. Concise footnotes help to clarify issues of translation or wording, refer to relevant passages in the Qur'an, or identify other scholars and historical figures mentioned. The excerpts are of a convenient length for classroom use.

Abu Hamid al-Ghazali (al-ga-ZALLY). *Qanun at-ta'wil* or *The Canons of Ta'wil*; also known as *Al-qanun al-kulli fit-ta'wil*. **In John Renard, ed., Windows on the House of Islam (Berkeley: University of California Press, 1998), 48–54.**

This excerpt, translated by Nicholas Heer, is taken from the midst of a long essay in which the great philosopher and theologian al-Ghazali levels a critique at various unacceptable or erroneous methods of interpreting scripture through the application of reason. He identifies five different approaches to reconciling apparent conflicts between scripture and reason, rejecting four of these and endorsing a balanced view that values both. He then offers three recommendations for comprehending the Qur'an in a rational way. Al-Ghazali wrote extensively on the theory of scripture interpretation and analyzed certain passages as exemplars of his method (see also chapter 7).

Taqi al-Din Ahmad ibn 'Abd al-Halim ibn Taymiyya (ibbin tic-MEE-yah). His name also appears as Taki al-Din, and as Taymiyah or Taymiya. *Muqaddima fi usul at-tafsir* or *Introductory Treatise on the Principles of Tafsir*. **In Renard, Windows, 35–43.**

Ibn Taymiyya was a Hanbali jurist and theologian with a strong commitment to law and his view of orthodoxy. A contentious individual, he expressed adamant opinions upon the errors of his time, incurring the wrath of his opponents and dying imprisoned in the Citadel at Damascus (see also chapter 4). The excerpt here, translated by Jane Dammen McAuliffe, proposes a method of interpreting the Qur'an by reference to itself first, then by means of the *sunna* (the custom or practice of the Prophet, believed by Muslims to be authoritative and inspired; see the discussion of the *sunna* in chapter 2). He discusses further sources: the Companions of the Prophet (among them Ibn 'Abbas), the Followers, the "Isra'iliyat" or Jewish and Christian narratives, and finally the role of *ra'y* or personal opinion. The excerpt serves as a sound introduction to many of the major sources of classical commentary.

Ibn Taymiyya. *Muqaddimah fu usul al-tafsir* or *An Introduction to the Principles of Tafseer.* **Translated by Muhammad Abdul Haq Ansari (Birmingham: Al-Hidayah, 1993).**

This more complete edition of Ibn Taymiyya's work is available in English, but it exists in very few library collections.

The Classical Age of Tafsir

AL-TABARI (d. 923)

Abu Ja'far Muhammad ibn Jarir al-Tabari (at-TOB-aree). His name also appears as Abu Dja'far Muhammad ibn Djarir al-Tabari. *Jami' al-bayan 'an ta'wil ay al-Qur'an* or *Comprehensive Clarification of the Interpretation of the Verses of the Qur'an.* Also known as *Jami' al-bayan fi tafsir al-Qur'an.*

The first mature work defining the classical age of *tafsir* was the *Jami' al-bayan* (also known simply as the *Tafsir*) by the historian and exegete al-Tabari. Born in the Caspian region, Tabari later lived and worked in Baghdad, where he became a foremost scholar not only in Qur'anic studies and history but also in Arabic grammar and lexicography, poetry, science, and law. His most important work is his history of the world (see chapter 5).

His commentary on the Qur'an, however, is also a turning-point text in Islamic scholarship. With extraordinary erudition, Tabari drew together, organized, and coherently presented a compendium of the contributions known to him from earlier interpreters, with their complete chain of transmitters. This encyclopedic collection includes the opinions of earlier commentators even if they repeat or contradict each other; Tabari's selection of *hadith* material is based mainly upon the reliability of its transmission and the authority of its originator. His collection is still used as a vast and rich storehouse for these earlier exegetes, whose work has in many cases otherwise been lost. The contributions of Ibn 'Abbas, for example, are known primarily through this collection.

Tabari does not merely catalog the work of others, however. He evaluates their opinions, criticizes their errors, and pronounces his own views, often in the form of a paraphrase or restatement of the Qur'anic text in a way that conveys what he believes to be its most authentic and accurate reading. In addition, Tabari analyzes the text word for word, making use of the work of philologists and grammarians to exhaust the semantic and syntactical implications of significant terms and phrases.

In a lengthy introduction, Tabari discusses his exegetical methods and the theory of Qur'anic hermeneutics in a rather argumentative fashion, as if responding to an interlocutor. His concern throughout the work is not just the preservation of past findings and practices, but the conscious formation and advance of the intellectual discipline of Qur'anic exegesis. "If Tabari's commentary stands at the end of the early period of *tafsir* with its concentration on Traditional exegesis, and marks a summation of the material available in his age, it also stands at the beginning of a period in which *tafsir* was to develop into a more critical and scholastic endeavor, with the refining of methodology and the establishing of the 'sciences of the Qur'an (*'ulum al-Qur'an*)' on a systematic basis."[2]

Al-Tabari, *Commentary on the Qur'an*. Translation and notes by John Cooper (Oxford: Oxford University Press, 1987).

This meticulously edited translation by John Cooper of Tabari's commentary was the first of five planned volumes, an abridgement of Tabari's very lengthy work. Unfortunately, the project has been discontinued by Oxford University Press. This volume contains Tabari's introduction, in which he makes extensive remarks about the aims and methods of Qur'anic exegesis, and Tabari's commentary on the Basmala (opening formula of the Qur'an) and on Sura 1 and Sura 2, verses 1–103. The translation of this volume is based upon the scholarly edition of Tabari's work in Arabic by Ahmad and Mahmud Shakir (Cairo: Dar al-Ma'arif, 1955–1969). It is helpful for readers of Arabic to have access to that edition, because numbers indicate where material omitted by Cooper may be found in Shakir and Shakir.

The abridgement is carefully marked to show the nature of the material omitted (e.g., certain *hadith* narratives, poetry quotations, long chains of transmitters). The wealth of exegetical transmission collected in Tabari's commentary has been for the most part retained, sometimes condensed, with repetitions minimized. All of the variant opinions deemed significant have been included. Grammatical and recitational detail has been reduced. Some of Tabari's own peripheral remarks are elided, and some passages are summarized and identified as such. All of the editorial additions, deletions, and adaptations are made completely evident to the reader.

Cooper has also sought to aid the reader with typographical cues and paragraphing to make the course of Tabari's arguments more visible. Headings such as "Question," "Objection," or "Reply" pepper the text, and "Tabari's

Opinion" is prominently noted. Each section begins with the Arabic text from the Qur'an in script and transliteration, then an English version from Arberry or Pickthall. Tabari's own interpretive paraphrase is highlighted. In addition, endnotes for each section clarify translation problems, explain terms, and add background material.

It should be noted that the richness of the scholarly apparatus in this edition may make it seem a bit daunting to the inexperienced reader, but it amply rewards one who takes the time to understand it. The translator's own introduction is also an informative essay about Tabari's work in the context of the history of Qur'anic commentary.

AL-ZAMAKHSHARI (d. 1144)
Abu al-Qasim Mahmud ibn 'Umar al-Zamakhshari (azza-MOK-sha-ree). *Al-kashshaf 'an haqa'iq ghawamid al-tanzil* **or** *Unveiler of the Realities (or Real Meanings) of the Secrets of the Revelation.* **His name also appears as Abu al-Kasim.**

While Tabari's primary achievement was his collection of tradition-based interpretations, the commentary of the Persian exegete al-Zamakhshari is an impressive example of the philological analysis of the Qur'an. He gave minute attention to the syntax and morphology of the text, explaining each departure from conventional word order or any other unusual stylistic or rhetorical feature. These characteristics of the Qur'an are understood by Zamakhshari to be evidence of its supreme inimitability or uniqueness. So acute were his observations on the Qur'an's Arabic text that his commentary is still valued by scholars for this information.

One factor limiting the acceptance of Zamakhshari's work among Muslims was his allegiance to the Mu'tazili movement and its theology. He asserted, for example, the Mu'tazili doctrine of the nature of the Qur'an as a created object, not an eternal one. Another limiting factor is that the linguistic refinement of his work may be hard for English speakers to appreciate.

In Kenneth Cragg, *The Mind of the Qur'an* (London: George Allen and Unwin, 1973), 65–69.

An excerpt from the *Kashshaf* in Cragg's own translation is incorporated into his analysis of the history of Islamic exegesis. The passage is Zamakhshari's commentary on Sura 90, "The Land." Cragg supplies an English version of the *sura* itself, then the commentary. He also provides a few footnotes pointing out places where the Arabic resists translation—for example, some double meanings or plays on words. He also omits some portions that are strictly linguistic in nature.

In Gätje, *The Qur'an and Its Exegesis* (Berkeley: University of California Press, 1976).

Gätje's very useful work is more than an anthology, but serves some of the purposes of one. It is composed of substantial excerpts from several of the major interpreters of the classical age of *tafsir*, including Zamakhshari. Gätje's work is organized by topic or theme, with an index of Qur'anic passages. An index of names and subjects is also provided, as well as a valuable, partly annotated bibliography. The endnotes for each chapter are very helpful and should not be overlooked. In addition, Gätje's introduction has enough content to be a good source of information without being overly technical or burdened with too much detail. It places *tafsir* in the context of Muslim intellectual history and defines much of the scholarly vocabulary one encounters in other works.

Substantial excerpts from Zamakhshari's *tafsir* are also available in Abdul's edition of Tabarsi's *Majma' al-bayan* and in the anthology *Classical Islam* (see below).

AL-RAZI (d. 1209)

Abu 'Abdallah Muhammad Fakhr al-Din al-Razi (focker-id-DEEN ar-ROZZI). *Mafatih al-ghayb* (*ghaib*) or *Keys of the Unseen* (or *Hidden*). Also known as *Al-tafsir al-kabir* or *The Great Commentary*.

The Persian-born philosopher and theologian Fakhr al-Din al-Razi was an opponent of Mu'tazili thought, as well as other movements he considered erroneous.[3] He was familiar with classical Greek thought and natural science through the discipline of Islamic learning known as *falsafa* or philosophy (see chapter 6) and was highly critical of some aspects of Avicennan thought; he endeavored to achieve a synthesis between rationality and revelation while defending orthodoxy and to employ the sacred text as a guide for human reason.[4]

Al-Razi's commentary is a huge work of more than thirty volumes, wide-ranging, packed with philosophical digression and argumentation. His method has been compared with the scholasticism of Thomas Aquinas (d. 1274).

In Norman Calder, Jawid Mojaddedi, and Andrew Rippin, *Classical Islam* (London; New York: Routledge, 2003), 121–27.

This superb new anthology contains a sizable excerpt from Al-Razi's *tafsir*—a highly significant passage as well, from Sura 98 ("Al-Bayyina"). Because the anthology contains excerpts from other major *mufassirun* on the same passage, it is possible to compare their treatment of this text. Expert translations of the primary material are joined with very concise but helpful introductory remarks and a careful selection of bibliographic references.

Further excerpts may be found in Gätje and Abdul, as well as Wheeler (*Prophets in the Quran*). In these works, material is organized thematically and the work of individual exegetes must be sought through the table of contents or index. In addition, Cragg provides some fairly lengthy quotations in the course of his discussion of al-Razi's work.

AL-BAYDAWI (d.c. 1286)

'Abdallah ibn 'Umar al-Baydawi (buy-DOW-ee). His name often appears as al-Baidawi. *Anwar al-tanzil wa asrar al-ta'wil* or *The Lights of the Revelation and the Secrets of the Interpretation.*

An enormously influential commentary was produced by another Persian exegete in the late thirteenth century (his death date is variously reported by historical sources). Baydawi's work is usually described as a condensation and adaptation of Zamakhshari's *Kashshaf*, relieved of its Mu'tazili tendencies. J. J. G. Jansen maintains that it also derives material from al-Razi's *Mafatih*. The Baydawi commentary seemed to supply the need for an orthodox and accessible vehicle for linguistic and philological information and analysis, and it became the standard exegetical textbook for many Islamic schools. Several "supercommentaries" were created by scholars adding glosses and annotations to Baydawi's work. Portions of the commentary are available in English editions.

Al-Baidawi. *Baidawi's Commentary on Surah 12 of the Qur'an.* Translated and edited by A. F. L. Beeston (Oxford: Clarendon Press, 1978).

This expert work is a meticulous translation of Baydawi's commentary on the twelfth *sura*, the story of the prophet and patriarch Joseph. Beeston's intention was to introduce the genre of classical *tafsir* to the European student working at an intermediate level of proficiency in Arabic. It is meant to form a bridge between an ordinary Arabic text and the highly technical, condensed, grammatically sophisticated style of classical *tafsir*. The idea was that the student could become familiar with the specialized discipline of *tafsir* through English before trying to tackle Baydawi and other exegetes in Arabic.

For this reason, Beeston's edition is merciless in its use of Qur'anic passages (and of grammatical terms) transliterated but *not* translated. The student who reads only English will find this very slow going, rather like reading a highly technical Bible commentary if one has not studied Hebrew or Greek. However, it has the great benefit of displaying the full complexity of the lexical and philological detail of classical *tafsir* and the prevalence of grammatical terms that have no European equivalent.

Beeston's lengthy endnotes often increase the overwhelming effect of all this linguistic complexity. But they can also be very useful to the English reader. Beeston expands or clarifies Baydawi's more obscure statements and points out places where Baydawi restates or contradicts Zamakhshari's remarks on the same passage. Beeston also mentions certain parallels with the Bible's account of the story of Joseph, sometimes with reference to biblical redaction and text criticism. (He also fully identifies persons mentioned in passing by Baydawi and directs the reader to relevant articles in the *Encyclopaedia of Islam.*) Beeston occasionally indicates flaws in the Fleischer Arabic edition upon which his translation is based and comments on other European-language renderings of the Qur'an (Blachère, Dawood, Bell, Arberry). Moreover, he notes any discrepancy in vocalizing or the numbering of verses in Sura 12 by Flügel and the Cairo edition. This adds up to an achievement in editing and annotating that sets a very high standard.

Al-Baydawi. *Chrestomathia Baidawiana: The Commentary of el-Baidawi on Sura III.* Translated and annotated by D. S. Margoliouth (London: Luzac, 1894).

Like Beeston's edition of Sura 12, this work by Margoliouth was intended for use by students of Arabic, in the Oxford Oriental School. This work, however, eschews even transliteration and supplies Arabic terms only in their original orthography. Like Beeston, Margoliouth has chosen a portion of the Qur'an of inherent interest to students of the Bible: Sura 3 contains several substantial passages mentioning Mary, Jesus, and the "People of the Book" (Jews and Christians).

The text consists of brief phrases from the Qur'an paraphrased in English, then Baydawi's explanatory comments in English translation. His comments focus on variant readings (where different vowel points are possible), supply anecdotes from the traditions, or introduce factual background information (for example, the definition of terms such as "full weight of gold" or "fine cattle"). Baydawi also may link the passage to others within the Qur'an that shed light upon it, or refer very briefly to the opinions of earlier authorities. He also includes explicit rejections of erroneous assertions by other commentators. All of these are typical features of classical commentaries with which the student must become familiar.

Endnotes (mainly on translation issues) are provided by the editor. The translation, while authoritative, employs an antiquated English prose not very agreeable to modern readers.

Al-Baidawi. A *Translation of Baidawi's Commentary on the First Sura of the Koran*. A thesis by Roswell Walker Caldwell (MA), submitted to the Kennedy School of Missions of the Hartford Seminary Foundation, 1933.

An English version of Baidawi's comments on the Basmala and Sura 1, with explanatory footnotes.

IBN KATHIR (d.c. 1373)

'Imad al-Din Isma'il ibn 'Umar ibn Kathir (ibbin ka-THEER). *Tafsir al-Qur'an al-'azim* or *Interpretation of the Mighty Qur'an*.

Remembered principally as an historian and an expert in the *hadith* literature (see chapter 5), Ibn Kathir also wrote a classical *tafsir*. The work is indebted to Tabari and is considered to stand in the same exegetical category, often called *tafsir bil-ma'thur* or tradition-based *tafsir* (as opposed to *tafsir bil-ra'y* or interpretation by opinion). Ibn Kathir, a student of Ibn Taymiyya, acquired an encyclopedic knowledge of the *hadith* narratives and their transmission and was highly regarded for his ability to assess their relevance and soundness. His work carefully selects, orders, and evaluates material from the traditional corpus and opinions of past commentators, displaying deliberate concern for the procedures and principles of exegesis.

In Andrew Rippin and Jan Knappert, *Textual Sources for the Study of Islam* (Chicago: University of Chicago Press, 1986), 47–49.

The excerpt from Ibn Kathir's commentary included in this collection of freshly translated primary source material is brief, but well chosen. It represents Ibn Kathir's treatment of a verse from Sura 33 of the Qur'an on Muhammad as the "seal" of the prophets. The passage exemplifies Ibn Kathir's use of several *hadith* narratives, with an evaluation of the soundness of each narrative's origin and transmission, and the exegete's own summary statement at the end.

Ibn Kathir. *Tafsir Ibn Kathir*. Abridged by a group of scholars under the supervision of Shaykh Safi-ur-Rahman al-Mubarakpuri (Riyadh: Darus-salam, 2000). 10 vols.

Although this is a new edition, it has a distinctly antiquated style. Nevertheless, the English prose is clear and readable, and the print quality is good. Qur'anic passages are given in English and the fully pointed Arabic text; bold headings have been added to guide the reader, and there are footnotes referencing the major *hadith* compendia, Tabari's commentary, and certain other primary sources. The editing is explicitly directive, as if addressed to students, and the abridgement was undertaken specifically to remove "weak *hadiths* and Israelitish stories"[5] from the text; one gets the impression of not so much an abridged version as an expurgated one.

In Brannon M. Wheeler, *Prophets in the Quran* (London: Continuum, 2002).

This interesting collection of quotations is topically arranged, with chapters on each of the persons designated as prophets in Islam. The chapter on Abraham, for example, presents Qur'anic passages that pertain to Abraham (in Wheeler's own translation), such as the annunciation of Isaac, or the establishment of the sanctuary at Mecca. Wheeler then provides quotations about the passages—from one sentence to a paragraph in length—from noted Muslim exegetes. Some of these are very scarce indeed in English, so it is helpful to have them represented in this volume. An index of Qur'an citations and an index of the Muslim commentators make it possible to track down material in those ways; there is also a general index for names and subjects mentioned. Wheeler also supplies a useful bibliographic essay.

The chief drawback to Wheeler's book is that the title of the source of each quotation is not identified. When Ibn Kathir is quoted, it is not clear from which of three documentary sources the quote is taken. Ibn Kathir's commentary is one of these sources, but his world history and his *Tales of the Prophets* are as well, so the reader is not sure whether a given quotation can be found in the commentary or the other works. This problem exists for each writer for whom more than one source appears in the list of works consulted.

Another Source

A popular edition of a substantial portion of Ibn Kathir's work has been published as *Tafseer Ibn Katheer: Juz' 'Amma*, translated and abridged by Sameh Strauch (Riyadh: International Islamic Publishing House, 2000). It contains his interpretation of the final or thirtieth segment of the Qur'an, comprising the last thirty-seven *suras*. The translation is accessible and interesting, but the work lacks a scholarly research apparatus.

Classical Shi'i Tafsir

AL-TABARSI (d. 1154)

Abu 'Ali al-Fadl ibn al Hasan al-Tabarsi (at-tuh-BAR-see). His name also appears as Amin al-Din (or Amin al-Islam) al-Tabrisi. *Majma' al-bayan li 'ulum al-Qur'an* or *Collection of the Explanation of the Sciences of the Qur'an.*

The prolific and erudite Shi'i scholar al-Tabarsi was a contemporary of al-Zamakhshari, and he had considerable respect for and sympathy with Mu'tazili exegetes. He stands on the shoulders of other prominent Shi'i *mufassirun*, such as al-Qummi (d. 939) and al-Tusi (d.c. 1067). Tabarsi's commentary is comprehensive and inclusive, reporting the opinions of authorities from various doctrinal or sectarian viewpoints. He was committed, however, to the particular concern in Shi'i theology with the unique legitimacy of 'Ali and his descendants as interpreters of scripture and to the Shi'i tendency toward allegorical or layered exegesis, with surface and deeper meanings.

In *The Qur'an: Shaykh Tabarsi's Commentary.* Translation and notes by Musa O. A. Abdul (Lahore: Sh. Muhammad Ashraf, 1977).

This clearly organized, interesting study of Tabarsi's great commentary was undertaken through a grant from the Rockefeller Foundation at the Institute of Islamic Studies at McGill University in Montreal. The first half contains biographical information about Tabarsi, an introduction to the *Majma' al-bayan* and Tabarsi's general intention and method, including a lengthy excerpt provided as a typical example of the commentary's contents, in English and Arabic. There is also an essay tracing the historical development of *tafsir* from the Companions through the twentieth century, then a comparison of the *Majma' al-bayan* with Zamakhshari's *Kashshaf*.

In the second half, Abdul delves into Tabarsi's discussion of three issues: the beatific vision, the imamate of 'Ali, and the problem of mortal sin. One or two verses of the Qur'an come first, then a substantial excerpt (three to six pages) from the *Majma' al-bayan*, first in Arabic, then in English translation. Abdul then provides excerpts from the *Kashshaf* and Fakhr al-Din al-Razi's *Mafatih*, again in Arabic first, then in Abdul's English translation. He follows each of these sets of excerpts with a brief summary in which he indicates the chief points of interpretation treated by these three great exegetes. He also discusses Western critical literature in these summaries, and sources are footnoted throughout. Finally, Abdul's volume provides a useful bibliography and index.

The excerpts incorporated here are long enough to give readers a good idea of each commentator's exegetical emphases and techniques. It is especially helpful to provide these passages in both English and Arabic for those who are able to compare them. Although the physical printing and manufacture of the book is inferior, this volume is a valuable source for Tabarsi in English, and for Zamakhshari and Razi as well. It may also serve as an example of one of the ways in which Muslim scholars appropriate and reexamine the *tafsir* of the medieval period for modern times.

Modern Qur'an Interpretation

The advent of the modern era brought enormous new challenges to the Muslim world, among them the development of nationalism versus European imperialism and increased contact with Western religions and philosophies, political and social systems, sciences, and technology. Classical *tafsir* had always studied the Qur'an as the foundation of Islamic law and theology using the tools of philology and the authoritative body of traditions. But this minute examination of linguistic detail and the doctrinal controversies of the past did not necessarily address the intense and demanding issues of the present. Also, a new generation of Muslims was being educated primarily in Western-oriented schools independent of the mosque, particularly the class of social and professional leaders and intellectuals.

MUHAMMAD 'ABDUH (d. 1905) and RASHID RIDA (d. 1935)
Muhammad 'Abduh (OB-dou) and Muhammad Rashid Rida (ra-SHEED RID-uh). *Tafsir al-Manar* or *The "Lighthouse" Commentary.* Also known as *Tafsir al-Qur'an al-hakim* or *Commentary on the Wise Qur'an.*

The first *mufassir* to confront these issues effectively was Muhammad 'Abduh. Classically trained at Al-Azhar University in Cairo, he responded to the influence of anticolonial activists (among them the fiery Jamal al-Din al-Afghani) and became involved in the resistance against the British occupation of Egypt in 1882. He began publishing his ideas in journals that reached younger people like Rashid Rida, who became 'Abduh's student and collaborator and eventually a mature and accomplished exegete.

Together, they published a new approach to *tafsir* in a public medium, the journal *Al-Manar* (*The Lighthouse*). This material—based upon 'Abduh's lectures and later greatly expanded and continued by Rashid Rida—became a major exegetical contribution, a turning-point text. The commentary departs from the previous practice of exhaustive semantic and syntactical analysis of isolated words or phrases of the Qur'an. Instead, verses are tackled in "meaningful units," and "the notion of context and integrity [of the pericope] enters as a hermeneutical principle."[6]

The work also critically engages the modern world's rationality and empiricism. The popular piety of their day was mired in what 'Abduh regarded as unproductive superstition, legend, and magical thinking; 'Abduh asserts that revelation and reason are compatible and that the divine truth of the Qur'an does not consist in its anticipation of or contradiction to the findings of modern natural sciences. Most significant, however, is the commentary's goal in interpreting the Qur'an as a source of moral guidance for the living of

Islam in practical terms in one's own social environment. Religious and educational reform (through a constructive, positive renewal of the community's self-understanding without sacrificing Islamic validity and commitment) became a key objective of contemporary *tafsir*.

It is worth noting that Muhammad 'Abduh and Rashid Rida were influential in the founding of the modern *salafiyya* reform movement, which explicitly recognizes its debt to the thought of Ibn Taymiyya. For a detailed definition of this movement and its principles, see the very helpful article by Emad Eldin Shahin, "Salafiyah," in the *Oxford Encyclopedia of the Modern Islamic World* (Oxford, 1995), v. 3: 463–69.

In Gätje, *The Qur'an and Its Exegesis*, 248–61.

This substantial excerpt is much to be valued, since very few sources exist for the *Al-Manar* commentary in English. 'Abduh actually published four commentaries, but this is the major work extended by Rashid Rida (to Sura 12:52), for which both exegetes are best known. The selection discusses the third verse of Sura 4 on the delicate subject of polygamy. The discourse displays a concern for the abuses of polygamy found in Egypt at the time, the poor education of women and their susceptibility to religious misinformation and error, the balanced partnership of man and woman in marriage, and the social values of functional families and protection for the vulnerable. A strong apologetic motive is evident in reply to perceived questioning of the practice by Western critics. This reading would lend itself well to classroom discussion.

MAWLANA MAWDUDI (d. 1979)

Sayyid Abul A'la Mawdudi (mao-DOO-di). His name may also be Anglicized as Syed Maududi or Maudoodi. *Tafhim al-Qur'an* or *Understanding the Qur'an*. He is often known by the honorific Mawlana or Maulana.

One of the most prominent exponents of revivalist discourse emerged in the turbulent climate of prepartition India. Amidst the powerful currents of communalism, nationalism, and secularism pushing forward competing visions for the future of the Muslim population of the subcontinent when British colonial rule ended, Mawdudi argued persuasively for the aim of an explicitly Islamic state. He was determined to see *shari'a* or Islamic law joined with political power, and he resisted any secular concept of a state that would adopt a national identity and constitution not founded upon Islam. When Pakistan came into being in 1947, it was Mawdudi who led the Jama'ati Islami organization in its campaign to establish an Islamic state and insisted that Pakistan's new constitution acknowledge an Islamic ideal of society and law.

His views led him into conflict with a succession of Pakistani governments, resulting in periods of imprisonment. Throughout this embattled era, however, Mawdudi continued to produce an extensive body of scholarly work of a high caliber, which has had an impact on revivalist or reformist thought not only in Pakistan but in the wider Islamic world.

For many years (1932–1979) Mawdudi edited the monthly magazine known as *Tarjuman al-Qur'an* (*Interpreter of the Qur'an*), in which his *tafsir* first began to appear in 1942. The first volume was published in book form in 1950 as *Tafhim al-Qur'an*, and the entire work was completed in six massive volumes in 1973. From its inception, the *Tafhim* was enormously popular and opened the Qur'an in a new way to Urdu speakers. Along with his pocket introduction to the faith, *Risala Diniyat* (*Towards Understanding Islam*), and over one hundred other works, it has established Mawdudi as a major figure in twentieth-century Islamic letters.

Mawdudi, *Towards Understanding the Qur'an*. Translated and edited by Zafar Ishaq Ansari (Leicester: Islamic Foundation, 1988–).

This fine edition of Mawdudi's *tafsir* in English boasts the express endorsement of the original author. Ansari has the ability to render the Urdu of Mawdudi's translation and commentary into a fluent, accurate, and highly readable English.

The format of the work will be familiar to students who have used scholarly Bible commentaries. Each *sura* is introduced by a brief explanation of its title, the circumstances of its revelation, its historical background or setting, and its primary subjects or themes. The Arabic text of the Qur'an is presented, with Mawdudi's own interpretive translation; then, copious footnotes provide Mawdudi's detailed observations and comments, anchored in the text. The comments reflect the exegete's overriding concern with faithful Muslim life in the modern era and are directed toward believers who have been raised and educated in contact with Western intellectual, political, and social environments.

A disappointment, perhaps, is Mawdudi's own introduction to the overall work in vol. 1. There is little evidence of a critical distance between the scholar and his subject; the introduction is essentially a statement of faith in the unique supremacy of the Qur'an as a faultless expression of divine revelation.

This edition is equipped with very useful reference helps: a general index (especially good for names), maps, biographical notes identifying persons mentioned in the commentary as well as the text, a glossary, and a translation of the Urdu edition's unusual subject index, which nearly does the work

of a scripture concordance. Ansari has also taken care to document all references to *hadith* and other *tafsir* sources and to supply English quotations in
their original wording.

Seven volumes of this valuable edition are now available in hardcover and
paperback through the Islamic Foundation in Leicester. Five of them were
examined for this review.

SAYYID QUTB (d. 1966)

**Sayyid Qutb (SYE-id KOOT-ub) Ibrahim Husayn Shadhili. His name of-
ten appears in a Westernized form using Qutb as a surname: Qutb, Sayyid.
Fi zilal al-Qur'an or *In the Shade (or Shadows) of the Qur'an.***

The undertaking of *tafsir* in the service of social change was moved many
steps further by Egypt's radical Islamist writer Sayyid Qutb. His mentor, Hassan
al-Banna (d. 1949), founder of the Muslim Brotherhood, was in his youth a student of Rashid Rida. But the aims of the Muslim Brotherhood went well beyond social or religious reform to resistance against corrupt political structures
and rejection of both Western influences and degenerate Muslim leaders; the
Brotherhood (*al-Ikhwan al-Muslimin*) took on the character of an outlawed rev-
olutionary or paramilitary organization.[7] Sayyid Qutb, who had derived from
Mawdudi a contempt for secular nationalism, became the primary theorist and
spokesman for the Brotherhood. As such, he publicly opposed Nasser's government. This activism led to his imprisonment, trial, torture, and execution
in 1966. But the influence of his prolific writing, including his powerful and
original *tafsir*, is still active in Islamist circles today.

**Sayyid Qutb. *In the Shade of the Qur'an.* Translated and edited by M. Adil
Salahi and Ashur A. Shamis (Leicester: Islamic Foundation, 1999–).**

Sayyid Qutb's extensive commentary was begun in 1951 and completed
during a long period of imprisonment in 1954–1964. The work is very popular in Egypt and beyond, and demand for access to it by English speakers is
strong.

The whole of the commentary comprises thirty volumes, but the first to
appear in English was the final part, covering the thirtieth section of the
Qur'an (Suras 78–114). Much of Sayyid Qutb's final volume had already appeared in English translation in *The Muslim* (journal of the Federation of
Student Islamic Societies in the United Kingdom and Ireland), so it could be
readily adapted to book form; the Muslim Welfare House published vol. 30
originally in 1979. The Islamic Foundation in Leicester continues to publish
additional portions translated by Salahi and Shamis, and vols. 1–8 are now
in print (fifteen volumes are planned).

The translators have produced an attractive and readable English version that could easily be employed in the classroom. They provide the Arabic text of each *sura*, then a rendering in polished modern English. Then follows the interpretation by Sayyid Qutb, in which highly technical detail is kept to a minimum, while attention is focused on an understanding of the implications of the passage. Sayyid Qutb occasionally refers to earlier exegetes, but more often he paraphrases narratives from the traditions to illustrate or explain the text. The very brief, highly concentrated Meccan *suras* are often rather cryptic unless the commentator supplies such information (e.g., Sura 105, "The Elephant").

Sayyid Qutb's hermeneutic serves the aim of reawakening the faith and obedience that empowered the first believers when "Islam assumed the leadership of humanity . . . [and] introduced a fresh understanding of life and its values, and of the whole world order,"[8] thereby attaining a fully realized Islamic *ummah* (community of believers). His interrogation of the text is driven by this objective. His sharpest criticism is directed toward "ex-Muslim peoples" who have slipped away from true Islam and back into "ignorance" or *jahiliyya* and thus deviated from an almost utopian ideal (see his interpretation of Sura 109, "The Disbelievers"). He rejects a rationalism that is reluctant to submit to the Qur'an's divinely revealed authority and any political system or theory that one may substitute for the centrality of Islam.

The agenda of a fundamentalist revival of Muslim nations and societies and the implementation of *shari'a* is indirect but perceptible in this portion of Sayyid Qutb's work and is more fully developed elsewhere.[9] The *tafsir* was partially revised (up to Sura 15) and its activist reputation rests upon that revised version.

This accessible English edition also contains an interesting foreword by Muhammad Qutb (the author's brother), an introduction by the author, and a somewhat helpful index.

'AISHA 'ABD AL-RAHMAN or BINT AL-SHATI (d. 1998)
'Aisha 'Abd al Rahman or Bint al-Shati (bint as-SHOTTI). *Al-tafsir al-bayani lil Qur'an al-karim* or *Rhetorical Exegesis of the Noble Qur'an.*

'Aisha 'Abd al-Rahman, another brilliant Egyptian exegete, is far better known by her pseudonym Bint al-Shati ("Daughter of the Shore"). She was born in 1912 and reached the peak of her creative productivity in the 1960s, and was therefore a contemporary of Sayyid Qutb. Her objective in the interpretation of scripture, however, was entirely different.

Her *tafsir* was based upon a fruitful collaboration with her husband Amin al-Khuli, a professor of exegesis who formulated a new approach to commentary inspired by Theodor Nöldeke's *Geschichte des Qorans* (1909). Amin al-Khuli developed what might be considered an historical-critical method of interpretation, founded upon the original setting and audience of the revelation and the way it was understood by those who first received it. The Qur'an's vocabulary and grammatical structure were seen as a part of its character as the exemplar of Arabic literature, as its vehicle for expression and meaning.

Bint al-Shati was a professor of Arabic language and literature at 'Ayn Shams University in Cairo and an authority on Arabic poetry, an essayist, critic, journalist, and published poet herself. She was uniquely positioned to apply Amin al-Khuli's theories in a literary and rhetorical study of the Qur'an. She was able to combine her knowledge of the Qur'an's chronology and context with an understanding of metaphor and symbolism, genre, emphasis, and literary techniques such as rhythm, assonance, and rhyme. Her work was well received, and later in her career she served as a professor of higher Qur'anic studies at al-Qarawiyin University in Fez, Morocco, and wrote a popular regular column in Cairo's newspaper *Al-Ahram*. Her unusual gifts produced an exegete able "to judge by literary criteria intelligently applied."[10]

In Cragg, *The Mind of the Qur'an*, 70–74, and in J. J. G. Jansen, *The Interpretation of the Qur'an in Modern Egypt* (Leiden: Brill, 1974), 68–76.

The first volume of Bint al-Shati's *tafsir* appeared in 1962 and the second in 1969. Together, they contain expositions of fourteen of the early Meccan *suras*. Unfortunately, this extraordinary work does not exist in any substantial form in English. Some of her other works are available in translation (see chapter 5), but not her *tafsir*. The studies by Cragg and Jansen incorporate enough direct quotes to give the reader a sense of her approach, and both dwell at some length on her analysis of Sura 93. An interesting body of secondary literature on her exegetical method is available.

Modern Shi'i Commentary

TABATABA'I (d. 1981)

Sayyid Muhammad Husayn Tabataba'i (tobba-tob-BUY-ee). He is also well known as 'Allameh (or 'Allamah) Tabataba'i. *Al-mizan fi tafsir al-Qur'an* or *The Scales [of Justice] in the Interpretation of the Qur'an*.

Among the great Persian scholars of the twentieth century, 'Allameh Tabataba'i was fully trained in law and philosophy in the Shi'i holy city of Najaf. He taught in Tabriz, then settled in Qum, where his reputation as a leading intellect and a deeply spiritual individual attracted many devoted students. Among them was Seyyed Hossein Nasr, known as a distinguished

Islamic scholar in his own right. Nasr brought the work of Tabataba'i to the attention of English-speaking audiences, making some of it available in Nasr's own translation.

Tabataba'i's many books cover a range of subject areas, including *tafsir*; his works in philosophy have become required reading in many Islamic schools. His philosophical thought and interest in spirituality led to an unusual collaboration with the French philosopher Henri Corbin, exploring comparative mysticism. They discussed classic mystical and gnostic texts belonging to the Christian, Hindu, Taoist, and Sufi traditions. An awareness of comparative religion is apparent in Tabataba'i's major works of Qur'anic exegesis.[11]

Tabataba'i. *Al-Mizan: An Exegesis of the Qur'an*. Translated by Sayyid Saeed (or Sa'id) Akhtar Rizvi. (Tehran: World Organization for Islamic Services, 1983–).

The first volume of this extensive work covers Sura 1 and the beginning of Sura 2. Indeed, the first four volumes are required to reach the end of Sura 2. Eleven volumes have now been published by the World Organization for Islamic Services in Tehran, and it seems that forty volumes are planned.

Tabataba'i reflects extensively on the aims and methods of *tafsir* in his preface, and offers more comment on this subject at the beginning of Sura 3, "The Family of Imran." He argues in favor of a Shi'i understanding of the Imams descended from the Prophet as authoritative interpreters of the Qur'an, and against a highly polemical or sectarian hermeneutic that attempts arbitrarily to impose philosophical or mystical precepts upon the text.

The exegete works his way slowly through each passage, discussing its vocabulary and syntax and comparing it with many other passages within the Qur'an. He raises rhetorical questions of a philosophical nature and answers them, quotes from Sunni and Shi'i traditions and from earlier exegetes (including Tabarsi), then offers his own conclusions. There are lengthy essays on topics suggested by the text: For example, a discussion of "The Miracle of the Qur'an" is placed within the exposition of Q. 2:22. These self-contained segments could easily be employed as readings for classroom use.

This edition does not contain a conventional index, but some reference helps are provided: a sort of thematic outline of the volume's contents, a chronological table of the twelve Imams, and lists of the authors and works mentioned in the book (mostly medieval Sunni and Shi'i sources, but including a few contemporary writers like Rashid Rida). Though printing errors are apparent, the English prose is competent and readable.

Current Issues in Hermeneutics

The classic patterns of Qur'an exegesis have been challenged in modern times by scholars willing to adopt very different approaches to the literature of Qur'an commentary and criticism. Fazlur Rahman's book *Major Themes of the Qur'an* (Minneapolis: Bibliotheca Islamica, 1980) slices through the usual scholarly preoccupations with chronology and sources to delineate the major theological content of the scripture as a whole. Mohammed Arkoun comes to grips with a secularist critique of the faith and its epistemology in *Rethinking Islam: Common Questions, Uncommon Answers* (Boulder: Westview Press, 1994).

Among the new critics of conventional hermeneutics is Amina Wadud. Her book *Qur'an and Woman: Rereading the Sacred Text from a Woman's Perpective* (Oxford: Oxford University Press, 1999) is a gender-inclusive approach to *tafsir* that consciously engages and analyzes traditional exegesis, its methods and assumptions. Asma Barlas is prepared to contest paternalistic readings of the text in *"Believing Women" in Islam: Unreading Patriarchal Interpretations of the Qur'an* (Austin: University of Texas Press, 2002) and to recover its thematic coherence, establishing the independence of the exegete from the medieval religious literature and its limitations.

A persuasive and accessible discussion of the issues involved in Qur'an interpretation today is provided by Farid Esack in his *Qur'an, Liberation and Pluralism* (Oxford: Oneworld, 1997). He explains the vocabulary and assumptions of exegesis as it has typically been practiced in the past, pointing out where the methodology has stopped short of an effective engagement with the text. A doctrine of Scripture as eternal, uncreated, and entirely free of human or historical contingency makes it impossible to consider issues of authorship or environment, condition or context—all basic to critical discourse on any document. The idea of the Qur'an as a product of human agency presents an unacceptable affront to the authority of Scripture as it has customarily been understood and enforced in Islamic orthodoxy.

Esack raises two classic concerns of Qur'anic study: *asbab al-nuzul* or information regarding the original setting or circumstances of a particular revelation, and *naskh* or the abrogation or clarification of an earlier passage by a later one. He connects these exegetical principles with the concept of progressive revelation and contemporary attempts to contextualize the meanings of the Qur'an, in a way that unleashes its power today—particularly for those who are living in marginalizing or oppressive conditions, in need of justice and a liberating grace. He views criticism as a corollary to praxis: "To understand the Qur'an in its historical context is not to confine its message to that context; rather, it is to understand its revealed meaning in a specific past context and then to be able to contextualize it in terms of contemporary reality."[12]

Esack also grounds the hermeneutical process in the contingencies of the exegete, who must be consciously aware of his or her personal, social, or political horizons and assumptions. Just as earlier exegetes had their own ideological affiliations and agendas (Shi'i, Mu'tazili, etc.) and did not hesitate to set forth these views, current interpreters engage the text, legitimately, through their own experience. "There is therefore no plausible reason why any particular generation should be the intellectual hostages of another . . . the emergence of *tafsir* as a science of Islam is itself proof of the creativity of exegetes who still continue to be inspired by, assimilate, elaborate upon and even reject the work of their predecessors . . . what is required of the interpreter today is a clear understanding of where he or she comes from, a statement of his or her baggage as the word of God is being approached."[13]

The Qur'an as a key to liberation for today's disempowered and exploited people is vividly demonstrated by Esack in this volume; his source notes and references make it clear that he is not alone in his concern. Esack's own context was the campaign against apartheid in South Africa, but he addresses issues of patriarchy, exclusion, and economic injustice on a wider scale, and asserts that the Qur'an can support and guide the active struggle for liberation. His views at this point may be considered out of the mainstream, but as Muslims increasingly encounter the challenges of pluralism and progressive values, this discussion is likely to carry on.

Notes

1. For a concise discussion of this issue, see the excellent article by Andrew Rippin, "Tafsir," *ER2*, v. 13: 8950–51.

2. John Cooper, ed. and trans., *Commentary on the Qur'an* (Oxford: Oxford University Press, 1987), xxiv.

3. For a concise account of the theological issues involved in the Mu'tazili and Ash'ari movements, see Albert Hourani, *A History of the Arab Peoples* (Cambridge, Mass.: Harvard University Press, 1991), 62–65; see also chapter 7.

4. R. Arnaldez, "Falsafa," *EI2*, v. 2: 773–74; compare Henri Corbin, *History of Islamic Philosophy* (London: Kegan Paul, 1993), 267–69.

5. Ibn Kathir, *Tafsir Ibn Kathir* (Riyadh: Darussalam, 2000), 5. From the publisher's note by Abdul-Malik Mujahid.

6. Jane D. McAuliffe, *Qur'anic Christians: An Analysis of Classical and Modern Exegesis* (New York: Cambridge University Press, 1991), 85. An interesting set of essays in apologetics by Rashid Rida that also appeared in *Al-Manar* has been translated and annotated by Simon A. Wood, in his dissertation *The Criticisms of the Christians and the Arguments of Islam* (Temple University, 2004).

7. The definitive study on the formative years of this movement is Richard P. Mitchell's *The Society of the Muslim Brothers* (Oxford; New York: Oxford University Press, 1993), originally published in 1969.

8. Sayyid Qutb, *In the Shade of the Qur'an* (Leicester: Islamic Foundation, 1999), v. 1: xxiii.

9. For a very succinct and vivid excerpt, see Andrew Rippin and Jan Knappert, *Textual Sources for the Study of Islam* (Chicago: University of Chicago Press), 179–84. A new translation of Sayyid Qutb's *Muqawwimat al-tasawwur al-Islami*, an extensive treatment of his fundamental ideas, has been published as *Basic Principles of Islamic Worldview* (North Haledon, N.J.: Islamic Publications International, 2005), translated by Rami David and edited by Hamid Algar.

10. Kenneth Cragg, *The Mind of the Qur'an* (London: Allen and Unwin, 1973), p. 74.

11. McAuliffe, *Qur'anic Christians*, 87.

12. Farid Esack, *Qur'an, Liberation and Pluralism: An Islamic Perspective of Interreligious Solidarity against Oppression* (Oxford: Oneworld, 1997, 2002), 61.

13. Esack, *Qur'an*, 62.

CHAPTER FOUR

~

Law and Legal Theory: Shari'a and Fiqh

The foundation of conformity with God's will for the faith community of Islam is the law. Obedience and submission to duly constituted authority, what is permitted and what is prohibited, standards of personal and social behavior—these concerns are existentially compelling, for the individual believer and for the larger units of society of which he or she is a part. As the obligations of religious law are established and enforced by the mechanisms of government, they become the basis of Islamic statecraft and political theory.

The divine law itself is understood to transcend human institutions: It is a revealed truth, the *shari'a* (sha-REE-ah). The word has been used to designate the entire message of a particular prophet and is nearly synonymous with the revealed religion as a whole: the straight path to be followed, the command of God for mankind.[1] As Kevin Reinhart has observed, specific statutes in Islamic communities are not legislated, they are interpreted—scholars trained in the religious lore and literature determine how the received truth is to be applied in particular situations.[2]

In the classical literature, the essential sources from which Islamic law is derived are the Qur'an itself and the *sunna*—the exemplary behavior of the Prophet as known through the *hadith* narratives (see chapter 2). The information in these sources was processed and applied to the concerns of community life through an approved process of reasoning, known as *ijtihad* (idge-tih-HAD). The tools employed in legal reasoning included *ijma'* (idge-MAA) or the consensus of knowledgeable interpreters, and the principle of analogy or *qiyas* (kee-YASS), by which a known legal standard could shed light upon a new problem.

The study of the law as a human activity, carried out by scholars, is called *fiqh* or *fikh* (FIK). The jurist who conducts this type of scholarship is a *faqih* or *fakih* (fa-KEEH); plural, *fuqaha'* (foo-ka-HAH). The science of jurisprudence has produced an enormous and highly complex literature; the mastery of this literature is a demanding intellectual challenge requiring many years of diligent study. The jurist, therefore, has held an exalted position in the Islamic community over the centuries, establishing the methods of the discipline and writing critical studies of its texts.

The formal product of legal interpretation in response to a specific question is known as a *fatwa* (FOT-wah); plural, *fatawa* (fot-TAH-wah); the scholar whose job it is to render such an interpretation is a *mufti* (MOOF-tee), to whom ordinary people and sultans alike would turn for definitive rulings on matters of law. The terms used for these authorities are not mutually exclusive: The same individual could be known as a *faqih*, a *mufti*, a *mujtahid* (one who undertakes *ijtihad*), or an *'alim* (a member of the community of scholars; plural, *'ulama'*). The rulings of a particularly eminent authority were often collected by his students or disciples and became part of the literature and heritage of jurisprudence.

As the study of the law took shape over time, there was a degree of geographical variation, as the customary practices and prevailing social patterns differed from place to place; local legal precedents and *hadith* sources produced a particular body of knowledge in Medina as opposed to that of Kufa or Damascus, for example. An exceptionally able and influential authority could also attract a set of students who emulated his individual style of reasoning. A discrete trend, discipline, or orientation of legal thought became defined as a *madhab* or *madhhab* (MODD-hob); the plural is often seen as *madhabs* or more properly as *madhahib* (mod-HAH-hib). Typically, they are known as "schools" of jurisprudence, though in a figurative sense—they did not exist originally as incorporated institutions, but as schools of thought.

By the mid-ninth century CE, several of these distinct legal disciplines were recognized, of which four gained primary importance. All four were respected as valid and orthodox understandings of religious law, and they held a substantial set of common doctrine. Major Islamic centers of learning would often include jurists of all four *madhabs* or legal disciplines. Believers customarily allied themselves with only one of the schools, usually the one dominant in their locality. In the course of Islamic history, the Shi'a also developed an authoritative approach to jurisprudence, often designated as the fifth school of legal interpretation.

The Hanafi School

The earliest of the four major *madhabs* began to form in the mid-eighth century CE around the noted scholar Nu'man ibn Thabit, known as Abu Hanifa (d. 767). Abu Hanifa (AH-boo ha-NEE-fa) worked in the city of Kufa as a dealer in silk fabric, while studying law and the *hadith* (hah-DEETH) or "traditions"—stories and sayings describing the exemplary behavior of the Prophet, one of the most important sources of legal knowledge. However, his doctrine is said to be less dependent upon the *hadith* narratives than some authorities would have it, and rather more inclined toward the use of informed personal judgment or *ra'y* (RAH-ee) and reasoning by analogy or *qiyas*. Because of this tendency, his school is sometimes referred to as the "People of Opinion," as opposed to the "People of Tradition"; some literature exaggerates this distinction for polemical purposes.

Abu Hanifa himself produced very little in writing, though certain texts have been attributed to him. His opinions and style of reasoning are known chiefly through the work of two of his very accomplished disciples: Abu Yusuf and al-Shaybani.

The Hanafi school of jurisprudence ultimately became the most pervasive and influential of the *madhabs*, favored by the 'Abbasid, Saljuq, and Ottoman rulers; it furnished the basis of the *Majalla* (also transliterated as *Majallah*, *Medjelle*, or *Mecelle*), the Ottoman civil code of 1869. Hanafi practice spread eastward through South and Central Asia and into China. In the Middle East, it remains the most recognized school among Sunni Muslims in Iraq, Syria, Lebanon, Jordan, Israel-Palestine, and Egypt. Its strong presence on the Indian subcontinent made it significant in the formation of "Anglo-Muhammadan" law.

ABU YUSUF (d. 798)

Ya'qub ibn Ibrahim al-Ansari al-Kufi, known as Abu Yusuf (AH-boo YOU-suff). His name may also appear as Yusuf (Abu) Ya'qub. *Kitab al-kharaj* or *al-kharadj*, or *Book of Taxation*. The title also appears as *Kitab al-risala fi al-kharaj ila al-Rashid*, or *Book of the Epistle [on the Subject of] Taxation [Addressed to] al-Rashid*.

The scholar Abu Yusuf regarded Abu Hanifa as his master, but his own career was so crucial for the development of the Hanafi school that he can truthfully be described as one of its founders. He and his own disciple, al-Shaybani, are known in Hanafi circles as *al-Sahiban* (the Two Companions).

Abu Yusuf trained in religious law and *hadith* in both Kufa and Medina. He served as a *qadi* (or *kadi*), a judge, in Baghdad under the legendary caliph Harun al-Rashid and was given the dignity of primary *qadi* and the authority to appoint other judges; he apparently made himself very useful to the caliph in the administration of imperial law and policy. He wrote a number of works that appear in the medieval bibliography the *Fihrist*; among these may be indicated a very early work of legal theory, which unfortunately has not survived. He also produced a *hadith* collection and studies of the recorded legal opinions of Abu Hanifa.

Abu Yusuf. *Abu Yusuf's Kitab al-Kharaj*. Translated and provided with an introduction and notes by A. Ben Shemesh (Leiden: Brill; London: Luzac, 1969).

This fine edition by Ben Shemesh is the third of a three-volume set of documents on the subject of *kharaj*, titled *Taxation in Islam*. The printed text of Abu Yusuf's *Kitab al kharaj* (Bulaq, 1885) contained other material dealing with history, criminal law, and administration, which the translator has omitted.

One might expect this topic to be exceedingly dry, but the lengthy introduction by Ben Shemesh is very informative, even entertaining. He explains carefully Abu Yusuf's role in the tension between the "People of Opinion" and the "People of Tradition" and Abu Yusuf's interpretive strategy toward the *hadith* in general. He then explains the development of a fiscal system during the 'Abbasid era, with attention to its impact upon the property of non-Muslims.

Abu Yusuf may have been specifically requested by the caliph Harun al-Rashid (addressed as "Commander of the Faithful") to create a systematic study of the religious duties and precepts pertaining to state revenue; however, the epistolary form may be merely a stylistic device. In any event, the opening "Exhortation" is an impressive and at times passionate appeal for order and justice, the responsibility of the monarch to the people and his accountability before God.

Abu Yusuf then presents detailed discussions of the distribution of property seized in war, pensions and wages, land grants, water sources, portions due of the yield of all crops and herds, and an illuminating section on the *jizya* or poll tax. The English prose is consistently articulate and straightforward, but one might appreciate a glossary for the many untranslatable terms. The book does include a brief bibliography, index of Qur'an quotations, a simple summary of legal maxims, and an index of names.

There is a highly technical discussion of Abu Yusuf's *Kitab al-kharaj* in Norman Calder's *Studies in Early Muslim Jurisprudence* (Oxford: Clarendon, 1993), 105–60; it contains some lengthy quotes in Calder's own translation.

AL-SHAYBANI (d.c. 804)

Abu 'Abdallah Muhammad ibn al-Hasan al-Shaybani (osh-shy-BAH-nee). He is often referred to as Muhammad ibn Hasan. *Kitab al-siyar*, or *Book [Defining] the Law of Nations.*

Of the three great founding scholars of the Hanafi school of law, al-Shaybani was the youngest; he grew up in Kufa and studied briefly with Abu Hanifa himself, then more extensively with Abu Yusuf. Something of a prodigy as a traditionist or scholar of *hadith*, he traveled to Medina to study with Malik ibn Anas and became responsible for transmitting one of the authoritative recensions of the latter's *Al-muwatta'*, with al-Shaybani's own annotations.

Al-Shaybani served as a judge for a time, but chiefly distinguished himself as a theorist and lecturer in Kufa and Baghdad. After the death of Abu Yusuf, he was regarded as the primary jurist of the Hanafi persuasion. His writings have preserved the opinions of all three founders, often in the form of discussion or a comparison of their legal reasoning.

Al-Shaybani. *The Islamic Law of Nations: Shaybani's Siyar.* Translated with an introduction, notes, and appendixes by Majid Khadduri (Baltimore: Johns Hopkins University Press, 1966).

The term *siyar* (SIH-yar), in this context, refers to what is conventionally called the "law of nations," or standards regulating the interaction of states and peoples. But it is important to recognize that in al-Shaybani's era, the entities in conflict were not modern nations, but rather the *dar al-islam* or body of believers and the *dar al-harb* (literally, "house of war") or non-Muslim peoples. Islamic law was personal and binding upon Muslims regardless of their location, but the concept of territoriality became important when Muslims carried out missions of conversion and conquest in non-Muslim areas.[3] The behavior of the Muslims in these foreign lands, the rights and obligations of the unbelievers, and the distribution of captives and plunder had to be defined and regulated by the category of law known as *siyar*.

This work, expertly translated and edited by Majid Khadduri, contains the full text in English of the chapters on *siyar* from al-Shaybani's *Kitab al-asl* (also titled *Kitab al-mabsut*).[4] The first section furnishes the text of fifty-four *hadiths*, with their complete chains of transmission, relating the conduct of the Prophet and other early Muslim leaders during military campaigns and their teachings specifying certain lawful and unlawful behavior in wartime. The second section of six chapters (the core of this work) is written in the form of a dialogue between Abu Yusuf and Abu Hanifa, exploring in great detail the principles that can be derived from the sources; the process of reasoning from known precedents to deal with new questions is evident. Most of the opinions are Abu Hanifa's, but addenda are contributed by Abu Yusuf and al-Shaybani. The level of detail is quite fascinating. In the third section, al-Shaybani summarizes much of the material already covered. The fourth section deals with the subject of taxation, particularly of non-Muslim populations in conquered territories, who must pay certain forms of tribute or tithes of property.

The inherent interest of this material today, when Muslims and non-Muslims may find themselves in a state of conflict or competition, is remarkable. Any discussion of *jihad* or *bellum justum* should perhaps consider the juncture in history when reflection upon the relationships of Islam with other peoples "introduced into Islamic learning a new concept of the *siyar* which transformed it from a narrative to a normative character";[5] that is, the point at which stories about the early Muslim conquests were turned into regulations or guidelines for the present and future.

Khadduri's excellent introduction sets forth very lucidly the issues involved, placing al-Shaybani's work and Hanafi doctrine in their historical and literary contexts. The edition is generously supplied with precise and pertinent footnotes, a scholarly translation and text-critical apparatus, a glossary, and an index.

AL-MARGHINANI (d. 1196)
Burhan al-Din 'Ali al-Marghinani (al-mar-gee-NAA-nee). His name also appears as 'Ali ibn Abu Bakr. The *Hidaya,* or *Guide*. The title may be spelled *Hidayah* or *Hedaya*.

Each generation produced its own jurists, who meticulously studied the works of their predecessors; often, these scholars would write critiques of and commentaries upon these earlier works, seeking to refine the arguments or determine current legal practice. Such a work was produced by the Hanafi jurist al-Marghinani. His important opus known al *Al-hidaya* (hid-DAY-ya) was considered the authoritative statement of Hanafi law for its time. It was created as an abridgement of his lengthy commentary on a work by al-Shaybani called *Al-jami' al-saghir*. The *Hidaya* was itself the subject of many later annotated editions, synopses, derivative works, and commentaries.

Al-Marghinani. *The Hedaya or Guide: A Commentary on the Mussulman Laws*. Translated by Charles Hamilton. 2nd ed. (Lahore: Premier Book House, 1975).

The second edition of Hamilton's translation, here reprinted, was originally published in 1870 (the first edition appeared in 1791) as a textbook for "students of the Inns of Court, who are qualifying themselves for call to the English Bar, with a view of practising in India."[6] It has been reduced from four volumes to one very dense and difficult tome in a two-column format, indistinctly printed in a tiny typeface. An index has been created that is sure to defeat any but the most motivated student of Victorian legal history. The translation itself is described rather uncharitably by F. H. Ruxton as "a chaos of prolixity and confusion"; the reader is tempted to agree with this assessment.[7] Nevertheless, the edition contains a feature that might assist those researching Hanafi law: a "Preliminary Discourse by the Translator," in which Hamilton summarizes the contents of each section and points out its most salient features.

India and Pakistan

The exercise of British imperial authority on the Indian subcontinent resulted in the development of a subset of literature on what was known as "Anglo-Muhammadan" law. The British chose to administer some territories indirectly, allowing Islamic law to govern many aspects of personal behavior. British bureaucrats oversaw Indian judges who would deal with family issues and certain criminal offenses; there was an attempt to codify Muslim custom according to the categories of European law. In 1911 Sir Abdur Rahim, a judge in the High Court of Judicature at Madras, published his *Principles of Mohammedan Jurisprudence*, explaining the sources and methods of Islamic law using a British barrister's vocabulary.

Some Muslims in India were dealing with British rule by detaching their pietistic ideology from the colonial state (the Deoband movement) or by adopting an independent modernism that accommodated itself to Western culture (Sayyid Ahmad Khan and the Aligarh experiment). Others pursued the aim of a separate Muslim state (Muhammad Iqbal) and, when British rule ended and Pakistan was formed, demanded for the new nation an expressly Islamist identity (see Abul A'la Mawdudi's *The Islamic Law and Constitution*, 1955). Also in 1955, Asaf Ali Asghar Fyzee published the second edition of his *Outlines of Muhammadan Law* (London: Oxford University Press); he called for a form of *ijtihad* that would analyze Islamic dogma through the prism of Western critical scholarship, establishing a secular civil law. As Francis Robinson observed, "The British Empire was the context in which many Muslims experienced the transition to modernity,"[8] and that transition was often a complex and difficult one.

The Maliki School

The factor of geography as a determinant of some features of the individual *madhabs* is particularly characteristic of the Maliki school. It began forming toward the end of the eighth century CE around the distinguished *faqih* and traditionist Malik ibn Anas (d. 795), commonly known as the Imam of Medina. He created the earliest surviving manual of jurisprudence, called *Al-muwatta'* or *Book of the Smoothed Path*; this turning-point text is dealt with in detail in chapter 2. In it, Malik recorded the customs and practices of the Muslim community at Medina on the performance of ritual and worship and on matters of general law. An eminent traditionist, Malik reports hundreds of *hadith* narratives concerning the Prophet and his Companions, using this material as evidence to support legal precepts, but the preeminent source for Malik's interpretation of the law is the *ijma'* or consensus of the authorities at Medina.

The pattern of enunciating norms in the two categories of *'ibadat* (rituals, prayer, acts of worship) and *mu'amalat* (social behavior) is characteristic of a type of legal literature known as *furu' al-fiqh* (fuh-ROO al-FIK) or "branches" of the law. The ritual topics come first in these works, signaling their importance: They include the norms for purification, prayer times and practices, the giving of alms or charity, fasting and the observance of Ramadan, and the pilgrimage to Mecca. They may also include *jihad*, as in the case of al-Shaybani's *Kitab al-asl*, discussed above. The norms for social behavior address the issues of family law, such as marriage, divorce, paternity, and inheritance; commercial activity, including contracts of sale and partnership, lending, gifts and bequests, the ownership of land and property, slaves and animals; criminal proceedings and penalties for murder, adultery, theft, and so on. Works of this genre ordinarily classified acts into five categories: obligatory, recommended, permitted, objectionable, and forbidden.

Malik's *Muwatta'* provides an account of the accepted practice of Medina on these issues and takes a moderate position on disputed points, effectively representing the consensus view. The Maliki school developed an extensive literature of descriptive and normative law according to the doctrine and methods of its founder. The influence of the school spread from the Hejaz to Andalusia (Muslim Spain) and the Maghreb and is still the dominant legal philosophy of Tunisia, Libya, Algeria, Morocco, and parts of West Africa; it is also well known in the Gulf states, and in Egypt and Sudan.

IBN ABI ZAYD (d. 996)

Ibn Abi Zayd (ibbin obbi-ZADE) al-Qayrawani, or Kayrawani. His name also appears as Ibn Abu Zayd or Zaid; he may be referred to as al-Qayrawani. The *Risala*, or *Epistle*.

The most important early collection of Maliki *fiqh* is the *Mudawwana al-kubra* of 'Abd al-Salam Sahnun (d. 854), which unfortunately is not available in English.[9] This major reference work inspired a large number of studies and commentaries, including two by Ibn Abi Zayd of Qayrawan, which was then a major center of commerce and learning in Tunisia. These two works have long served as the backbone of *fiqh* instruction in North Africa.

Ibn Abi Zayd was the acknowledged leader of the Maliki school of law in his city of origin and attracted numerous students. His studies of Sahnun's work, his collections of legal decisions, and his tireless efforts to counteract what he considered to be the errors and excesses of his time established his reputation. His best-known work was the treatise known as *Risala*, also titled *Bakurat al-sa'd* or *Beginnings of Happiness*.

Ibn Abi Zayd. *First Steps in Muslim Jurisprudence: Consisting of Excerpts from Bakurat al-sa'd of Ibn Abu Zayd.* **Translated by Alexander David Russell and Abdullah al-Ma'mun Suhrawardy (London: Luzac, 1963).**

Russell and Suhrawardy prepared this abridged version of the *Bakurat* in 1906, with more than one purpose in mind. They saw it as an appropriate text for intermediate students of Arabic, particularly those in training for British administrative positions in Egypt or Muslim India; indeed, the brevity and simplicity of the work would enhance its value as a teaching tool. They also intended it to provide a handbook or ready reference to colonial legal officers and administrators in West Africa, where the Maliki *madhab* predominated. They also hoped it might be useful to Arabic speakers learning the English language.

This edition simply enumerates some of Ibn Abi Zayd's formulaic dicta upon issues of family law, civil status, gifts and bequests, and guardianship, setting a concise translation on the facing page to the Arabic text. Footnotes employ some information from the classic commentaries, identify Qur'an passages, and offer basic explanatory remarks; appendixes provide much more detail on the application of these precepts in typical legal procedures. There is a simple but helpful index.

A more modern English translation by Hajj Abdalhaqq and Aisha Bewley of portions of the *Risala* can be found online at ourworld.compuserve.com/homepages/ABewley/Page 17.html.

Ibn Abi Zayd. *A Madinan View: On the Sunnah, Courtesy, Wisdom, Battles and History.* **Translated by Abdassamad Clarke (London: Ta-Ha, 1999).**

Ibn Abi Zayd's *Kitab al-jami'* (*Comprehensive Book*), composed as a part of his abridgement of Sahnun, has been translated and published in this popular edition by Ta-Ha. This edition is not intended for scholarly research, but to be "of use to people engaged and active in rebuilding Madinan societies in our age."[10] It conceives of the early Muslim community of Medina as a paragon of obedience to the Prophet and transmission of his *sunna*; the prefatory material and chapter endnotes directly address the distinctive Maliki view of the *hadith* corpus and its interpretation, particularly in certain sections of chapters 1 and 4. The majority of the material in this volume consists of pronouncements by Malik ibn Anas and his replies to specific queries regarding details of religious observation and daily life.

The book is also supplied with an index and an interesting annotated bibliography; there is an alphabetized roster of persons mentioned in the text, with hagiographical accounts of their lives.

SIDI KHALIL (d. 1365)

Khalil ibn Ishaq (or Ishak) ibn Musa ibn Shu'ayb. He is commonly called Khalil ibn Ishaq (ka-LEEL ibbin iss-HOCK) or by honorific as Sidi Khalil (SEE-dee ka-LEEL). The *Mukhtasar* or *Summary*.

The literature of *furu' al-fiqh* was developed through the years in two typical forms: the composing of a *mukhtasar* or concise epitome of legal doctrine, and the formation of a *mabsut*, a voluminous and inclusive work enlarging upon themes of law, citing numerous cases and precedents, discussing and justifying certain positions or opinions and refuting others. A condensed summary or epitome of Maliki law, based upon Sahnun's fundamental work *Al-mudawwana al-kubra*, was created in Cairo in the fourteenth century by the highly respected jurist Khalil ibn Ishaq and became the ubiquitous Maliki text for teaching and reference in North and West Africa. It provides an accurate synopsis of standards, principles, and doctrines needed to rule on specific questions both in the area of ritual or worship and in social or interpersonal relations.

Khalil ibn Ishaq was born in Cairo, studied in Medina, and adopted the Maliki legal philosophy. He rose to great distinction in Cairo as the foremost among religious scholars, producing a number of substantial commentaries. The manuscript of his *Mukhtasar* (mook-TOSS-ar) was only about one-third complete at the time of his death, but it was finished by his disciples using his extensive notes and drafts.

Sidi Khalil. A *Manual of the Law of Marriage from the Mukhtasar of Sidi Khalil*. Translated by Alexander David Russell and Abdullah al-Ma'mun Suhrawardy (Lahore: Law Publishing, 1979).

The original date of publication of this work is unknown, but it must be contemporary with the same translators' edition of Ibn Abi Zayd described above. The design of the work is itemized, and almost interlinear: A very brief segment of the text is printed in fully pointed Arabic, and the translation appears immediately afterward. Often, several sentences in English are required to convey the meaning of two or three words in Khalil's highly condensed prose. The translators' additions are marked off with brackets. Abundant footnotes (according to the preface, these are derived mainly from classical commentaries upon this work) try to explain or clarify Khalil's often cryptic pronouncements. Only those chapters from the *Mukhtasar* dealing with family law have been included here.

The baroque complexity of medieval Muslim marriage is reflected in this excerpt: the intricate conditions of family law in an environment of routine polygamy and concubinage, arranged marriage, foster parenting, frequent divorce, remarriage, multiple sibling relationships and inheritance, and paternity or consanguinity issues. Spouses of Christian, Jewish, or Magian origin add further concerns. Another interesting element is the nature of oath-taking, imprecation, repudiation, "injurious assimilation," or verbal damages, in which a man's formal statements have the force of law.

The translation aims for a controlled, literal accuracy and is not fluent or readable, but nevertheless rewards careful study. The book is supplied with a detailed and very helpful index.

Sidi Khalil. *Maliki Law: Being a Summary from the French Translation of the Mukhtasar of Sidi Khalil*. Translated by F. H. Ruxton (Westport, Conn.: Hyperion, 1980).

Administrative concerns in Maliki West Africa inspired the British colonial authorities to produce this version of Khalil's *Mukhtasar* in 1916. The preface is specifically addressed to fellow imperial officers functioning in an executive capacity in Nigeria and is meant to help them understand the beliefs and behaviors of their native subjects; as Ruxton puts it, "The more we can grasp the inward significance of motives and acts, the more sympathetically, and therefore more efficiently, we shall be enabled to administer Muhammedan peoples."[11]

Ruxton's translation is based upon Nicolas Perron's six-volume French edition (1848–1852), which was itself compiled from Khalil's Arabic text and the contents of several huge commentaries. In Perron's own edition, the material intercalated from the commentaries was marked off with brackets, but Ruxton has abandoned these, so in the English edition the reader is unable to tell which part of the text is Khalil's and which is commentary. Also, Ruxton ruthlessly abridges the text, eliminating any material he judges to be of a strictly religious nature: details of ritual ablution, prayer, pilgrimage, vows and imprecations, apostasy, and so on—material of no practical value to a colonial administrator but of great interest to a student of medieval literature, law, or religion. He also expunges information on any customs not practiced in West Africa.

These editorial decisions limit the work's usefulness in some respects. However, the English prose is straightforward and readable, there are some helpful footnotes (from Perron), and the volume has a glossary and an excellent index.

The Shafi'i School

In the early stages of the development of the science of jurisprudence, the process of *ijtihad* (idge-tih-HAD) or systematic interpretation was still fluid; every scholar recognized the preeminent authority of the Qur'an, of course, but the emphasis placed upon the other roots or sources of the law was under discussion. The relative importance of the *sunna* as preserved in the *hadith*, the consensus of scholarly opinion in a given area, the degree to which one might rely upon one's own judgment, analogical reasoning, or certain other principles—this valuation formed the basis of a category of legal literature known as the *usul al-fiqh* (oss-SOOL al-FIK) or "roots" of the law. Careful attention to methodology was required to produce a defensible interpretation; *ijtihad* connotes, as Norman Calder puts it, "the exertion of the utmost possible effort to discover, on the basis of revelation interpreted in the light of all the rules, the ruling on a particular juristic question."[12] The scholarly works that form the genre of *usul al-fiqh* are meant to define those rules by which the revelation is understood and applied.

The turning-point text in this genre, understood to be the earliest surviving work in the discipline of *usul al-fiqh*, is the celebrated *Risala* of Muhammad ibn Idris al-Shafi'i. (It is possible that Abu Yusuf or another early scholar tried to address this subject; but if so, those works have been lost.) Al-Shafi'i was born in Gaza but grew up in the Hejaz, where he was thoroughly trained in the Qur'an and in the *hadith* corpus; he is said to have memorized the *Muwatta'* of Malik ibn Anas by the age of ten. While yet a young man, he went to Medina and became a student of Malik's; he also studied under the Hanafi jurist al-Shaybani. Therefore, his knowledge of the doctrine and methods of both contemporary schools of jurisprudence was exceptional, and he clearly possessed the kind of penetrating intelligence that was able to assess and critique their underlying assumptions.

In about 814 CE, al-Shafi'i moved to Cairo (Fustat) and established himself as an eminent but controversial figure. His independence of Maliki thought—and some critical remarks he made in writing about Malik's philosophy and methods—generated considerable antipathy against him. But he attracted numerous devoted disciples, and in time a separate *madhab* or juristic discipline became recognized with al-Shafi'i as its eponym. Some of the notable scholars affiliated with this legal orientation were al-Tabari (d. 923), al-Shirazi (d. 1083), Nizam al-Mulk (d. 1092), al-Razi (d. 1209), al-Nawawi (d. 1277), al-Suyuti (d. 1505), and the great philosopher al-Ghazali (d. 1111), whose treatise *Al-mustasfa* is among the historic texts of this school.[13] The Shafi'i *madhab* established itself well in Egypt and developed a strong following in the Middle East, the Indian subcontinent, and in Malaysia and Indonesia.

AL-SHAFI'I (d. 820)
Abu 'Abdallah Muhammad ibn Idris al-Shafi'i (ash-SHAA-fi-ee). *Kitab al-risala fi usul al-fiqh* or *Book of the Epistle on the Sources of Jurisprudence*; often called simply *Risala*.

A *risala* (ris-SAL-ah) is a type of literary convention in which an essay or monograph is addressed to someone in the form of an epistle or letter. It is often translated as "treatise," and in fact there is little in the character of correspondence about most *risala* works.

Some authorities believe that al-Shafi'i composed his *Risala* at the request of the traditionist 'Abd al-Rahman ibn Mahdi of Basra, who felt the need for a guide to the authoritative sources of *fiqh* and the proper methods of applying them. In it, al-Shafi'i first discusses, in an engrossing way, the balanced relationship of revelation and reasoning. Then (beginning in chapter 5), he argues forcefully for the priority of two sources of jurisprudence: the Qur'an and the *sunna*—specifically, the *sunna* of the Prophet: his exemplary behavior, his words and deeds, his responses to questions and problems put to him, and his approval or disapproval of the behavior of others. Al-Shafi'i enjoins obedience to the Prophet upon all believers as a religious duty and affirms that the Prophet's *sunna* is divinely inspired, a channel of revelation second only to the Qur'an itself. He also defines with unprecedented clarity the nature of the legal rules and principles within the Qur'an, another noteworthy contribution of the *Risala*.

The primary vehicle for a knowledge of the *sunna* is the body of traditions known as *hadith* (see chapter 2). Therefore, legal rulings would need to be documented by well-attested *hadith* sayings and narratives originating with the Prophet, not merely by the custom or precedent approved by the scholarly consensus of Medina, as Malik allowed, nor yet by the exercise of individual judgment or *ra'y*, as endorsed by Abu Hanifa. These sources and others (especially *qiyas* or analogical reasoning) could be employed to a certain extent, but only with a cognizance of the "overriding authority" of the *sunna* and the traditions.[14]

Al-Shafi'i composed other important works, including a substantial *Kitab al-umm*[15] and a *Kitab ahkam al-Qur'an*. But the originality and impact of the *Risala* can be summed up in the words of Majid Khadduri: "No other jurist seems to have discussed the subject [of *usul al-fiqh*] in so coherent and systematic a manner, and the *Risala* appears to be the first complete and well-organized survey of the *usul*, their interrelationship, and how the detailed rules and decisions were derived from the authoritative sources."[16] However, the work encountered initial resistance from other authorities, particularly those who recognized in it a departure from the two regnant legal philosophies of his time. Eventually, it had the effect of constricting the interpretation of the law to the ancient documentary sources and discouraging latitude or diversity in the methods of legal reasoning.

Al-Shafi'i. *Islamic Jurisprudence: Shafi'i's Risala*. Translated with an introduction, notes and appendixes by Majid Khadduri (Baltimore: Johns Hopkins University Press, 1961).

This authoritative critical edition of the *Risala* is widely available in library collections. In addition, several excerpts are available in microform as part of the *Islamfiche* collection. A second edition was produced by the Islamic Texts Society under the title *Imam Muhammad ibn Idris al-Shafi'i's al-Risala fi Usul al-Fiqh: Treatise on the Foundations of Islamic Jurisprudence* (1987; reprinted 1997). It has a somewhat expanded index and corrigenda; the volume is compact, nicely printed and formatted, with clear enumeration, subheadings, and footnotes.

Khadduri has created a precise and carefully annotated translation, working from several of the best Arabic manuscripts and critical editions. He provides a lengthy and articulate introduction that places the life and work of al-Shafi'i in their historical context and analyzes the composition, structure, substance, and argument of the *Risala*, its vocabulary and fundamental ideas. He also explains the formation of the text over time (an early version of the *Risala* was evidently composed before al-Shafi'i emigrated to Egypt). Useful appendixes are included: an alphabetical listing of the transmitters of *hadith* mentioned in the text, bibliographies of primary sources and modern works, and a glossary.

AL-NAWAWI (d. 1277)
Muhyi al-Din Abu Zakariyya Yahya ibn Sharaf al-Din al-Nawawi (an-NA-wa-wee). *Minhaj al-talibin* or *Road of Seekers*. The title may also be spelled *Minhadj*.

An eminent traditionist, al-Nawawi is widely known as the composer of one of the most enduring succinct collections of *hadith*, his *arba'in* or "forty" (see chapter 2). But he was also of fundamental importance as a jurist, the creator of the *Minhaj al-talibin*. This work was accepted as the authoritative statement of Shafi'i law; two major commentaries were written upon it in the sixteenth century, Ibn Hajar's *Tuhfa* and al-Ramli's *Nihaya*. These two works in turn became the basis for juristic ruling by the scholars of the Shafi'i *madhab* into the twentieth century.

Al-Nawawi. *Minhaj et Talibin: A Manual of Muhammadan Law* According to the School of Shafi'i. Translated into English from the French edition of L. W. C. Van den Berg by E. C. Howard (Lahore: Law Publishing, 1977).

This important work of *fiqh* is available to the English reader in a derivative version in this reprint (originally published in 1914). Van den Berg's French translation was made not from the *Minhaj* itself but from the two later commentaries of Ibn Hajar and al-Ramli; scholars have found fault with that edition. Howard then translated the French into English, but without any critical or scholarly apparatus. There is a simple glossary of Arabic terms and an index.

Al-Nawawi. *Al-Nawawi's Manual of Islam.* Translated by Nuh Ha Mim Keller (Cambridge: Islamic Texts Society, 1996).

Another work by al-Nawawi, *Al-maqasid* or *The Objectives*, serves some of the purposes of the *mukhtasar* works described above: It is a brief synopsis or ready reference to the practical requirements of worship and behavior. In this popular edition, it is combined with copious notes taken from another work of the Shafi'i school, *'Umdat al-salik* or *The Reliance of the Traveller*. The text is distinguished from the notes by parentheses and other symbols.

Al-Nawawi. *Al-majmu' sharh al-muhaddab* and *Fatawa*. In Norman Calder, Jawid Mojaddedi, and Andrew Rippin, *Classical Islam* (London; New York: Routledge, 2003), 192–201.

Two well-chosen and expertly translated selections from the *fiqh* works of al-Nawawi are included in this critical anthology. In the first excerpt, al-Nawawi defines the attainments and traits of a qualified *mufti*—one who is able to interpret the legal sources properly and issue an authoritative *fatwa* or ruling (plural, *fatawa*) in response to a specific question. The second excerpt contains some examples of al-Nawawi's own *fatawa* on a variety of topics, with enough of the reasoning and use of sources to exemplify his methods. The editors have supplied biographical information, introductory remarks, precise bibliographic references, and suggestions for further reading. These selections are particularly suitable for classroom discussion.

The Hanbali School

The great Imam of Baghdad, Ahmad ibn Hanbal, was considered in his own time not a *faqih* or jurist at all, but rather a *muhaddith* or traditionist; evidence indicates that he regarded himself this way as well. He did not create any separate work on the subject of jurisprudence. His major life's work was his *Musnad*, meaning "supported" or "attested," an impressive collection of nearly thirty thousand *hadith* narratives (see the discussion of this work in chapter 2). In *musnad* works, the traditions are arranged under the names of their original narrators, rather than by topic.

Ahmad ibn Hanbal's legacy is defined in another way as well, by his *Masa'il* or responses (or *responsa*); these are substantial collections created by his followers recording his replies to specific legal questions put to him in public or private seminars. The work of recording and transmitting these responses was the impetus for the formation of a *madhab* that reflected the orientation and opinions of its eponym.

Ibn Hanbal recognized as legitimate "roots" of the law (*usul al-fiqh*) only the Qur'an and the Sunna of the Prophet, with the *fatawa* or rulings of the Companions as an authoritative source of interpretation. The earliest believers, particularly the four "rightly guided" caliphs, knew and understood the revelation better than any later interpreters; therefore, all forms of *bid'a* (BID-aa) or innovation were to be avoided, *ra'y* or personal opinion explicitly rejected, and allegorical reasoning excluded as much as possible. This deeply conservative tendency was to become significant in the philosophy of later Hanbali thinkers, leading to a particular commitment to the concept of the caliphate, and to what Henri Laoust has called "a slightly fanaticized turbulence" and an "extravagant literalism"[17] in the "pious and militant tradition of Hanbalism."[18]

The Hanbali school eventually gained adherents in many parts of the Middle East but is most prominent on the Arabian Peninsula, especially in Saudi Arabia and the Gulf (Qatar).

AHMAD IBN HANBAL (d. 855)
Abu 'Abdallah Ahmad ibn Muhammad ibn Hanbal (ibbin HAHN-bal). The *Masa'il* or *Responses*.

Although the purpose of these *masa'il* works was to record and preserve the legal discourse of Ahmad ibn Hanbal, the documents themselves were

written by his followers, among them his son 'Abdallah (who was also instrumental in composing the *Musnad*), the famed traditionist Abu Dawud al-
Sijistani (see chapter 2), and Ishaq ibn Mansur al-Kausaj (d. 865). 'Abdallah
and Abu Dawud created compendia of small anecdotes, beginning, "I heard
Ahmad say . . ." or "I asked my father about . . ." Often, there is a dialogue
or exchange, with someone asking follow-up questions. Sometimes, it is clear
that the questioning is taking place in a group setting. The compilation by
al-Kausaj also features the opinions of another prominent scholar, the jurist
Ishaq ibn Rahwayh (d. 853), in the style of an extended discussion or debate.

Ahmad ibn Hanbal. *Chapters on Marriage and Divorce: Responses of Ibn
Hanbal and Ibn Rahwayh.* Translated with introduction and notes by Susan A. Spectorsky (Austin: University of Texas Press, 1993).

Spectorsky has selected, from the three *masa'il* works mentioned above,
those portions dealing with the topics of marriage and divorce, with all of
their casuistic complexity. She has created precisely documented and annotated scholarly translations of these works, with relevant text-critical detail.
A carefully crafted introduction explains the nature of the material and the
editorial decisions made, then analyzes the contents of the three works under topical headings. The translator's footnotes are as absorbing as the text
itself. She connects the text continually with the Qur'an, many other ancient sources, and modern secondary literature. Appendixes provide further
information on the manuscripts, a bibliography, index of names, a Qur'an index, and a glossary-index of topics and terms.

This edition is so well done that one can find only minute faults: In the
glossary/index, a few terms are not defined (e.g., *hadd*, *li'an*, *tamlik*), and some
definitions offered may be too limited for the reader with no knowledge of
Arabic.

IBN TAYMIYYA (d. 1328)

Taqi al-Din Ahmad ibn 'Abd al-Halim ibn Taymiyya (ibbin tie-MEE-yah).
His name also appears as Taki al-Din; it may be spelled as Ibn Taymiyah
or Taymiya, or other variants. *Kitab al-siyasa al-shar'iyya* or *Book of Legal Politics*.

The life of the great Hanbali jurist Ibn Taymiyya was turbulent in a number of ways. His career of writing and teaching in Damascus and Cairo was
disordered by episodes of warfare against the invading Mongols and those
thought to be collaborating with them, battles with Crusaders in Syria, periods of imprisonment on various political charges, and constant theological
controversy over Mu'tazili teachings, Shi'i tenets of faith, and certain Sufi or

mystical doctrines, and other philosophies, particularly those of Ibn al-'Arabi and Ibn Sina (see chapters 6 and 8).

He was quick to denounce perceived instances of *bid'a* or innovation and maintained a fervent allegiance to the *salaf* (SAL-aff), often translated as "ancestors," "ancients," or "predecessors," meaning the earliest Companions of the Prophet. He envisioned the early Muslim community at Medina (recorded by Malik) as the ideal embodiment of faith and obedience, from which later generations had departed. His reputation as a reformer stems from this radicalism in its strict sense, a desire to return to the original essence of the faith. This commitment entails a degree of detachment from the body of later legal interpretation created by the four *madhabs*, a position that was not appreciated by his fellow jurists. But it was Ibn Taymiyya who formulated what became a fundamental principle of the Hanbali school: that there are no binding obligations other than what Allah has specifically required and nothing unlawful except that which Allah has prohibited (in the Qur'an and the *sunna*). His teaching about *tawhid* or the absolute unity of God also had a powerful influence upon later Hanbalis.

Ibn Taymiyya's student Ibn Qayyim al-Jawziyya (d. 1350; his name also appears as Ibn Kayyim al-Djawziyya) became a master of Hanbali law and doctrine in his own right, with a reformist orientation. He composed a number of influential works, including an important study of *usul al-fiqh*. Some of his theological writings are available in English (see chapter 7), but not his works of *fiqh*.

Ibn Taymiyya. *Ibn Taimiyya on Public and Private Law in Islam, or Public Policy in Islamic Jurisprudence.* Translated by Omar A. Farrukh (Beirut: Khayats, 1966).

The principal concern of Ibn Taymiyya's *Al-siyasa al-shar'iyya* is the nature of leadership and authority, the relationship of the ruler to the ruled. He addresses princely or political authority as well as that of learned jurists. The work begins with a long essay on the proper aims of public policy, defining the responsibilities of the man in office, from viceroys and judges and army commanders down to scribes, tax accountants, teachers, village leaders, post office clerks, even guards and blacksmiths. All of these should regard their roles as a public trust. The exercise of authority by the ruler and obedience by the ruled has a single objective: to establish the religious life of the whole people, for religious and civil affairs are one.

Following the introductory essay, Ibn Taymiyya discusses a number of specific matters of public policy, with a heavy emphasis on criminal penalties and punishments. There are other more theoretical portions of considerable interest, such as the chapters on counsel, the necessity for authority, and his concept of reform.

This significant text deserves better translation and editing than it has received here. The English prose is neither fluent nor precise; textual information is scanty, and the footnotes, glossary, and index are inadequate.

Ibn Taymiyya. *The Madinan Way: The Soundness of the Basic Premises of the School of the People of Medina.* Translated by Aisha Bewley; edited by Abdalhaqq Bewley (London: Ta-Ha, 2000).

Even for a popular paperback, this little volume is short of basic information; it is not clear which treatise has been translated here, or from what manuscript or published text. Nevertheless, the material is quite interesting. Ibn Taymiyya covers a great deal of ground in a brief and informal discourse, commenting on all of the prominent *fuqaha'* of the four schools and their methods, the validity of the basic *hadith* sources, the relative authority of the various Companions and *salaf*, and the superior soundness of the Medinan position on disputed issues. However, the lack of translation and source notes dictates caution about the accuracy of passages that seem like paraphrase; for example, "When knowledge of the Book and the *sunna* has the upper hand, and the sword follows it, then the business of Islam is established" (p. 88). Despite Bewley's experience as a translator, this edition does not inspire confidence.

Other Sources

A number of other texts by Ibn Taymiyya outside the realm of *fiqh* are available in English, some of them in excellent editions; for example, *Ibn Taimiya's Struggle Against Popular Religion, with an Annotated Translation of His Kitab iqtida' as-sirat al-mustaqim mukhalafat ashab al-jahim* by Muhammad Umar Memon (The Hague; Paris: Mouton, 1976), including a treatise on the so-called cult of saints in the Sufi tradition, primarily a work of theology. In the fields of education, ethics, and economics, studies of Ibn Taymiyya's works and translations of certain texts can be obtained, including *Public Duties in Islam: The Institution of the Hisba* (*Al-hisbah fi al-Islam*), translated by Muhtar Holland; edited by Khurshid Ahmad (Leicester: Islamic Foundation, 1982).

IBN 'ABD AL-WAHHAB (d. 1792)

Muhammad ibn 'Abd al-Wahhab (ibbin obd alwa-HAB). *Kitab al-tawhid or Book of the Unity [of God].*

The trend of Hanbali reformism took a more extreme turn with the appearance of a charismatic youth in Central Arabia in the mid-eighteenth century.

Growing up in Najd in the family of a Hanbali scholar, Ibn 'Abd al-Wahhab began to react to what he perceived as the degenerate and polytheistic practices of that era. The veneration of the tombs and shrines of holy persons (especially Sufi and Shi'i figures), a belief in their intercession, interest in occult magic, and the worship of sacred caves, trees, stones, and the like had become ingrained in popular religion; a speculative mysticism and an uncritical acceptance of the accretions and digressions of medieval scholarship had caused Islam to depart from its early purity and simplicity.

Influenced by his study of Ibn Taymiyya and other Hanbali reformers, Ibn 'Abd al-Wahhab denounced these innovations and errors, often aggressively. He wrote a forceful manifesto rejecting these practices and insisting upon the doctrine of *tawhid* (tao-HEED), the absolute sole divinity of God, to whom nothing should be compared, attached, or equated. The assigning of any partner or competitor to God is polytheism or *shirk*, the primary mortal sin. Ibn 'Abd al-Wahhab reinforced this point with a campaign of destruction against the tombs of holy persons and other sacred objects. He also led a revival of ancient practices, such as stoning to death for adultery, and set aside the authority of contemporary religious scholars and *fuqaha'* to return to an idealized original image or concept of orthodox Islam.

In 1744, Ibn 'Abd al-Wahhab formed a pact with the local leader in Dar'iya (near Riyadh), Muhammad ibn Sa'ud, and they undertook a *jihad* to establish and expand a territory governed upon Wahhabi principles. This territory spread to Riyadh, then Mecca and Medina, and eventually most of the Arabian Peninsula; the Sa'udi dynasty has retained its fusion with this puritanical strain of Hanbali doctrine (what Fazlur Rahman has called "the right wing of orthodoxy"[19]) into the modern era.

Ibn 'Abd al-Wahhab. *Kitab at-Tauhid.* **Translated by the Compilation and Research Department, supervised by Abdul Malik Mujahid (Riyadh: Dar-us-Salam Publications, 1996).**

Because the message of Ibn 'Abd al-Wahhab remains the focus of much attention among certain Islamic renewal movements today, a number of his works are available in some form in English. However, this edition suffers a bit from the proselytical zeal of its publishers. The introduction is an encomium to Ibn 'Abd al-Wahhab and the *da'wa* or missionary call of Islam; the writers were unable to produce this material in fluent, idiomatic English, and its information is dubious.

Nevertheless, the editors have made a good decision in printing the full text of passages from the Qur'an and the *hadith*, both in Arabic and in English. They have also created comprehensible, somewhat expanded versions of the author's "Important Issues of the Chapter," very brief observations that indicate the lessons to be learned from the quotations provided. There are no editorial notes or scholarly apparatus, but parenthetical remarks are meant to aid in interpretation.

Ibn 'Abd al-Wahhab. *Kitab al Tawhid: Essay on the Unicity of Allah, or What Is Due to Allah from His Creatures.* Translated by Isma'il Raji al-Faruqi (Riyadh: International Islamic Publishing House, 1991).

The introduction to this edition is highly polemical, but indicative of the enthusiasm generated by Ibn 'Abd al-Wahhab's work in certain circles today. The translation of the text itself is rather awkward. Chapters often begin with a brief out-of-context Qur'an quotation, or allusions to several Qur'an passages densely packed together (helpful footnotes identify the passages), which are almost unintelligible in their abbreviated form. The *hadith* narratives in each chapter are easier to understand, as they are quoted in full (but without chains of transmission). The observations at the end of each chapter, called here "Further Issues," are extremely succinct; sometimes, a word of explanation or a footnote is offered.

There is a useful glossary, an index of Qur'anic passages, and a names index.

The Ja'fari School

The four orthodox *madhabs* described up to this point were not the only interpretations of *fiqh* that developed into distinct schools of thought; others formed and gradually disappeared, and the Shi'a began to define their own patterns of reasoning and sources of jurisprudence. The primary Shi'i school takes its name from Ja'far al-Sadiq (jah-FAR os-sud-DEEK), the Sixth Imam (d. 765), the most important originator of law in Imami or "Twelver" Shi'ism.

As the legitimate and inspired successors to the Prophet, the Imams themselves are considered an authoritative source for *fiqh*, along with the Qur'an and the *sunna*. The consensus of scholarly opinion (*ijma'*) and various legal methods are admissible insofar as they are in accord with the teachings of the Imams. The four great canonical *hadith* collections of the Shi'a consist to a large extent of traditions originating with the Imams, so these provide an essential documentary source for Shi'i jurisprudence (see chapter 2). The process of *ijtihad*, or systematic interpretation based upon disciplined reasoning, was needed to derive specific laws from these sources and to pronounce verdicts in juridical proceedings.

A fully trained and qualified individual who has attained the intellectual and spiritual mastery needed to perform *ijtihad* is known as a *mujtahid*. The most virtuous and learned *mujtahids* are recognized as models to imitate; in the absence of the Hidden Imam, they provide the best possible guidance for their followers, and obedience to them is viewed as a religious obligation. These individuals may be invested with the power of government as well. In the Islamic Republic of Iran, the religious authority of the jurists has been united with the political authority of the state through the adoption of the postrevolutionary constitution of 1979.[20]

There are also large populations of Ja'fari adherents in Iraq and Lebanon; though numerous, they were politically marginalized for many years and developed an authority structure in parallel to the Sunni or Sunni/Maronite state.

AL-HURR AL-'AMILI (d. 1699)

Muhammad ibn al-Hasan, known as al-Hurr al-'Amili (al-HOOR al-AAM-ilee). *Tafsil wasa'il al-Shi'a ila ahkam al-shari'a* or *Wasa'il al-Shi'a,* or *Legal Methods of the Shi'a.*

Toward the end of the seventeenth century, a respected *shaykh* at Mashhad in Persia began work on a monumental compilation of *hadith* that took him twenty years to complete. Al-Hurr al-'Amili was primarily a traditionist and favored the methodology of those who placed great emphasis on the *hadith* as the determinant of law; his juristic philosophy fell into disfavor, but his *hadith* collection became established as an eminent reference work in Shi'i jurisprudence. In it, he combines the contents of the four canonical books of traditions, along with *hadith* narratives dealing with legal issues from other important sources, and organizes them according to their juristic applicability, in a pattern similar to standard works of *furu' al-fiqh.*

In addition to this well-established text, al-Hurr al-'Amili created a collection of *hadith qudsi,* biographical works detailing the lives of noted Persian scholars, and some literature highly critical of Sufism.

Al-Hurr al-'Amili. *Combat with the Self.* Translated by Nazmina A. Virjee (London: Islamic College for Advanced Studies Press, 2003).

Among the many volumes of this scholar's primary work, the *Wasa'il al-Shi'a,* there is a substantial section on the topic of *jihad,* comprising two divisions. One focuses on *jihad* against the enemy, meaning holy war versus the opponents of Islam, and the other on *jihad* against errors and faults in oneself, in the sense of striving or struggling toward greater obedience, wisdom, and holiness. In a well-known *hadith* narrative, the Prophet endorses this effort of "combat with the self" as the greater jihad—presumably, more challenging and more significant than a struggle against external enemies.

Virjee has produced a carefully crafted, attractive, and readable translation of the portion known as Jihad al-nafs (jih-HAHD an-NAFS) or Combat with the Self, using a critical edition published in Beirut in 1993. Small segments consist entirely of hadiths on various obligatory or recommended behaviors and traits, or prohibited ones; the documentary source of each hadith or quotation is noted, and the originator of each saying is identified (without a complete chain of transmission). Virjee uses brackets to designate translation issues or words added for the sake of clarity. She also supplies a convenient glossary and a limited bibliography and index.

MUGHNIYYA (d. 1979)

Muhammad Jawad Mughniyya (moog-NEE-ah). His name may appear as Mughaniyah or Maghniya. Al-fiqh 'alal madhahib al-khamsah or Jurisprudence of the Five Major Schools.

In 1904, Muhammad Jawad Mughniyya was born in southern Lebanon and orphaned by the age of ten. He managed to get to Najaf in Iraq and obtain training in theology and fiqh; he was appointed to the shari'a court in Beirut with jurisdiction over Shi'i affairs. A contemporary of Ruhollah Khomeini, he pursued a somewhat different political theory; he accepted the supremacy of the Imams and the leadership role of the jurist in their absence, but argued that the jurist is not entitled to exercise the direct authority of government and should function in an advisory capacity, as in the 1906 Persian constitution.

Muhammad Jawad Mughniyya. Encyclopedia of Islamic Law: A Compendium of the Views of the Major Schools. Adapted by Laleh Bakhtiar; introduction by Kevin Reinhart (Chicago: ABC/Kazi, 1996).

This interesting work itemizes many of the topics normally found in works of furu' al-fiqh and then brings together under each heading the teachings of all five of the major madhabs. For example, in a section on choosing a leader for public prayer (pt. 2.8.4.), there is a brief summary of the Hanafi criteria for selecting a worthy individual, then the Maliki, Hanbali, Shafi'i, and Ja'fari methods. In Reinhart's informative introduction, he observes that the structure of this work displays both the unity and diversity of normative Islamic legal opinion; there is agreement about what issues are important, yet a degree of pluralism in the way the issues are sorted out. Bakhtiar's adaptation of this work is furnished with very extensive editorial and bibliographic notes; there is a helpful glossary and a general index.

IMAM KHOMEINI (d. 1989)

Ruhollah Khomeini (ko-may-NEE). His name may also appear as Ruh Allah or Ruhullah Khumayni, with an honorific Ayatollah or Imam. *Huku-mat-i Islami* or *Islamic Government.*

Born in 1902 in a small town near Tehran, Khomeini was sent as a young man to study in Qum, which was then becoming a center for the revival of Islamic learning in Iran. He excelled in ethics and philosophy with an interest in spirituality and mysticism. But the repressive rule of the Pahlavi monarchs of Iran and their attempt to neutralize Islam as the basis of Persian culture and society soon radicalized Khomeini, and he became a well-known critic of the Shah's regime. By 1963, the Shah and the religious leadership were locked in a deadly struggle, and Khomeini was arrested; massive demonstrations took place demanding his release, and he was exiled from Iran in 1964. He continued to inspire the resistance from abroad until the Shah's overthrow in 1979, when Khomeini returned to Iran to direct the establishment of the new Islamic Republic.

The theory of *wilayat al-faqih* or government by the jurist was developed by Khomeini in his seminal work *Hukumat-i Islami*, based on a series of lectures he presented at Najaf in 1970. The lectures argue for the responsibility of the *fuqaha'* to accept the leadership of a fully Islamic state in Iran, purged of the tyranny and corruption of the Shah's rule. The work is full of close reasoning and scholarly substance, yet it retains the stirring immediacy of a call to arms. Its principles were incorporated into Articles 107–112 of Iran's 1979 Constitution.

Khomeini. *Islam and Revolution: Writings and Declarations of Imam Khomeini.* Translated and annotated by Hamid Algar (Berkeley: Mizan Press, 1981).

This collection of Khomeini's lectures, public addresses, and interviews contains the full text of his *Hukumat-i Islami*, beautifully translated from Farsi and supplied with very helpful and detailed annotations by Hamid Algar. The intelligence, authority, and passion of an individual who had the power to direct a popular revolution are transmitted clearly even through the medium of another language. The other works included in the volume are also very interesting; an appendix provides an example of some of Khomeini's *fatawa* or juridical rulings in response to specific questions. The book is also furnished with a useful index.

Ethics

The study of ethics in Islam is based in more than one category of religious thought, mainly *falsafa* or philosophy, *kalam* or theology, and *fiqh*. The term generally used to convey the idea of ethics is *akhlaq* (ock-LOCK), connoting one's character or inner disposition. The task of ethics is customarily understood as the development of virtuous or noble persons, those who have cultivated within themselves the kind of manners and behaviors exemplified by the Prophet; there is a sense that personal perfection in holiness is an attainable ideal for which the believer should strive. As in the more general realm of law and legal theory, the Qur'an and the *sunna* of the Prophet (or the Imams) as known through the *hadith* narratives constitute the fundamental sources of knowledge, to be systematically interpreted using the approved methods of legal reasoning.[21] The work described above by al-Hurr al-'Amili, *Combat with the Self*, is a good example of *akhlaq* as a subset of *fiqh*.

In modern times, the conduct of ethical discourse has moved assertively into the political and social spheres. Trained jurists may be asked to rule not just on personal issues but also public ones; Muhammad 'Abduh and Rashid Rida, for example, issued *fatawa* dealing with political questions. Sayyid Ahmad Khan concerned himself with the role of human moral behavior in society. Sayyid Qutb and Abul A'la Mawdudi have argued passionately for the political application of religious faith. Ruhollah Khomeini was a respected authority on *akhlaq* who taught the principle of a close integration between a profound personal spirituality and the struggle for social and political justice.

The role in society of Muslim minorities and immigrant populations creates further complex issues, often multicultural ones. Problems in medical ethics, gender equality, and just war theory have focused the attention of many contemporary interpreters of Islamic law, sometimes under great pressure; statements by Muhammad Hussein Fadlallah (a leader of Lebanon's Hizbollah) on terrorism and kidnappings offer a case in point.[22] Recent rulings on whether Muslim soldiers in the U.S. Army might serve in the 2001 Afghanistan campaign present another example.

Legal and ethical issues in the contemporary public arena are often ambiguous and controversial, and opinion in the Muslim world covers an enormous range. The literature is extensive and merits careful study.

Law and Society in the Modern Era

Modern works in Islamic law, ethics, and government are very much more accessible and comprehensible to the English reader than the classic works described in this chapter. Many were initially produced in French or English, as the formulation of Islamic law and public policy has increasingly been undertaken by Muslims living in Europe or North America, or working in dialogue with Western scholarship. The catalog of any academic library will quickly yield numerous titles that analyze modern works in their cultural and political contexts. The spectrum of modern legal discourse is fascinating, and its implications for Muslims and their neighbors, both locally and globally, could hardly be more significant.

Some especially well-edited and useful anthologies of twentieth-century and contemporary primary sources in Islamic law and political theory are mentioned briefly below.

Islam in Transition: Muslim Perspectives. Edited by John J. Donohue and John L. Esposito (New York; Oxford: Oxford University Press, 1982).

Brief, focused selections from a very wide variety of political and doctrinal standpoints; helpful prefatory remarks in each topical division; includes statements by Jamal al-Din al-Afghani, Muhammad 'Abduh, Rashid Rida, 'Ali 'Abd al-Raziq, Sayyid Ahmad Khan, Muhammad Iqbal, Hassan al-Banna, Abul A'la Mawdudi, Sayyid Qutb, Khurshid Ahmad, 'Ali Shari'ati, and many others.

Liberal Islam: A Sourcebook. Edited by Charles Kurzman (New York; Oxford: Oxford University Press, 1998).

A substantial introduction and a helpful prefatory paragraph with every selection; well-chosen material, clearly organized and carefully annotated; a valuable glossary, Qur'an index, and names index; includes excerpts from 'Ali 'Abd al-Raziq, Muhammad Sa'id al-Ashmawi, Muhammad Iqbal, Fatima Mernissi, Amina Wadud-Muhsin, 'Ali Shari'ati, Yusuf al-Qaradawi, Mohamed Arkoun, Abdul-Karim Soroush, and many others.

Modernist Islam, 1840–1940: A Sourcebook. Edited by Charles Kurzman (New York; Oxford: Oxford University Press, 2002).

A companion volume to the one mentioned above, again beautifully edited, with many of the same features and attributes; includes selections from Muhammad 'Abduh, Rashid Rida, Jamal al-Din al-Afghani, Chiragh 'Ali, Sayyid Ahmad Khan, Muhammad Iqbal, and many others.

Modernist and Fundamentalist Debates in Islam: A Reader. Edited by Mansoor Moaddel and Kamran Talattof (New York: Palgrave Macmillan, 2000).

An extremely helpful and convenient two-part introduction, summarizing the viewpoints of each contributor; includes some historic documents as well as excerpts from individuals; annotations, bibliographical references, and an index; includes selections from Jamal al-Din al-Afghani, Chiragh 'Ali, Muhammad 'Abduh, 'Ali 'Abd al-Raziq, Sayyid Ahmad Khan, Abul A'la Mawdudi, Sayyid Qutb, 'Ali Shari'ati, Ruhollah Khomeini, and many others.

Progressive Muslims: On Justice, Gender and Pluralism. Edited by Omid Safi (Oxford: Oneworld, 2003).

Challenging essays from contemporary contributors; an incisive and forthright introduction by the editor; an especially good set of recommendations for further reading, listing current publications and websites; a well-crafted index; includes intriguing work by Khaled Abou el-Fadl, Farid Esack, Amina Wadud, Scott Kugle (Siraj al-Haqq), and others.

Notes

1. Fazlur Rahman presents a subtle discussion of the way the word has been used over time in his *Islam* (Chicago; London: University of Chicago Press, 1979), 100–9.

2. Laleh Bakhtiar, *Encyclopedia of Islamic Law* (Chicago: ABC/Kazi, 1996); from the introduction by Kevin Reinhart.

3. Majid Khadduri, *The Islamic Law of Nations: Shaybani's Siyar* (Baltimore: Johns Hopkins University Press, 1966), 51–52.

4. For further information on the *Kitab al-asl* as a whole, see Norman Calder, *Studies in Early Muslim Jurisprudence* (Oxford: Clarendon, 1993), 39–53.

5. Khadduri, *Islamic Law of Nations*, 39.

6. Charles Hamilton, *The Hedaya or Guide: A Commentary on the Mussulman Laws* (Lahore: Premier Book House, 1975), iv. From the "Advertisement to the Second Edition," by Standish Grove Grady.

7. F. H. Ruxton, *Maliki Law* (Westport, Conn.: Hyperion, 1980), 10.

8. Francis Robinson, "The British Empire and the Muslim World," *The Oxford History of the British Empire* (Oxford, 1999), v. 4: 398.

9. An analysis of Sahnun's *Mudawwana* can be found in Calder's *Studies*, 1–19; a lengthy quotation is included.

10. Abdassamad Clarke, *A Madinan View* (London: Ta-Ha, 1999); from the translator's introduction.

11. F. H. Ruxton, *Maliki Law*, v.

12. Normal Calder, "Law: Legal Thought and Jurisprudence," OEMIW, v. 2: 452.

13. A translation of vol. 1 of this work is included in a dissertation by Ahmad Zaki Mansur Hammad, *Abu Hamid al-Ghazali's Juristic Doctrine in Al-mustasfa min 'ilm al-usul* (Chicago: University of Chicago Press, 1987).

14. Majid Khadduri, *Islamic Jurisprudence: Shafi'i's Risala*, 24; see also his discussion on pages 35–40.

15. Calder discusses the *Kitab al-umm* and provides a lengthy excerpt in *Studies*, 67–85.

16. Khadduri, *Islamic Jurisprudence*, 40–41.

17. Henri Laoust, "Ahmad ibn Hanbal," *EI2*, v. 1: 274.

18. Laoust, "Hanabila," *EI2*, v. 3: 160.

19. Rahman, *Islam*, 194.

20. The definitive study on this subject is *The Just Ruler (al-sultan al-adil) in Shi'ite Islam: The Comprehensive Authority of the Jurist in Imamite Jurisprudence* by Abdulaziz Abdulhussein Sachedina (New York; Oxford: Oxford University Press, 1988).

An interesting twentieth-century textbook of Shi'i *usul al-fiqh* by Muhammad Baqir al-Sadr has been published as *Principles of Islamic Jurisprudence* (London: ICAS, 2003), translated by Arif Abdul Hussain and Hamid Algar.

21. A valuable set of six articles on foundational ethical concepts in Islam is found in *Journal of Religious Ethics* 11, no. 2 (Fall 1983).

22. John Kelsay, *Islam and War: A Study in Comparative Ethics* (Louisville, Ky.: Westminster/John Knox, 1993), 108–10.

CHAPTER FIVE

~

History and Historiography: Ta'rikh

The written history of Islam is above all a sacred history, a *Heilsgeschichte*: an account of divine salvific activity on the human plane, the working-out of God's plan to reveal and effect His will on earth. This plan is understood to begin with Adam and the creation of the world and to move through a succession of messengers to the final "seal" of the prophets, Muhammad, and the ultimate revelation of the Qur'an. The universal histories of the medieval era depict this God's-eye view of human events and evaluate the behavior of the actors of the past based upon their religious virtue and conformity with the *shari'a* or divine law.

Nevertheless, the writing of history or *ta'rikh* (tah-REEK) was not regarded as a formal religious science, like the work of the traditionist, the jurist, or the exegete. It was undertaken by scholars almost as a sideline, and often in the service of another objective: For example, the development of extremely accurate and detailed biographical dictionaries was stimulated by the need to document the reliability of the transmitters of the *hadith* or narrative traditions. It is astonishing, therefore, to encounter the very impressive work of these scholars, who created narrative, biographical, and critical products of the greatest importance for historical study.

Certain works of the early Islamic period focus entirely upon the life and leadership of the Prophet Muhammad; this body of literature is known as the *sira* (SEE-rah), often translated "biography." It encompasses many different types of materials: miracle stories and legends, speeches and sermons, some written documents (such as letters and treaties between Muhammad and certain

Arab tribes or foreign rulers), poetry, genealogies, paraphrases or interpretations of Qur'anic passages and reports of the circumstances in which they were revealed (*asbab al-nuzul*), and an important genre known as *maghazi* (mah-GAZZY), which comprises accounts of the military campaigns of Muhammad and his Companions. The *sira* literature does not have the status of holy scripture, but it is a valued part of popular devotion and apologetics.

The *hadith*-based approach to history as the compilation of transmitted traditions began to yield in the ninth century CE to the influence of a somewhat more literary historical discourse, with the growth of the prose genre known as *adab* (ADD-abb). The word suggests education or cultural training and connotes a literature that exemplifies and encourages civilized conduct, especially in the courtly milieu. This was not simply a secular form of history, since the king was viewed as God's appointed agent of authority and the cornerstone of the social hierarchy, but the emphasis shifted from the theological significance of events to the political and cultural. A virtuous ruler was an example of pragmatic wisdom and the art of governance; however, many anecdotes were not so much edifying as entertaining. Some court histories were composed in Arabic, but Persia provided the language and the cultural setting for many of these works; in Ottoman times, Turkish came to the fore.

There is a tension in Islamic historical materials between the more legendary and rhetorical elements and the objective of strict accuracy in the genealogical, annalistic, and biographical information. The verification of an *isnad* (the chain of transmission of a *hadith* narrative) called for great attention to literal detail. Biographical records were formed into *tabaqat* (tobba-KOTT), meaning "generations" or "classes," carefully compiled rosters of persons in certain categories: scholars in a particular city or province, grammarians, poets, physicians, astronomers, jurists belonging to the recognized schools of jurisprudence, Sufi masters, and so on. These works represent a considerable intellectual investment in historical precision. Yet at the same time, an enthusiasm for the miraculous and the fantastic helped to shape the historian's image of reality.

H. A. R. Gibb remarks (in a haughty tone) of Islamic history, "During its apprenticeship to the science of *hadith*, the native credulousness and romanticism of Arabic memories of the past had been schooled by a certain empiricism and respect for critical standards which are the essential conditions for any genuine historiography."[1] Khalidi indicates that the *adab*-based court histories and their progeny may, in fact, have contributed much more than the *hadith*-based sacred histories toward this end.[2] Gibb acknowledges that these conditions eventually produced one of the world's most original and perceptive analytical historiographers, Ibn Khaldun (d. 1406), and asserts that Ibn

Khaldun was able to achieve his critical standpoint without relinquishing his Islamic orthodoxy,[3] a point debated by other scholars. However one interprets its development, reading this literature today requires a respect for the quality and credibility of its scholarship, as well as an awareness of its nature as the product of a faith community and of its own time and place.

Because of its interest to Western scholars over many years, a great deal of Islamic historical literature exists in English translation. This chapter features a sampling of significant and representative editions.

IBN SA'D (d. 845)

Abu 'Abdallah Muhammad ibn Sa'd (ibbin SAHD). *Kitab al-tabaqat al-kabir* or *The Large Book of Classes*; that is, *The Great Biographical Encyclopedia*. He is also known as Muhammad ibn Sa'd, or Katib al-Waqidi.

The earliest major extant work of Islamic biography was created by the traditionist Ibn Sa'd, with the aim of providing definitive information on all known transmitters of *hadith*. Born at Basra, he traveled to study with several noted authorities; he settled in Baghdad and became an assistant to the traditionist Muhammad ibn 'Umar al-Waqidi (author of a surviving *maghazi* text). There is some scholarly dispute as to which of these two writers deserves greater credit for creating "the classification scheme of *tabaqat* which proved influential and lasting in every religious discipline."[4] Ibn Sa'd was also a trained jurist, though his career was shadowed by legal decisions that favored the Mu'tazili doctrine of the created Qur'an (under pressure from the Caliph al-Ma'mun).

The *Tabaqat* is considered to be a landmark of its genre, extending to eight volumes in the Arabic edition printed at Leiden (1904–1921). The first two volumes convey *hadith* narratives detailing the life of the Prophet, forming an important contribution to the *sira* literature. After that, he classifies the narrators and transmitters of the traditions geographically, chronologically, genealogically, professionally (e.g., jurists or *fuqaha'*), and in terms of the point at which they embraced Islam—what is sometimes called their "seniority." The entries on the Companions are substantial, but become shorter as they deal with lesser persons. The work contains information on more than 4,250 individuals, including about six hundred women, up to the author's own time.

Ibn Sa'd. *Kitab al-tabaqat al-kabir*. Translated by S. Moinul Haq and H. K. Ghazanfar (Karachi: Pakistan Historical Society, 1967). 2 vols.

The editors of these volumes have produced a solid example of *hadith*-based historiography in all of its meticulous detail—not simplified or streamlined in any way. Full chains of transmission are supplied for every narrative (including not only names but also modes of transmission), and the reader is urged to study these carefully to evaluate their reliability. These two volumes contain mostly *sira* and *maghazi* material, but the last sixty pages of the second volume provide more typical *tabaqat* entries about several of the learned Companions. It appears that this project was never completed, leaving these volumes out of context and without indexes; they stand nevertheless as an authentic example of their genre.

Ibn Sa'd. *The Men of Madina: Volume One.* Translated by Aisha Bewley (London: Ta-Ha, 1997).

This attractive book is the work of the accomplished and prolific translator who produced the *Muwatta'* of Malik ibn Anas (see chapter 2). The title is a bit confusing, because this is a translation of vol. 7 of the *Tabaqat*, which covers the scholars and leaders of Iraq, Khurasan, Syria, and Egypt. Bewley has already produced *The Men of Madina: Volume Two* (London: Ta-Ha, 2000), encompassing vol. 5 of the *Tabaqat*, which actually does cover Medina. A third volume is planned for the contents of vol. 6, which covers Kufa. She has also translated vol. 8 and published it as *The Women of Madina* (London: Ta-Ha, 1995, 1997).

The simplified format of this volume gives a clear idea of the reference character of the *tabaqat*: Brief entries under individual names are collected in well-defined categories. No more than one source is named for each unit of information, and there are only a few footnotes. Bewley has provided a helpful (if somewhat partisan) introduction, including a convenient chronology of events for 622–861 CE; there is also a basic map, a glossary, and an index.

Other Sources

The anthology *Classical Islam* (London: Routledge, 2003), 27–35, contains excerpts from al-Waqidi's *Kitab al-maghazi* and the *Tabaqat* of Ibn Sa'd, along with helpful introductory remarks about each scholar. The portion from Ibn Sa'd consists of *hadiths* concerning the Prophet's wives and is a better example of a *sira* work than of the biographical entries characteristic of *tabaqat*.

As time passed, it became impractical to compile collective biographies of the entire house of Islam, and separate references were created: one for the Shafi'i jurists, one for Persian poets, another for members of a certain Sufi order, and so on. Some of these were local or regional, such as the *Ta'rikh Baghdad* prepared by al-Khatib al-Baghdadi (d. 1071) as a resource for traditionists. Material from the geographical introduction to this work (not the biographical information) in English is available in microform as part of the *Islamfiche* collection and in Jacob Lassner's *The Topography of Baghdad in the*

Early Middle Ages: Text and Studies (Detroit: Wayne State University Press, 1970); some biographical entries are found quoted or excerpted in other works, such as Richard J. McCarthy's *The Theology of al-Ash'ari* (Beirut: Imprimerie Catholique, 1953), 139–41.

The biographer Ibn Khallikan (d. 1282) used a different criterion: He excluded the Companions, caliphs, and major narrators of *hadiths* whose lives were already well documented and chose instead persons of outstanding achievement in various fields for his *Wafayat al-a'yan* or *Deaths of the Notables* (also known as *Tabaqat al-a'yan*). This work is available as *Ibn Khallikan's Biographical Dictionary*, translated by William MacGuckin de Slane (Beirut: Librairie du Liban, 1970), a reprint of the 1842 edition.

AL-TABARI (d. 923)

Abu Ja'far Muhammad ibn Jarir al-Tabari (at-TOB-aree). His name also appears as Abu Dja'far Muhammad ibn Djarir al-Tabari. *Ta'rikh al-rusul wa al-muluk* **or** *History of the Prophets and the Kings.*

Few scholars have been as influential in their fields as Abu Ja'far al-Tabari. His great work of Qur'an exegesis, the *Tafsir*, is discussed in chapter 3. His universal history is without question a turning-point text in the literature of Islam; many such histories were produced before Tabari,[5] but later scholars considered his *Ta'rikh* the definitive treatment of its subject. They abridged it, supplemented it, extracted from it, and commented upon it, but rarely attempted to surpass it. Khalidi has called him "the imam of *hadith* historiography," and explains that for Tabari, "knowledge of the past cannot be deduced or inferred; it can only be transmitted."[6]

Tabari begins his vast work with a discourse upon time and eternity, and the duration of the world—the number of years believed to have elapsed since the Creation. He then develops the idea of natural theology, or how the observable world is understood as a revelation of the nature of God; then he addresses the concept of predestination, the Pen that writes whatever is going to be (*al qadar*). The six-day process of creation is detailed, culminating in the appearance of Adam and reflection upon the nature of the human being, the origin of corruption and disobedience, and humanity's place in the created universe. Elements from Persian mythology are included. His treatment of prophets and patriarchs familiar from biblical narratives is of obvious interest in the study of comparative religion: vol. 2 relates the stories of Noah, Job, Jacob and Esau, Abraham, Isaac, Lot, and Joseph, and vol. 3 those of Moses and Aaron, Joshua, Samuel, Saul, David, and Solomon.

After the period of mythic prehistory, Tabari deals very extensively with the Sassanian kings of pre-Islamic Persia, the life of Muhammad (composed of important *sira* and *maghazi* material), and the first four "rightly guided" Caliphs, the Umayyads and the 'Abbasids up to the year 915 CE. He moves very carefully through controversial material; for example, information dealing with the *fitna* or civil war and the murder of the Caliph 'Uthman in 656 CE.

Tabari's method is similar to that of his *Tafsir*: He assembles an enormous amount of *hadith* material (narratives are recorded with their complete chains of transmission) and information from other sources, compiling them in a topical arrangement; for the Islamic era, the work is organized by chronology. Where there are fragmentary or contradictory accounts, he usually includes them all, one after another, and sometimes pronounces his opinion on which is most likely to be correct. The presence of the author in the first person is often subtle, but perceptible, and he has placed his own stamp on this vast body of material.

Al-Tabari. *The History of al-Tabari*. Edited by Ihsan 'Abbas, C. E. Bosworth, Jacob Lassner, and Franz Rosenthal; general editor, Ehsan Yar-Shater (Albany: State University of New York Press, 1985–).

This extraordinary critical edition is the work of a generation of outstanding scholars in Arabic language and Islamic studies, among them W. Montgomery Watt, G. H. A. Juynboll, R. Stephen Humphreys, and Jane Dammen McAuliffe, to name only a few. Several volumes are the work of C. E. Bosworth, and the eminent Semitics authority Franz Rosenthal prepared the extremely detailed information on the life and works of Abu Ja'far al-Tabari in vol. 1. Also in the first volume is a preface by the general editor, specifying the precise standards and conventions employed in this project. The entire edition comprises thirty-nine volumes of translation, abundant and meticulous critical notes, bibliographies of works cited, and indexes. The editors endeavored to divide Tabari's huge work into meaningful units that can be studied separately; these volumes are usually cataloged in library collections by their individual titles, with *The History of al-Tabari* as the series title.

AL-MAS'UDI (d. 956)
Abu al-Hassan 'Ali ibn al-Hussain al-Mas'udi (almass-OOD-ee). *Muruj al-dhahab wa ma'adin al-jawhar* or *Meadows of Gold and Mines of Jewels*. The title may also appear as *Murudj*.

Al-Mas'udi grew up in Baghdad and apparently became a man of independent means, very well read and well traveled. His intense curiosity led him to explore the anthropology and natural history of Persia, India, Palestine, Syria, and Turkey, the Caspian and Caucasus regions, and Egypt; he also gathered a great deal of information about China, Byzantium, and Western Europe from other travelers. He particularly sought out minority populations with distinctive beliefs and customs, such as the Zoroastrians, Sabians, and Samaritans. He had a keen interest in the history, geography, and cultures of non-Islamic lands, unusual among Muslim historians. His writings encompassed every conceivable subject, from law and philosophy and political theory to astronomy, medicine, and botany. Of the thirty or more works he is known to have produced, the *Muruj* (moo-ROODGE) and a *Kitab al-Tanbih* or *Book of Notification* have survived.

The works of al-Mas'udi reflect his Imami (or "Twelver") Shi'i faith and certain Mu'tazili doctrines. But he is known to have consulted and cited a wide range of more than 160 written sources, including translations of Plato, Aristotle, Ptolemy, and Persian literature. His work has an expansive and humanistic quality that seems suited to "the sophisticated reading public of Baghdad and Cairo [who] could appreciate Mas'udi's lively blend of dynastic history, anecdote and general encyclopedia."[7]

Al-Mas'udi. *The Meadows of Gold: The Abbasids*. Translated and edited by Paul Lunde and Caroline Stone (London: Kegan Paul, 1989).

Lunde and Stone have approached the *Muruj* with a literary sensibility, as a work of art, not merely an impersonal chronicle of events. Their abridgement emphasizes the color and drama of al-Mas'udi's tales and includes his numerous digressions into poetry and witty anecdote. Each selection is keyed to the two full editions of the *Muruj*: the Arabic/French edition of Barbier de Meynard and the Charles Pellat edition in Arabic of 1974 (also being published at the time in French). This wise decision makes it possible for the multilingual reader to locate the entire passage in context. The editors also note which passages have been omitted.

Their English prose is vivid, natural, and aesthetically pleasing; explanatory notes are marked with an asterisk and placed at the end, along with a glossary, bibliography, and index. Two historical maps are printed within the covers of the book.

The volume examined covers the 'Abbasid dynasty, and was the first of a projected three-volume set, which was expected to cover the pre-Islamic period and the Umayyads. However, it seems that the remaining volumes were not produced.

Excerpts from the *Muruj* are also available in Reynold A. Nicholson's *Translations of Eastern Poetry and Prose* (Cambridge: Cambridge University Press, 1922), 64–78, in a somewhat old-fashioned style.

NIZAM AL-MULK (d. 1092)
Abu 'Ali al-Hasan ibn 'Ali, known as Nizam al-Mulk (nih-ZAHM al-MOOLK). *Siyar al-muluk*, or [The] *Conduct of Kings*; also known by the Persian title *Siyasat-nama* or *Siyaset-nameh*, The Book of Government.

The author of the greatest of the court histories in Persian, Nizam al-Mulk, did not merely record events—he lived them and to some extent directed them. As vizier to the Sultan Alp Arslan and his successor, Malikshah, Nizam al-Mulk was himself responsible for the administration of the Saljuq (or Seljuk) empire at the peak of its power. He served Alp Arslan as an adviser or court functionary while the latter was governor of Khurasan province; when the reigning Sultan died without leaving a direct heir, Alp Arslan seized the throne and Nizam al-Mulk displaced the former vizier, who ended up exiled and murdered. The Saljuq court was a place of violence and intrigue, and Nizam al-Mulk was one of its most powerful actors for thirty years. It seems ironic, then, that the young Sultan Malikshah (who succeeded his assassinated father at the age of eighteen) asked him to compose a treatise on the art of government.

Nizam al-Mulk did not fully complete the requested work before he himself was assassinated on the way to Baghdad with Malikshah; the manuscript was held in the hands of a figure known as The Librarian, who published it some years later. Malikshah himself died shortly after his vizier, and the Saljuq dynasty fell into disarray.

Nizam al-Mulk. *The Book of Government, or Rules for Kings: The Siyar al-Muluk, or Siyasat-nama of Nizam al-Mulk.* 3rd ed. Translated by Hubert Darke (Richmond, Surrey, UK: Curzon, 2002).

The *Siyar al-muluk* (SIH-yar al-moo-LUKE) is one of a genre of Persian works known as "mirrors for princes" or *Fürstenspiegel*; it is structured as a book of practical advice to the ruler in fifty thematic chapters, assembled from a multitude of sayings and anecdotes taken from diverse sources. These anecdotes are meant to be instructive and entertaining, but not strictly accurate as history. Longer episodes are frankly legendary; Darke observes that "they represent some of the earliest prose fiction in the Persian language."[8] Some of the later chapters of the work are thought to be more historical in nature (secs. 44–47).

Hubert Darke prepared this critical translation from a newly discovered document called "the Nakhjivani manuscript of Tabriz"; evidently, it was far more authentic and free of interpolations than those previously known and is believed to be close to Nizam al-Mulk's autograph. The Persian text of it first appeared in printed form in 1968. The first edition of Darke's translation was published in 1960, the second, in 1978; this new publication is cataloged as a third edition, but it appears to be a reprint of the second.

The book is attractively formatted and bound, the translation disciplined and readable; there are detailed chapter headings and subheadings to ease navigation, a bibliography, and an index. Darke has provided helpful endnotes clarifying translation issues, supplying background information, and referencing both medieval and modern works.

An excerpt from Darke's translation is available in James Kritzeck's *Anthology of Islamic Literature* (New York: Holt, Rinehart, and Winston, 1964), 153–59.

IBN AL-ATHIR (d. 1233)

'Izz al-Din Abu al-Hasan 'Ali ibn Muhammad, known as Ibn al-Athir (ibbin ala-THEER). *Al-kamil fi al-ta'rikh* or *The Complete [Book of] History.*

Born in Mosul into the family of a local government official, Ibn al-Athir was the second of three highly talented brothers, who were fated to live in interesting times. He studied in Mecca and Baghdad, but in 1186 went to Syria to fight with the great Salah al-Din (Saladin) in his campaigns against the Crusaders; he was present at the siege of the Krak des Chevaliers. His brother Diya' al-Din served in the caliph's court, and apparently his father and brothers were in a position to obtain useful political information.

At some point he settled down and devoted himself to scholarly work, particularly the study of *hadith*, and compiled two biographical dictionaries concerned with *hadith* transmitters. He then wrote a history of the courtly dynasty with which his family had been associated (the *Ta'rikh al-bahir fi al-dawla al-atabakiyya* or *The Resplendent History of the Atabeg Dynasty*) and finally, an immense universal history, the *Kamil* (pronounced like the word "camel"), which has been described as "the high point of Muslim annalistic historiography"[9] and as "one of the most impressive achievements of premodern historiography in any culture."[10] His work is distinguished by its consistent, coherent, and astute point of view and literary style and is considered a valuable perspective on the Saljuq era in particular.

Ibn al-Athir. *The Annals of the Saljuq Turks: Selections from al-Kamil fi'l-Ta'rikh of 'Izz al-Din Ibn al-Athir*. Translated and annotated by D. S. Richards (London: RoutledgeCurzon, 2002).

Ibn al-Athir's account begins with the Creation, as is typical of universal histories, and relies on Tabari's *Ta'rikh* up to the year 915. This particular volume covers the period of the Turkic Saljuq dynasty from the year 1029 through the reigns of the Sultans Tughril Beg and Alp Arslan to the end of the reign of Malikshah and the death of Nizam al-Mulk. Richards has selected material from the ninth and tenth volumes of Thornberg's Arabic/Latin edition of the *Kamil*, published in Beirut. He has coordinated his selections with the complete edition by page number and provided brief indications of the content of all omitted material.

The annalistic structure imposes rigid limits on the narrative, but is easy to follow, and every incident is given a descriptive heading. Some of the most interesting incidents in each year appear in the sections headed "Miscellaneous Events." Ibn al-Athir's accounts are rich with detail, if rather dry, and Richards's scholarly translation is precise but articulate and readable. Generous footnotes provide translation data, background information, and comparative material from other medieval sources. Richards has also provided a very helpful, informative introduction and considerable insight into debate within the modern scholarly community about the sources used by Ibn al-Athir, the accuracy of his account of events, and the value of his editorial and historiographical contributions. The volume also includes a bibliography and very necessary indexes of personal, tribal, and geographical names.

Other Sources

Richards has also produced a translation of the important and interesting biography of Saladin by Baha' al-Din ibn Shaddad (d. 1235), a contemporary of Ibn al-Athir and also connected with the Atabeg court. His work is titled *Al-nawadir al-sultaniyya fi al-mahasin al-yusufiyya* and is often cited as *Sirat Salah al-Din*. Richards's translation was published as *The Rare and Excellent History of Saladin* (Aldershot, UK: Ashgate, 2001) as part of the Crusade Texts in Translation series. The work offers detailed descriptions of military engagements, weapons, and tactics, and insights into the administration and diplomatic relations of both the Muslim and Crusader forces, using contemporary documents.

Francesco Gabrieli translated sizable portions of the *Sirat Salah al-Din* into Italian and included them in a very useful anthology, which was then translated into English and published as *Arab Historians of the Crusades* (Berkeley: University of California Press, 1969), often reprinted and available in many libraries.

IBN BATTUTA (d.c. 1369)

Shams al-Din Abu 'Abdallah Muhammad ibn 'Abdallah, known as Ibn Battuta (ibbin buh-TOO-tah) or Batuta. *Tuhfat al-nuzzar fi ghara'ib al-amsar wa 'aja'ib al-asfar* or A Gift to Those Interested in the Curiosities of the Cities and the Marvels of the Ways; his work is often known simply as the *Rihla*, or *Travel(s)*.

The duty of every Muslim to undertake the pilgrimage (or *hajj*) to Mecca at least once in a lifetime stimulated the growth of a kind of travel industry in Islam. During the *hajj* season, numbers of pilgrims could travel together in caravans and stop at shelters established for that purpose along their way;

traders likewise made use of these travel routes. There was also a strong tradition of traveling to learn from noted authorities, especially in the study of *hadith*. Accounts of these often eventful journeys were shared, and a literature of travel memoir developed. These accounts were not formal religious literature and rarely took on the character of a scientific geography, anthropology, or history. They tended to be works in the nature of an art form or entertainment medium. Nevertheless, they often contain most interesting material on the way foreign places were perceived and experienced by a particular visitor at the time.

The master of the *rihla* (RIH-lah) or travel narrative as a literary enterprise was the somewhat eccentric Ibn Battuta. Raised in Tangiers and trained as a Maliki jurist, he set off to complete the pilgrimage to Mecca in 1325 and began a lifetime of adventure travel. He was fascinated by the wonder-working and ecstatic rituals of mystics and dervishes and became an honorary member of several different Sufi orders, using the network of religious scholars and brotherhoods to facilitate his journeys.[11] His colorful first-person narrative often verges into the fantastic, giving it an almost Swiftian quality, and ranges from episodes of luxury and honor at the court of a noble to running for his life in rags and tatters from a gang of assassins. Upon Ibn Battuta's return to Morocco, the book was composed from his dictation (and supplemented from other sources) by a court scholar, Ibn Juzayy.

Ibn Battuta. *Ibn Battuta: Travels in Asia and Africa, 1325–1354*. Translated by H. A. R. Gibb. London: Routledge and Kegan Paul, 1929 (reprinted 1983).

The classic version in English of the *Rihla* is that of H. A. R. Gibb, which first appeared in this abridged edition while the entire text was being translated by Gibb under the auspices of the Hakluyt Society, working from the authoritative Arabic edition by Defrémery and Sanguinetti. The whole work was completed in four volumes in 1971, with additional annotations by C. F. Beckingham (reissued 1994), titled *The Travels of Ibn Battuta, A.D. 1325–1354*. An index to the entire four-volume set was prepared by A. D. H. Bivar and published in 2000.

Gibb produced a scholarly but readable translation, aiming to capture the informality and colloquialism of the original. A substantial section of elaborate notes clarifies many geographical details, vocabulary issues, and cultural data. The volume also contains indexes for personal and geographical names, plus some maps and illustrations.

An excerpt from Gibb's translation is available in James Kritzeck's *Anthology of Islamic Literature* (New York: Holt, Rinehart, and Winston, 1964), 262–66.

Other Sources

Another prodigious traveler who left a valuable account of his observations was Shams al-Din al-Muqaddasi (or Mukaddasi; d.c. 995). His *Ahsan al-taqasim fi ma'rifat al-aqalim* has been translated by Basil Anthony Collins and published as *The Best Divisions for Knowledge of the Regions* by the Centre for Muslim Contribution to Civilization (Reading, UK: Garnet, 1994, 2001). Unlike Ibn Battuta, he attempted a deliberate and systematic geography of Islam, carefully categorizing the provinces, their cities, and smaller units using an original vocabulary and describing not just the physical features of the landscape but also the social, economic, and political life of the populations. The work's design failed to make an impact on later scholars, but its information provides an image of the Islamic world toward the end of the tenth century.

IBN KATHIR (d.c. 1373)

'Imad al-Din Isma'il ibn 'Umar ibn Kathir (ibbin ka-THEER). *Al-bidaya wa al-nihaya* or *The Beginning and the End; or, Earlier and Later Developments.*

The Syrian scholar Ibn Kathir was originally trained in jurisprudence by a Shafi'i instructor, but was soon attracted to the teaching of the great jurist Ibn Taymiyya (d. 1328). Ibn Kathir was a versatile and ambitious writer who created a huge compilation of *hadith* known as *Kitab al-Jami'*, an important *tafsir* or commentary on the Qur'an (see chapter 3), the beginning of a planned treatise on the law, and a number of other works. But his most important achievement was his enormous history of Islam; the Arabic printing from the 1930s stretches to fourteen volumes.

Ibn Kathir's method in his history is similar to that of the traditionist, or *hadith* scholar. He relies upon the authoritative *hadith* sources, such as al-Bukhari, Muslim, and Ahmad ibn Hanbal, and he tends to place related traditions one after another even if they differ only in details of vocabulary. The effect is one of sequential anecdote rather than a coherent or unified narrative. He has gathered this material and information from other sources into thematic sections, within the overall chronological structure.

Ibn Kathir. *The Life of the Prophet Muhammad: A Translation of al-Sira al-Nabawiyya.* Translated from the Arabic printed text of Mustafa 'Abd al-Wahid by Trevor Le Gassick (Reading, UK: Garnet, 1998–2000). 4 vols.

The first portions of Ibn Kathir's history constitute an impressive example of the *sira* literature, or biography of the Prophet, and include many of the genre types characteristic of *sira*: poetry, sermons and prayers, genealogical information and other rosters of tribes and persons, and a major component of *maghazi* (accounts of the Prophet's military expeditions).[12] The editor, 'Abd al-Wahid, is credited with the task of deriving this material from Ibn Kathir's *Bidaya* and forming it into an independent unit. This unit was published in four handsome volumes as part of the Great Books of Islamic Civilization project by the Centre for Muslim Contribution to Civilization in Qatar.

The first volume covers the Prophet's ancestors, his birth and childhood, his call to prophethood, and the early revelations. Vol. 2 contains the "Night Journey," Muhammad's marriage to 'Aisha, and the significant events surrounding the emigration to Medina. Vol. 3 relates the battles and struggles to preserve and extend the new community and culminates in the conquest of Mecca. In the fourth volume, the new community matures and becomes established; details of the Prophet's daily life and the circumstances of his death are described. Each volume is furnished with a glossary and index.

IBN KHALDUN (d. 1406)
Wali al-Din Abu Zayd 'Abd al-Rahman ibn Muhammad ibn Khaldun (ib-bin koll-DOON). *Kitab al-'ibar wa diwan al-mubtada wa al-khabar* or *Book of Instructive Examples and Archive of Early and Later Events*; the initial portions of this work are often cited and published separately as the *Muqaddima* or *Introduction* (or *Prolegomena*).

An entire literature of scholarly interpretation has developed around the work of the North African historian Ibn Khaldun; he has been characterized in a variety of ways, but is widely regarded as one of the most original and significant thinkers in any culture, and as the creator of a true turning-point text. His universal history, the *Kitab al-'ibar* (IB-bar), and especially the philosophical reflection that introduces it, the *Muqaddima* (moo-KOD-dim-ah), has been described as a progenitor of the academic discipline of sociology and certainly represents an extraordinary achievement in critical historiography.

It is all the more surprising that Ibn Khaldun could have produced such a work while leading a very insecure life, bobbing like a cork on a tumultuous tide of events, often in imminent danger and suffering incalculable loss. He was born in Tunis into a scholarly family close to the Hafsid court and received a sound classical education in the Islamic sciences and Maliki law, but was orphaned by an outbreak of plague when he was only seventeen years old. He migrated to Fez and was able to use his scholarly skills to gain a position at the Marinid court and began a career of moving nimbly from the employ of one feudal warlord to another, always in an atmosphere of treachery and violence; accused of plotting against a certain emir, he spent some years in prison, but usually managed to shift his allegiances successfully with the fortunes of war. He survived for several years at the court in Granada (in Muslim Spain), where he acquired diplomatic experience in dealing with the likes of Pedro the Cruel of Castile, then absconded once again under threatening circumstances for North Africa.

In 1375, he was able to withdraw from political pressures long enough to complete a draft of his *Muqaddima* and *'Ibar*, and devote himself to teaching. But his enemies made things difficult for him, and under the pretext of making the pilgrimage to Mecca, he relocated in 1382 to Cairo, where he was able to establish himself as a Maliki jurist and judge. He sent for his family to join him, only to lose them all in a tragic shipwreck off the coast of Egypt. In 1400, he was carried off to Syria with an expedition meant to defend Damascus from the Mongol invader Timur-Lang (Tamerlane) and became a key negotiator in the effort to surrender the city, which was then sacked and burned by the invader. Ibn Khaldun's extensive contacts with the Mongol court are preserved in his *Al-ta'rif bi Ibn Khaldun wa rihlatuhu gharbhan wa sharqan* or *Information Concerning Ibn Khaldun and His Travels in the Occident and Orient*, an exceptional document in a scholarly tradition that rarely produced works of autobiography. Portions of this work have been edited and translated by Walter Joseph Fischel and published as *Ibn Khaldun and Tamerlane: Their Historic Meeting in Damascus, 1401 AD* (Berkeley: University of California Press, 1952).

It is chiefly the *'Ibar*, and especially the *Muqaddima*, that has so deeply impressed Western scholars. In it, many seem to perceive a critique of human events that foreshadows their own favorite styles of historical or social discourse: an expression of Enlightenment positivism or empiricism, a manifesto of dialectical materialism or class struggle, a Machiavellian drama, an account of the evolutionary competition for survival or social Darwinism, a literary exercise in the multivalent use of language, a pioneering work in economics, social psychology, education, geography, ethics, philosophy—even metaphysics. A few scholars stress his Islamic orthodoxy and foundation in jurisprudence.

Ibn Khaldun was himself well aware of the originality of his own approach and clearly states his intention to establish a new critical discipline, an *'ilm al-'umran* or science of social organization. He undertook to analyze the ways in which human beings come together to form effective units that allow them to cope with their physical environment and provide for their daily needs, while progressing from a tribal or nomadic existence to a highly developed and specialized urban society, economy, and political structure.

In social groups that attain particular success or dominance over others, Ibn Khaldun was conscious of a quality he called *'asabiyya* (ossa-BEE-yah), variously translated as "group feeling," "collective will," or "social solidarity." The cohesiveness of a nomadic tribe with strong blood ties is an instance of *'asabiyya*, and this quality may enable the group to develop itself into a powerful people with a dynastic leadership, a productive economy, and a culture proficient in the arts and sciences; however, the leisure and luxury such development brings with it tend to lead to that society's eventual disintegration and decay. Ibn Khaldun's eventful life had prepared him to reflect upon the struggles of successive warlord states, the concept of *siyasa* or political administration and governance, the relationship between temporal power and virtue, and the phenomenon of a late-medieval Arab Islamic world in a state of chaos and senility. His account of history unfolds his theories and illustrates them with *'ibar* ("lessons" or "instructive examples") from the past, while perceptively commenting upon the historicity of the records and reports, their use as evidence and related problems of epistemology, and the interpretations of earlier historians (especially Tabari and Mas'udi).

Ibn Khaldun's unique work was unable to gain traction with his peers or successors or to inspire a distinct movement or school of thought; nevertheless, it gained a receptive audience in Renaissance and modern Europe and eventually also in the Islamic world. Today, progressive Muslims tend to view him as an exemplar of rationality, insight, and intellectual freedom and to associate his work with efforts to create an authentically Islamic culture of democracy, civil society, and human rights.

Ibn Khaldun. *The Muqaddimah: An Introduction to History*. Translated and introduced by Franz Rosenthal; abridged and edited by N. J. Dawood; with a new introduction by Bruce B. Lawrence (Princeton, N.J.: Princeton University Press, 2005).

The most pervasive scholarly edition of the *Muqaddima* is based upon the very substantial three-volume translation by Franz Rosenthal published in 1958, working from various printed and manuscript sources. Dawood condensed the work into one volume and first published that version in 1967. Since then, it has remained a staple on the syllabi of Islamic studies courses and is available in most academic libraries.

Rosenthal's translation has been criticized for an excessive literalism, a pedantic or plodding quality; his introduction, however, explains clearly the strategy underlying his approach. One need only investigate a freer, more interpretive translation (such as Issawi's) to gain an appreciation for the discipline and accuracy of Rosenthal's work.

This 2005 edition provides three different introductions, all of them worthy of attention. Excisions by Dawood from Ibn Khaldun's text are indicated, but their contents are not summarized; the general nature of this material is described in his introduction. Footnotes are kept to a minimum, but they are always sharply focused and informative. There is a very helpful index (a bibliography is found in vol. 3 of the second unabridged edition).

Other Sources

A text as interesting as the *Muqaddima* could not fail to attract a number of translators; normally, however, a few favorite excerpts are chosen, rearranged, or presented out of context, which poorly conveys the character of the complete work. Some excerpts are available in R. A. Nicholson's *Translations of Eastern Poetry and Prose* (Cambridge: Cambridge University Press, 1922). A larger but still very idiosyncratic and eclectic collection of passages was published by Charles Issawi as *An Arab Philosophy of History: Selections from the Prolegomena of Ibn Khaldun of Tunis* (London: John Murray, 1950).

AL-SUYUTI (d. 1505)

Jalal al-Din Abul-Fadl 'Abd al-Rahman ibn Abi Bakr al-Suyuti (as-suh-YOO-tee). *Ta'rikh al-khulafa'* or *History of the Caliphs.*

The historical works of al-Suyuti, according to his own stated plan, were meant to draw material from the annalistic histories and *hadith* sources and reorganize it into narrative biographies of various classes of persons: the prophets, the Companions, the mystics, the poets, and all of the caliphs from the Prophet's first successor up to Suyuti's own time. Suyuti was an indefatigable compiler of works in almost every department of learning, tirelessly repackaging information into hundreds of different units, perhaps partly for the sake of having his own name associated with all of them.

Al-Suyuti had a remarkable ability to offend and antagonize his contemporaries, and a universal reputation for arrogance, competitiveness, and self-promotion. The son of a Persian jurist in Cairo, he began teaching Shafi'i law at the age of eighteen; he studied jurisprudence, *hadith*, and Qur'anic exegesis voraciously, then branched into other fields, always attempting to exceed other scholars in industry and erudition. He succeeded in producing some five hundred works, more than any other Islamic scholar; in them, he preserved the legacy of numerous earlier writers whose works have subsequently been lost.

Al-Suyuti. *History of the Caliphs by Jalalu'ddin a's Suyuti.* Translated by H. S. Jarrett (Karachi: Karimsons, 1977).

This reproduction of Major Jarrett's 1881 translation (originally published in Calcutta by the Asiatic Society) suffers, as do many of its kind, from poor production quality: paper, binding, and print clarity. It also resides firmly in the Victorian realm of formality and antique expression, with much use of "verily," "say thee unto him," and "when thou rememberest thy brother," and so on.

Jarrett's lengthy introduction is rather dense, but contains some intriguing material about al-Suyuti and his work from the man himself and his contemporaries. The *hadith* narratives (with at least one source mentioned), poems, sayings, and anecdotes al-Suyuti has collected are often worth reading; there are very important incidents (such as the *hadith* from Bukhari on the collection of the Qur'an into a single text under the Caliph Abu Bakr) balanced by the insignificant but interesting lives of obscure caliphs like Suleyman ibn 'Abd al-Malik.

The edition is heavily annotated; Jarrett handles the Arabic text carefully and calls attention to linguistic problems, comparing his reading with other translations. Footnotes also provide considerable information about each one of the countless persons mentioned in the text and clarify many points of law and cultural allusions. There is a names index and a helpful chart of the names and dates of the caliphs in succession from 632 to 1497 CE.

A translation in rather flat modern English of a portion of al-Suyuti's *Ta'rikh* is found in the anthology *Classical Islam* (New York: Routledge, 2003), 83–87. It relates the circumstances surrounding the murder of the Caliph 'Uthman.

The Ottoman Era

The tradition of courtly literature in various Islamic dominions was an ancient one, often predating Islam itself; the king's desire for a tribute to his regime and its dynasty produced epic poetry, legend, and flattering annalistic accounts (e.g., the "Sultan-Pasha chronicles" of the eighteenth century) [13] What is less well known is that these histories often made appropriate use of documentary sources: public and personal records, correspondence, government edicts, speeches or addresses, treaties, announcements of the appointments of various officials, administrative orders, legal briefs and verdicts, contracts of marriage in prominent families, deeds of property, wills and bequests (especially of a *waqf* or religious endowment), census information, economic data, and similar material. Franz Rosenthal observes of one such work: "Such documents as we find [in it] are the exact equivalent of the official papers of modern foreign ministries; reading them gave the contemporary Muslim student the same insight into history-in-the-making at his time which the modern student is wont to expect in the documented memoirs of one of the statesmen of our time."[14]

In the Ottoman era, the sheer scope and sweep of a vast centralized empire demanded the formation of detailed and well-ordered administrative archives. These documents were not collected with the aim of creating literature, but to meet the functional information needs of the imperial bureaucracy. The study of the documentary records of this era is the work of the scholarly specialist, but any reader interested in history will find them fascinating, and some are available in English; for example, in Justin McCarthy's *The Arab World, Turkey and the Balkans (1878–1914): A Handbook of Historical Statistics* (Boston: G. K. Hall, 1982).

First-person memoirs and narrative histories, sometimes based upon personal journals, are also extant from Ottoman times. Analytical or critical histories are few, especially in Ottoman Egypt, which experienced a decline in historical writing. Among the most interesting developments during this period is the literature generated by the collision of Islamic nations with the European colonial powers, especially France and England, prefiguring the political and cultural conflicts of the present day.

AL-JABARTI (d.c. 1825)

'Abd al-Rahman ibn Hasan al-Jabarti (al-job-BAR-tee). His name also appears as al-Djabarti. *Ta'rikh muddat al-faransawiyya fi misr* or *History of the Time Period of the French in Egypt*; the title may appear as *Ta'rikh muddat al-faransis bi misr.*

Napoleon Bonaparte's stunning invasion of Egypt in June 1798, and the three-year occupation that followed, is often referenced as the point at which the Middle East first met the modern West in the form of an advanced military power. Napoleon quickly defeated the Mamluk forces, deposed the Ottoman governors, took possession of Cairo, and announced his intention to colonize Egypt. But the French had far more in mind: They had brought with them an extraordinary team of 150 archaeologists, historians, geographers, architects, artists, linguists, natural scientists, and other experts whose job it was to study Egypt and "render it completely open, to make it totally accessible to European scrutiny," and to produce "that great collective appropriation of one country by another, the *Description de l'Égypte*."[15]

The Hanafi scholar al-Jabarti was an eyewitness to these watershed political and cultural events, and he recorded his personal observations in several different works. He wrote an initial impression of the first seven months of the occupation, known as the *Muddat*, meaning span of time (see the full title above). He produced a second work praising the Ottomans and rejecting the French (known as the *Mazhar al-taqdis* or *Religious Conduct*), and a third more comprehensive and dispassionate history of Egypt from 1688 to 1821, in which the period of French influence figures prominently, his *'Aja'ib al-athar fi al-tarajim wa al-akhbar* or *Marvels of the Reports of the Biographies and the Histories*. The *'Aja'ib al-athar* has been described as "the last great work in a traditional mold," using the established chronicle/biography style and methods of the medieval era.[16] An excerpt from this work, translated by William Shepard, is found in the anthology *Windows on the House of Islam* (Berkeley: University of California Press, 1998), 141–44; an interesting selection translated by Ibrahim Abdel Akher is in James Kritzeck's anthology *Modern Islamic Literature* (New York: Holt, 1970), 12–16.

Al-Jabarti. *Napoleon in Egypt: Al-Jabarti's Chronicle of the First Seven Months of the French Occupation, 1798*. Translated by S. Moreh; edited by Robert L. Tignor (Princeton, N.J.: M. Wiener, 1993).

This convenient edition binds together three different works that shed a great deal of light on each other. The first of them is al-Jabarti's *Muddat*, in a well-crafted and readable translation, capturing the immediacy of this first-person account. With this work is printed a first-person view from the French side, by Napoleon's secretary Antoine Fauvelet de Bourienne. The third work included is a critical commentary upon the French cultural assault on Egypt and its implications for both East and West, an excerpt from Edward Said's landmark study *Orientalism* (first published by Pantheon Books in 1978).

The book includes endnotes, information about the writers and translators, and an introduction by Robert L. Tignor; it also includes many intriguing illustrations and maps, which unfortunately are rather poorly reproduced.

History and Its Study in the Modern Era

Historical writing in the Islamic world in the modern era has been influenced by two powerful forces: the impressive and complex literature of the classical period and the legacy of colonial and postcolonial discourse. If the writing of history is fundamentally an exploration of meaning and identity, then the rich lore of Islamic tradition and the experience of rapid social and cultural change initiated by contact with Europe provided a great deal of material for such exploration.

For example, one of the last individuals to serve as official court historian under the Ottoman sultans was Ahmed Cevdet Pasha (d. 1895), who directed the preparation of the *Majalla* (or *Mecelle*), the Ottoman civil code of 1869. The code was an effort to apply a Hanafi interpretation of Islamic law to the needs of a nineteenth-century imperial administration while resisting pressure to adopt the French civil code. He was also a translator of Ibn Khaldun's

Muqaddima into Turkish. Cevdet Pasha wrote a fairly traditional court chronicle of the years 1774–1826, but made extensive use of European as well as Ottoman documents and displayed a keen interest in the Khaldunian critique of historical and social development and decline.[17]

Other writers attempted to bring the methods of twentieth-century literary and textual criticism to bear upon the sacred records of early Islamic history. The Egyptian novelist and critic Taha Husayn, again strongly influenced by Ibn Khaldun, rejected the authenticity of important pre-Islamic poetry, with implications for other ancient texts. Muhammad Husayn Haykal reinterpreted the *sira* literature in his biography of the Prophet, *Hayat Muhammad* (1934). Drawing from the classic sources (the Qur'an, the *Tabaqat* of Ibn Sa'd, Waqidi's *Maghazi*, etc.), and committed to a traditional Islamic piety, Haykal nevertheless argued for openness to Western scholarship and criticism as a way to combat intellectual lethargy and conservatism, and actively engaged the work of Orientalist scholars. The literary critic and exegete 'Aisha 'Abd al-Rahman (known as Bint al-Shati) developed the same sources into a creative paraphrase called *Nisa' al-Nabi* or *Wives of the Prophet*, again combining traditional piety with a humanistic and aesthetic sensibility. This very popular work, published in 1959, was followed by volumes on the daughters of the Prophet in 1963 and Muhammad's mother in 1966.

In the Shi'i world, eminent cleric 'Allameh Tabataba'i addressed himself to the history of the succession to the Prophet, the caliphate, and the early generations of Islam in his *Shi'ite Islam*, translated by Seyyed Hossein Nasr (Albany: State University of New York Press, 1975). Ahmad Kasravi of the University of Tehran also dealt specifically with the history of Shi'ism in his lectures and books. Issues of the legitimacy of the early and medieval institutions of authority and the credibility of ancient sources are never far from the surface in work of this nature.

Other academic historians, such as Mohamed Anis, Philip S. Khoury, Albert Hourani, 'Abdallah Laroui, Tarif Khalidi, and Tayeb al-Hibri have continued to probe these issues from the standpoint of the scholarly interpreter and critic. In recent years, fundamentalist movements and other political pressures in the Islamic world have made the work of understanding the past a sensitive and challenging task.

Notes

1. Hamilton A. R. Gibb, "Ta'rikh," *Studies on the Civilization of Islam* (Boston: Beacon Press, 1962), 117.

2. See the discussion of history and *adab* in Tarif Khalidi's *Arabic Historical Thought in the Classical Period* (Cambridge: Cambridge University Press, 1994), 83–95.

3. See Gibb, "The Islamic Background of Ibn Khaldun's Political Theory," 166–75 in *Studies*.

4. *Classical Islam: A Sourcebook of Religious Literature*, edited and translated by Norman Calder, Jawid Mojaddedi, and Andrew Rippin (London; New York: Routledge, 2003), 30.

5. Compare the early history *Kitab futuh al-buldan* by Ahmad ibn Yahya Baladhuri, translated by Philip Khuri Hitti and Francis Murgotten and published as *The Origins of the Islamic State* (New York: AMS Press, 1968), reprint of the 1916 edition.

6. Khalidi, *Arabic Historical Thought*, 74.

7. Al-Mas'udi, *The Meadows of Gold*, translated and edited by Paul Lunde and Caroline Stone (London: Kegan Paul, 1989), 15, from the translators' introduction. There is a concise but informative article by Julia Bray placing al-Mas'udi and other writers in the context of *adab* in *Medieval Islamic Civilization: An Encyclopedia*, edited by Josef W. Meri (New York: Routledge, 2006), v. 1: 13–14.

8. Nizam al-Mulk, *The Book of Government, or Rules for Kings*, 3rd ed., translated by Hubert Darke (Richmond, Surrey, UK: Curzon, 2002), xvi, from the translator's introduction.

9. Franz Rosenthal, "Ibn al-Athir," *EI2*, v. 3: 724.

10. R. S. Humphreys, "Ta'rikh," *EI2*, v. 10: 279.

11. See the article by Ian Richard Netton, "Myth, Miracle and Magic in the *Rihla* of Ibn Battuta," *Journal of Semitic Studies* 29, v. 1 (Spr 1984): 131–40.

12. The "Book of Military Expeditions" is found in the second volume of this edition, but further campaigns appear in vol. 3. For other examples in English of *maghazi* texts, see Ibn Sa'd and al-Waqidi, above.

13. See, for example, *Eighteenth Century Egypt: The Arabic Manuscript Sources*, edited by Daniel Crecelius (Claremont, Calif.: Regina Books, 1990) or *Al-Damurdashi's Chronicle of Egypt, 1688–1755*, translated and edited by Daniel Crecelius and 'Abd al-Wahhab Bakr Muhammad (Leiden. Brill, 1991).

14. Franz Rosenthal, *A History of Muslim Historiography*, 2nd ed. (Leiden: Brill, 1968), 121.

15. Edward Said, "Orientalism: The Cultural Consequences of the French Preoccupation with Egypt," in *Napoleon in Egypt* (Princeton, N.J.: Markus Wiener, 1993), 171 and 173.

16. R. S. Humphreys, "Historiography," *OLMIW*, v. 2: 115.

17. Humphreys, "Historiography," 116.

CHAPTER SIX

~

Philosophy: Falsafa

The revelation of God in the text of the Qur'an and the preservation of the Prophet's example and teaching in the text of the *hadith* narratives determined the course of early Islamic scholarship. The interpretation and application of these texts was the work of linguists, exegetes, traditionists, and jurists. Doctrinal theology, known as *kalam* (ka-LAMM), concerned itself with understanding the implications of what had been revealed and transmitted.

During the 'Abbasid dynasty, however, a new current of thought entered the Islamic world through contact with the philosophy of classical Greece and Greco-Roman Alexandria. The word *falsafa* (fall-SOFFA) is an Arabic form of the Greek *philosophia*, the love of wisdom, or philosophy. The Arabic word *hikma* (HICK-mah) or wisdom was also closely associated with this type of knowledge, which encompassed not only logic, dialectic, and abstract reasoning, but also mathematics (algebra, geometry), medicine, and all of the natural sciences, including physics, astronomy, and chemistry, and even their occult forms, astrology and alchemy.[1]

An effort to translate Greek or Syriac scientific information into accurate Arabic began in earnest with the caliphate of the 'Abbasids in 750 CE and was encouraged by the active support and resources of the court of al-Ma'-mun (813–833 CE). Along with the medical and scientific texts of scholars like Galen, Ptolemy, and Euclid came the philosophical works of Aristotle, Plato, and Plotinus, stimulating a rethinking of the place of human beings in the cosmos and the qualities and characteristics of human knowledge.

Translations of these texts soon led to the writing of commentaries upon them and then to original essays and treatises exploring the potential of this

new form of discourse. One who undertook this study and created its literature was known as a *faylasuf* (fay-la-SOOF); plural, *falasifa* (fa-LASS-iffa).
These thinkers and writers may be identified in modern scholarly discussion
as Neoplatonists, or as Peripatetics, in reference to the ancient Athenian
school of Aristotle. Corbin calls them "the Hellenizing philosophers"; Fakhry
speaks of "the Islamic philosophical school."[2]

The work of the *falasifa* appealed to some, but very much offended others,
who regarded this line of inquiry as a departure from established Islamic orthodoxy and an intellectual error. The philosophical emphasis on the powers of the human intellect or *'aql* (OCK-ul) was seen by some as a threat to
the supremacy of the revealed and transmitted sources of knowledge or *naql*
(NOCK-ul). The Sunni theologian Abul-Hassan al-Ash'ari (d. 935) considered certain assumptions of the philosophers to contradict divine sovereignty
and justice and to present unacceptable implications for ethics. A stronger
rejection of *falsafa* from the ranks of Ash'ari *kalam* came from the great jurist
and theologian Abu Hamid al-Ghazali (d. 1111), who undertook a step-by-
step refutation of Neoplatonic metaphysical theories he found to be contrary
to Islam (see below and chapter 7).

It would be misleading to assert that *falsafa* belongs to the Shi'a and *kalam*
to Sunni orthodoxy, especially since firm distinctions between these two
communities were not consistently observed during the period in which the
Neoplatonic philosophers were most active. But it is true that the concepts
and vocabulary characteristic of *falsafa* penetrated deeply into Shi'i (particularly Isma'ili) theology and that some of the more militant and legalistic of
Sunni theologians (such as Ibn Taymiyya) emphatically rejected it.

The impact of the Islamic Neoplatonists upon medieval European theology and philosophy, as well as upon mathematical and scientific learning,
deserves attention. Many of the early translators of the classical texts were
Syriac-speaking Nestorian, Monophysite, or Jacobite Christians, familiar
with the great theological corpus of Christian Alexandria; others were
Sabaeans or Persians of a Hellenistic or gnostic background. The migration
of their ideas into Latin Christianity through the Islamic philosophers is notable. Strong ties also developed with the medieval Jewish philosophers.
Comparable arguments for the existence of God are found in the works of
Ibn Sina, Maimonides, and the scholastic theologian Thomas Aquinas[3]; the
similar theoretical problems of the three scripturally based faiths and their
concerns with ethics, politics, and law, the disposition of the soul in eternity,
and the concepts of salvation and free will created important areas of com-
monality, distinctiveness, and dialogue among them.

AL-KINDI (d.c. 870)

Abu Yusuf Ya'qub ibn Ishaq al-Kindi (al-KINDY). *Fi al-falsafa al-ula* or *On First Philosophy.*

The first of the great thinkers of the Islamic philosophical school, al-Kindi, was himself engaged in supporting the effort to translate classical learning into Arabic and was attached to the court of the 'Abbasid caliphs, including al-Ma'mun. Born about 800 CE in Kufa, he became known as "The Philosopher of the Arabs"; he had a somewhat complex connection with the Mu'tazili movement and the persecution or *mihna* against its opponents undertaken by the caliphs at the time.

Al-Kindi had access to several key works by Plato and Aristotle, including the *Metaphysics*, and a *Theology* erroneously attributed to Aristotle that became very influential among the Islamic philosophers. He apparently also knew the work of Epictetus, Proclus, and John Philoponus, and the Christian philosophy of Alexandria; he was equally interested in Euclid, Ptolemy, and Archimedes. Al-Kindi produced more than 250 works, of which a few survive, writing extensively in pharmacology and medicine, astronomy and navigation, music, physics (especially optics), and the manufacture of certain materials, such as mirrored glass.

A pioneer in the field, al-Kindi began with a defense of philosophy itself, arguing for the value of knowledge obtained through the application of human reason. At the same time, he recognized the validity of the divine inspiration of the prophets and suggested that rational inquiry can help to explain or interpret the often condensed and cryptic language of revelation. He asserted that an honest effort by the philosopher to attain the truth will necessarily lead to the True One or the First Truth, and that an Aristotelian concept of causality is compatible with the revealed faith.

Al-Kindi accepts from Aristotle the "four causes" as the basis of metaphysical knowledge: the material, the formal, the efficient (or moving), and the final—and the "four questions" that inquire into them: "the whether, the what, the which and the why." He also acknowledges the cumulative nature of learning and the debt of later philosophers to those who have pursued an understanding of the truth, and rejects the accusation that such pursuit is tainted by blasphemy, "for the knowledge of truth involves the knowledge of the divine."[4]

Al-Kindi. *Al-Kindi's Metaphysics: A Translation of Ya'qub ibn Ishaq al-Kindi's Treatise "On First Philosophy"(Fi al-falsafa al-ula) with Introduction and Commentary.* **Translated and edited by Alfred L. Ivry (Albany: State University of New York Press, 1974).**

Al-Kindi's elegant and intriguing treatise is only about sixty pages long; the rest of this two-hundred-page volume is packed with critical data and expert interpretation. Ivry provides a quick overview of the state of scholarly study on al-Kindi and his work and basic biographical information about him. A careful explanation of the manuscript and text sources accompanies a brief summary and analysis of the content of the treatise, written in blessedly intelligible prose. Ivry has also produced an essay on the controversial relationship between al-Kindi and the doctrine of the Mu'tazila, which has been variously understood by scholars. All of this material is substantiated by extensive endnotes, offering a wealth of references to other ancient sources as well as to the modern scholarly literature.

Footnotes in the translation section are reserved for manuscript and textual problems. Discussion of the language and meanings of Fi al-falsafa al-ula, the sources al-Kindi used, how his statements compare with those of Aristotle on a particular issue, and many other concerns are dealt with in very detailed notes in a section headed "Commentary." The commentary is linked to the translation by means of an ornate page-and-line numbering system (the page numbers refer to the text, not the book). This information is of value mainly to the specialist; for one thing, it assumes a reading knowledge of both Arabic and Greek.

The volume also includes an extensive bibliography, a names index, and an index of the Aristotelian sources mentioned in the course of Ivry's discussion.

AL-FARABI (d. 950)

Abu Nasr Muhammad al-Farabi (al-fa-RAA-bee). *Kitab ara' ahl al-madina al-fadila* or *Book of the Opinions of the Citizens of the Virtuous* (or *Excellent*) *City*. His name appears as Alfarabius in medieval Latin; he is also known as Abu Nasr or in Latin, Avennasar.

The adoption of classical philosophy into the Islamic cultural milieu was first undertaken by al-Kindi and by the physican Abu Bakr Muhammad al-Razi (d.c. 930), known in Latin sources as Razes or Rhazes. But by far the most influential of the early philosophers was al-Farabi, often called the "Second Teacher" (after Aristotle). Born of Turkish origin at Farab (north of Samarkand), he lived and worked most of his life in Baghdad and Syria; he was taught by certain prominent Christian scholars of the Nestorian and Jacobite persuasions, heirs to the theology of Greco-Roman Alexandria. He had an extensive knowledge of Platonic and Aristotelian texts, as well as the scientific corpus of Galen, Ptolemy, and others. His works included important commentaries, one of which survives in its entirety (a commentary upon Aristotle's *De Interpretatione*). Al-Farabi also created a body of work setting forth his own philosophical approaches, including some significant works of political theory.

Al-Farabi moved beyond al-Kindi's view of philosophy as a valuable means of understanding or explaining revelation. He boldly argued that reason should govern human life as the divine mind oversees the universe, and that only philosophical truth is universally valid. Prophets possess the faculty of imagination or *fantasia*, with which they can represent the truth symbolically in a way that the ordinary nonphilosopher can comprehend. This imaginative activity, familiar to us in sleep and dreaming, occupies a creative level of the mind between sense perception and rational thought. Exceptional persons who are able to convey primary rational concepts through the secondary symbolic vehicle of religion are the philosopher-prophets (such as Muhammad). Because different cultures have their own languages and symbols, the world produces a variety of religions, or popular representations of philosophical truth.[5]

God is understood by al-Farabi as the source of the first intelligence, from which reality emanates in a complex hierarchy of being. The perfect individual, the philosopher, is naturally the ruler of the perfect city and society, in accord with the harmonious and rational cosmological order. Immortality is attained only by elite souls who have reached a state of incorporeal virtue. Marmura describes al-Farabi's political theory as essentially Platonic, deriving ultimately from Plato's *Republic* and *Laws*.

Al-Farabi's work had a direct and lasting influence upon later Islamic philosophers, including Ibn Sina, Ibn Bajja, Ibn Tufayl, and Ibn Rushd, and on writers in other disciplines, such as the historians al-Mas'udi and Ibn Khaldun, and in other religious traditions. Maimonides had a high regard for his work, and in Latin it was known to the scholastic theologians of the medieval period and the philosophers of the Italian Renaissance.[6] He is also regarded as the foremost scholar of musical theory in medieval Islam; the ethnomusicologist George Dimitri Sawa has called attention to al-Farabi's contribution to this aspect of cultural history.[7]

Al-Farabi. *Al-Farabi on the Perfect State: Abu Nasr al-Farabi's Mabadi' ara' ahl al-madina al-fadila*. A revised text with introduction, translation, and commentary by Richard Walzer (Oxford: Clarendon, 1985).

An eminent authority on Greek and Arabic philosophical texts, Richard Walzer, has taken great pains to examine all the manuscripts of al-Farabi's *Ara'* (also known as *Al-madina*) and to produce this meticulous critical edition. The handwritten Arabic text (with manuscript footnotes) is published here, with the English translation on each facing page. Walzer's very lengthy and detailed section-by-section commentary follows. An extensive scholarly bibliography is provided and indexes to the ancient and medieval authors mentioned, to Greek vocabulary, to Arabic vocabulary, and to subjects, concepts, and historical persons and movements discussed in the commentary.

The work begins with a summary (probably the work of an early student or editor) that gives the reader an idea of al-Farabi's train of thought. He sets forth a complete schema of the natural world as the result of emanation and cognition, causing the cosmic intelligences, the heavenly bodies, then material existents, species of living things, the human body, the soul and intellect, virtue and vice. Al-Farabi discusses revelation and representation, then begins to explain human society, and the nature of the excellent (or virtuous) city and the excellent ruler; he contrasts them with ignorant or erring cities and rulers. The virtuous city achieves knowledge of true happiness, while the corrupt seeks the false goals of safety, wealth, pleasure, power, or lawless autonomy.

Al-Farabi. *The Political Regime.* **Translated by Fauzi M. Najjar. In** *Medieval Political Philosophy: A Sourcebook,* **edited by Ralph Lerner and Muhsin Mahdi (Toronto: Collier-Macmillan, 1963), 31–57.**

Al-Farabi's political themes and concepts are also discussed in his *Al-siyasa al-madaniyya* or *The Political Regime* (this work is also known as *The Six Principles of Beings*), in a rather more succinct and readable form than in Walzer's edition. A substantial excerpt from this work is available in Lerner and Mahdi's excellent anthology. The anthology also contains readings from other important works by al-Farabi: *Ihsa' al-'ulum* or *The Enumeration of the Sciences, Tahsil al-sa'ada* or *The Attainment of Happiness,* and al-Farabi's summary of Plato's *Laws.*

Al-Farabi. *The Political Writings.* **Translated and annotated by Charles E. Butterworth (Ithaca, N.Y.: Cornell University Press, 2001).**

This fine new translation of al-Farabi's *Fusul al-madani* or *Aphorisms of the Statesman* (here titled *Selected Aphorisms*) is based upon newly discovered manuscripts that were not available when an earlier English translation was made (published by D. M. Dunlop as *Aphorisms of the Statesman* by Cambridge University Press in 1961). Butterworth has combined polished English prose with informative introductory remarks and precisely focused footnotes; he has also provided two useful glossaries and a basic index. The book also contains a new translation of an excerpt from *Enumeration of the Sciences* and two other important works by al-Farabi: *Kitab al-milla* or *Book of Religion,* and *Kitab al-jami' bayn ra'yay al-hakimayn Aflatun al-ilahi wa Aristutalis* or *Book of the Harmonization Between the Opinions of the Two Philosophers, Plato the Divine and Aristotle.*

Al-Farabi. *Al-Farabi's Philosophy of Plato and Aristotle*. Rev. ed. Translated and edited by Muhsin Mahdi (Ithaca, N.Y.: Cornell University Press, 1969).

Muhsin Mahdi, a leading authority on Islamic philosophy, brings together in this critical edition the three parts of al-Farabi's trilogy *Falsafat Aflatun wa Aristutalis* or *The Philosophy of Plato and Aristotle*. The first part is *The Attainment of Happiness* (portions of this translation are also available in the Lerner and Mahdi anthology); parts II and III are his *Philosophy of Plato* and *Philosophy of Aristotle*. Mahdi supplies detailed translation and manuscript notes; two substantial introductions are provided, but there is no line-by-line commentary upon the text.

Al-Farabi. *Al-Farabi's Commentary and Short Treatise on Aristotle's* De Interpretatione. Translated with an introduction and notes by F. W. Zimmermann (Oxford: Oxford University Press, 1981).

Al-Farabi wrote scholarly commentaries upon many of Aristotle's writings on logic; this one, known as *De Interpretatione* (*Peri Hermeneias*), is the second of the six parts of the *Organon*, coming between the *Categories* and the *Prior Analytics*. It is a study of the semantic value of the parts of an assertion, statements of subject and predicate, basic categorical statements in their square of opposition, and the problem of future contingencies.[8] Zimmermann has provided a lengthy and highly technical introduction, attacking the linguistic problems in both Greek and transliterated Arabic; footnotes throughout the text supply further detail. There are indexes of Greek and Arabic terms and an elaborate general index.

Other Sources

A selection from al-Farabi's treatise *Fi al-'aql* (*Concerning the Intellect*) is provided in *Philosophy in the Middle Ages: The Christian, Islamic and Jewish Traditions*, edited by Arthur Hyman and James J. Walsh, 2nd ed. (Indianapolis: Hackett, 1973). In the same volume is reprinted an excerpt from Muhsin Mahdi's translation of *The Attainment of Happiness*. Three selections from al-Farabi's works, including the *Kitab al-burhan* (a paraphrase of Aristotle's *Analytica posteriora*) can be found in the excellent scholarly collection compiled by Seyyed Hossein Nasr and Mehdi Aminrazavi, *An Anthology of Philosophy in Persia* (Oxford: Oxford University Press, 1999); the introductory materials and notes in this edition are especially helpful.

IBN SINA (d. 1037)

Abu 'Ali al-Husayn ibn 'Abdallah ibn Sina (ibbin SEE-nah). *Kitab al-shifa'* or *Book of Healing*. His name appears in Latin texts as Avicenna; he is sometimes known as Abu 'Ali.

The great Persian physician and philosopher who would become known as *al-Shaykh al Ra'is* ("The Most Learned One") flourished during a period of great literary and scientific achievement under the Buyid dynasty (932–1062 CE). He was born near Bukhara into an Isma'ili or "Sevener" Shi'i family; he excelled in the study of medicine and served as physician to sultans and princes. Exposure to court intrigue led to periods of great instability in his life; he seems to have been blessed with extraordinary physical strength and powers of memory and concentration and was able despite his difficulties to create an enormous body of highly original and influential work.

Perhaps the ultimate example of the medieval philosopher as master of all disciplines, Ibn Sina wrote important works on linguistics and logic, politics and sociology, astronomy, zoology and botany, psychology, poetry, physics (especially velocity, momentum, and projectile motion), geology and minerals, and of course, medicine. He wrote the most significant work in the history of the field, his *Qanun fi al-tibb* (*The Canon of Medicine*), which was translated eighty-seven times into Western languages and served as the fundamental text for the teaching of medicine in Europe well into the seventeenth century; his use of hypothesis and empirical information to establish proofs is basic to the scientific method.[9]

Ibn Sina pursued the ideal of a synthesis of knowledge based upon the Neoplatonic concept of an emanative cosmology and a rational, well-ordered hierarchy of being, like al-Farabi, and in a similar way proposes a tie between intuition and prophetic inspiration. He accepted the Aristotelian understanding of causality, but develops a different view of necessary versus contingent being, essence and existence, that later found its way into the discussions of the Western scholastic theologians. He also moved toward a mysticism and a gnostic view of wisdom that foreshadows the Illuminationist doctrine of Suhrawardi and Mulla Sadra. In his encyclopedic work *Kitab al-shifa'* (*Book of Healing*), he surveys the whole range of Greco-Islamic learning; Ibn Sina's own abridgement of this comprehensive work was titled *Kitab al-najat* (*Book of Salvation* or *Deliverance*).[10]

Ibn Sina. *Healing: Metaphysics X.* Translated by Michael E. Marmura. In Lerner and Mahdi, eds., *Medieval Political Philosophy*, 98–111.

Some important selections from Ibn Sina's *Kitab al-shifa'* are available in English translation in the Lerner and Mahdi anthology. The *Shifa'* consists of four parts, on logic, physics, mathematics, and metaphysics, or "divine science": The selections, ably translated by Marmura, come from the tenth part of the *Metaphysics*. Ibn Sina defines the role of prophet as lawgiver, to dispense justice in society and to establish a religion suitable for the tutelage of common persons (the "vulgar") in acts of worship and obedience. The legislator's objectives in organizing city life, marriage, the roles of women and children, and the offices of caliph and imam are dealt with. The anthology also includes valuable excerpts from Ibn Sina's *Fi ithbat al-nubuwwat* (*On the Proof of Prophecy*) commenting specifically on the revelation to Muhammad, and his *Fi aqsam al-'ulum al-'aqliyya* or *On the Divisions of the Rational Sciences*.

Two other brief excerpts from the *Shifa'* can be found in the Hyman and Walsh anthology: a portion from *Metaphysics I* on the important distinction between necessary and possible (or contingent) existence and one from *Metaphysics VI* on Aristotelian causality.

Ibn Sina. *Avicenna on Theology.* Translated and edited by Arthur J. Arberry (London: John Murray, 1951).

Some portions of the *Kitab al-najat* (Ibn Sina's abridged version of his *Shifa'*) are presented here, in a rather dated translation, together with other excerpts from Ibn Sina's works. This popular edition lacks the critical apparatus and bibliographical information needed for further study.

Ibn Sina. *Avicenna's Psychology.* Translated and edited by Fazlur Rahman (Westport, Conn.: Hyperion Press, 1981).

A far more substantial portion of the *Kitab al-najat* is contained in this critical edition by Fazlur Rahman (a reprint of the 1952 edition). It comes from the sixth section of the second part, the *Physics*; known as the *Nafs*, it contains very important material on the nature of the human mind and soul: the intellect and epistemology, the faculty of intuition and its role in prophecy, sensory perception and imagination, the immortality of the soul, and the nature of the Active Intelligence, "an eternal self-thinking thought" (p. 115). Rahman includes a rather difficult introduction and an even more difficult commentary in the form of extensive endnotes, assuming a specialist's knowledge of Arabic and Greek.

Ibn Sina. *The Metaphysica of Avicenna.* A critical translation-commentary and analysis by Parviz Morewedge (New York: Columbia University Press, 1973).

Ibn Sina created yet another summary or epitome of his work, this time in Persian (his mother tongue), at the request of the prince 'Ala' al-Dawla. The work is called *Danish nama-i 'ala'i* or *Book of Scientific Knowledge for 'Ala'*; it consists of the four major sections on logic, physics, metaphysics, and mathematics (the last part compiled by Ibn Sina's student al-Juzjani). The entire *Metaphysics* is here presented in a scholarly translation, so it has the advantage of constituting a complete line of argument. The volume includes precise critical notes on the text and then a much more discursive and explanatory commentary, unfolding Ibn Sina's whole metaphysical system. A glossary provides not merely verbal equivalents, but substantial definitions of terms and references to context; there are also names and subject indexes.

Ibn Sina. *Remarks and Admonitions: Part One, Logic.* Translated and edited by Shams Constantine Inati (Toronto: Pontifical Institute of Mediaeval Studies, 1984).

Ibn Sina's four-part schema takes on a different format in his *Kitab al-isharat wa al-tanbihat* (*Book of Remarks and Admonitions*). Here, the philosopher briefly states his views as "remarks," then occasionally warns of possible misunderstandings, the "admonitions" or "delusions." This critical edition covers only part I of the work, that concerning logic. Inati supplies an introductory analysis of the work, numerous footnotes, and a limited bibliography and index.

Other Sources

Some of Ibn Sina's other works have appeared in English translation, offering insight into the impressive range of his activity and erudition. The first part of his landmark work *Qanun fi al-tibb* or *The Canon of Medicine* was translated by a physician, O. Cameron Gruner (New York: Augustus M. Kelley, 1970; reprint of the 1930 edition).[11] It contains a fascinating blend of astute clinical observation and medieval interpretation. Ibn Sina also produced literary works, both fiction and poetry, and literary criticism. A translation of his Persian treatise *Mi'raj nama* or *Book of the Prophet Muhammad's Ascent to Heaven* was published by Peter Heath, with a scholarly discussion of Ibn Sina's cosmology and understanding of symbolism, imagery, and allegory (Philadelphia: University of Pennsylvania Press, 1992). Ibn Sina's commentary on Aristotle's *Poetics* was published in a critical translation by Ismail M. Dahiyat (Leiden: Brill, 1974). Also, an interesting autobiography, and its continuation by al-Juzjani, is available in a critical bilingual edition with extensive scholarly annotation by William E. Gohlman as *The Life of Ibn Sina* (Albany: State University of New York Press, 1974). Valuable selections from eight different works by Ibn Sina can be found in the Nasr and Aminrazavi anthology.

IBN BAJJAH (d. 1138)

Abu Bakr Muhammad ibn Yahya ibn al-Sa'igh ibn Bajjah (ibbin BOD-ja). *Tadbir al-mutawahhid* or *Regimen* (or *Governance*) *of the Solitary*. His name also appears as Ibn Bajah, Bajja, or Badjdja; in Latin sources he is known as Avempace. Some sources refer to him as Abu Bakr ibn al-Sa'igh or al-Sayigh; he may also be known as al-Andalusi.

A forceful blow against the Neoplatonist philosophers was struck in 1095 by the great jurist and theologian al-Ghazali. He wrote devastating critiques of *falsafa*, including *Tahafut al-falasifa* or *Incoherence of the Philosophers*, in which he explicitly refutes twenty fundamental theories of the Neoplatonists, exposing them as heretical innovations in conflict with Islamic orthodoxy (excerpts in English from these statements can be found in the Hyman and Walsh anthology).[12] The caliphate during the Saljuq (or Seljuk) era endorsed the teaching of *kalam* in Islamic schools rather than *falsafa*; this and the condemnation by al-Ghazali caused the influence of the philosophers to diminish in much of the Muslim world.

However, a younger contemporary of al-Ghazali in Islamic Spain (the Andalus) was to initiate a revival of Neoplatonist thought there and in the Maghreb. Born in Saragossa, Ibn Bajjah served the Berber governor there as vizier, and lived in Seville, Granada, and Oran before dying at an early age in Fez (possibly of poisoning). Like the great *falasifa* before him, Ibn Bajjah applied himself to the study of medicine, mathematics, astronomy, and music. He wrote of the ultimate aim of human life as an ascent through the hierarchy of being posited by the Neoplatonist cosmogony of emanation toward a contact or conjunction (*ittisal*) of the soul with the Active Intellect; many of his works are incomplete, however, and very little is available in English.

Ibn Bajjah. *Governance of the Solitary*. Translated by Lawrence Berman. In Lerner and Mahdi, eds., *Medieval Political Philosophy*, 122–33.

Apparently on the model of al-Farabi's *Al-madina* or *Al-siyasa al-madaniyya*, Ibn Bajjah reflects upon the role of the philosopher in the erring or corrupt cities. Al-Farabi proposed that the virtuous man who finds himself in the unfavorable environment of an ignorant city should emigrate to a more excellent one. Ibn Bajjah suggests that in a world in which no enlightened cities exist, the philosopher must govern only himself, as an isolated individual or "stranger," pursuing his spiritual happiness in the midst of corporeal existence. The work was left unfinished by Ibn Bajjah, and the five brief excerpts in Berman's translation have a disjointed and awkward quality, but are nevertheless of interest.

IBN TUFAYL (d.c. 1185)

Abu Bakr Muhammad ibn 'Abd al-Malik ibn Tufayl (ibbin too-FALE). *Hayy ibn Yaqzan* or *The Living, Son of The Awake*. His name may be spelled as Tufail; he appears in Latin texts as Abubacer or Avuvacer (Abu Bakr); he is also sometimes known as al-Andalusi.

Like his predecessor Ibn Bajjah, Ibn Tufayl was a scientist and philosopher of Islamic Spain, born near Granada; he became court physician to the Almohad ruler Abu Ya'qub Yusuf in Marrakesh. He acknowledged the influence of the earlier Neoplatonists, especially Ibn Sina, and it was from him that he took the inspiration for his metaphysical tale *Hayy ibn Yaqzan*. He is said to have produced works on medicine, natural science, and philosophy, of which only this intriguing story survives.

In the story, a baby boy called Hayy ibn Yaqzan is found alone on a tropical island and is raised by a doe as her fawn. As he grows up, the process of his learning and reasoning is described. He acquires practical and manual skills, then begins to reflect upon the meaning of his experiences as he encounters death, and fire, the anatomy of living things, the movement of the heavens, form and cause, the idea of God, and he immerses himself in the mystical contemplation of the divine. Eventually, another human being, a pious young man named Absal (or Asal), comes to the island in search of contemplative solitude; he meets Hayy, teaches him language, and finds that Hayy has arrived at an authentic knowledge of divine truth. Absal explains the religious tradition of Islam, and they realize that it is a symbolic representation of the same metaphysical realities Hayy has discovered; Absal explains that the Prophet cloaked truth in these representational terms because most human beings were not equipped to grasp it otherwise. The two of them travel to Absal's people, where Hayy tries to share with them his philosophical knowledge, but the people are not able to accept it. He urges them to stay within the bounds of their revealed religion, while Hayy and Absal go back to the unpopulated island and devote themselves to the mystical apprehension of divine truth.

Some lengthy excerpts from this work, in a translation by George N. Atiyeh, can be found in the Lerner and Mahdi anthology; omitted parts of the tale are summarized.

Ibn Tufayl. *Ibn Tufayl's Hayy ibn Yaqzan*. **Translated with introduction and notes by Lenn Evan Goodman (New York: Twayne, 1972).**

Goodman has prepared a rather pedestrian but readable translation of this tale, with extensive critical notes tying the text to ancient and modern sources, paying particular attention to pertinent Sufi teachings and the contributions of other Neoplatonists. He identifies allusions to the Qur'an and explains their relevance, and takes care to refer specifically to Ghazali's views on every point. Less helpful is the long and somewhat digressive introduction.

Ibn Tufayl. *The History of Hayy ibn Yaqzan*. Translated by Simon Ockley; revised and edited by A. S. Fulton (London: Chapman and Hall, 1929).

This antiquated translation was first published by Simon Ockley in 1708. Fulton has corrected Ockley's "liberties" by comparison with the standard Arabic text by Gauthier. He was apparently unable to transform the prose from its Bunyanesque style (which, one must admit, has a certain charm).

IBN RUSHD (d. 1198)
Abu al-Walid Muhammad ibn Ahmad ibn Rushd (ibbin ROOSHD). *Tahafut al-tahafut* or *Incoherence of "The Incoherence."* His name appears in Latin texts as Averroes or Averroës.

The greatest philosopher of the Andalus was without a doubt Ibn Rushd. As a young man, he was introduced by his senior colleague Ibn Tufayl to the Almohad emir Abu Ya'qub Yusuf and succeeded the former as court physician. The emir was a patron of philosophy and desired summaries and explanations of Aristotle's teachings; Ibn Tufayl nominated Ibn Rushd as the man to create them.

But before being trained in science, medicine, and philosophy, Ibn Rushd received a thorough education in *hadith* criticism, jurisprudence, and *kalam*. Born in Cordova, he was raised in a family distinguished by Islamic learning: his grandfather and father were both Maliki jurists and judges, and he himself served as a *qadi* or judge and wrote on Islamic law. Ibn Rushd was uniquely prepared to turn his discriminating eye upon the ancients, the theologians, and the philosophers alike.

It was Ibn Rushd who undertook a systematic response to al-Ghazali's challenge to the principles of *falsafa*. Ibn Rushd was himself very critical of the ideas of Ibn Sina; he chose to defend philosophy by returning to fundamental Aristotelian theories and reinterpreting them, expressly rejecting certain Avicennan modifications. He dissolved Ibn Sina's Neoplatonic emanative scheme, which posited a very remote God at the top of an eternal and unapproachable heavenly hierarchy, and proposed an understanding of creation as God's continual contact with and transformation of the material universe, the ongoing metaphysical cause of the physical order. This doctrine would allow for God's immediate knowledge of the particulars of our world of finite living things. He dismissed al-Ghazali's accusation of *takfir* (declaring someone to be in a state of unbelief) against the philosophers and explained that religious and philosophical discourse must be carried on in separate contexts, since only the philosopher is prepared for discussion on the demonstrative or apodictic level, while theologians and jurists are concerned with dialectical or rhetorical discourse within the religious tradition. Ibn Rushd was nevertheless accused in 1195 of a departure from orthodoxy; he was exiled and his works were banned, but he was able to find sanctuary in Marrakesh, where he died in 1198.

The majority of his work took the form of commentaries upon the classic texts of Aristotle and Plato (also Ptolemy, Galen, and others). He wrote in several characteristic formats: a brief summary of a certain work or "short commentary"; a more discursive interpretation or "middle commentary"; and a lengthy section-by-section study of a text, known as a "major commentary" or *tafsir*. It was through these important works that Ibn Rushd had an impact upon the Western scholastics and Renaissance philosophers and earned the title "The Great Commentator." Some of these works are no longer extant in Arabic, only in their Latin or Hebrew translations.

Ibn Rushd. *Averroes on the Harmony of Religion and Philosophy.* **A translation with introduction and notes by George F. Hourani (London: Luzac, 1976). The title varies slightly in library catalog records.**

Ibn Rushd presented his response to al-Ghazali's critique of *falsafa* in a set of three works: his *Fasl al-maqal* (often translated as *Decisive Treatise*); his *Kashf 'an manahij al-adilla* or *Expositions of the Methods of Proof*; and his *Tahafut*, discussed below. Hourani has provided an expert translation of the entire *Fasl* in this small volume, including its addendum or appendix known as *Damima*, and an important extract from the *Kashf*.

In the *Fasl al-maqal*, Ibn Rushd argues three principal points: The law does not prohibit philosophical study but in fact makes it obligatory. Philosophy contains nothing opposed to Islam. And, a philosophical understanding of authoritative religious texts should not be taught to ordinary believers because more appropriate methods exist for instructing them in the faith. Arnaldez points out that Ibn Rushd employs the technical vocabulary of the jurists, grammarians, Qur'an commentators, and theologians but manipulates these ideas within the conceptual or logical framework developed by the Greeks.[13]

The *Damima* explains God's knowledge of particulars in the material universe, one of the key elements of Ghazali's charge of heresy against the philosophers. The selection from the *Kashf* (also referred to as the *Manahij*) deals directly with the issue of resurrection and immortality, again a very sensitive point upon which the philosophers were vulnerable to the accusation of *takfir* (tock-FEER), a finding of heresy or unbelief.

These significant texts have received scrupulous attention by Hourani, working from his own edition of the Arabic documents and that of Marcus J. Müller (1859). Hourani is able at all times to control both minute details and larger meanings or implications, and to discuss the issues within the framework of Islamic religion, not just in philosophical terms. He has provided an informative and lucid introduction, and the text is linked to extensive and precise endnotes. There is also a brief bibliography and a glossary/index. Hourani's translation alone, without the other features, is included in the Lerner and Mahdi anthology.

Ibn Rushd. *Averroes' Tahafut al-tahafut* [or] *The Incoherence of the Incoherence*. Translated with introduction and notes by Simon van den Bergh (London: Luzac, for the E. J. W. Gibb Memorial Trust, 1954). 2 vols.

This is considered the standard scholarly translation and critical edition of Ibn Rushd's important treatise *Tahafut al-tahafut*, or *The Incoherence of* [al-Ghazali's] "*The Incoherence* [*of the Philosophers*]," based upon the Arabic text edited by Maurice Bouyges. An admirably concise and intelligible introduction provides an overview of the dispute between Ghazali and the *falasifa*, and of the response by Ibn Rushd to his critique. The *Tahafut* has a perfectly obvious organizational plan: Ibn Rushd takes on Ghazali's twenty arguments, one by one, quoting from the theologian's remarks and then presenting his rebuttal. The back-and-forth motion is constant, like a tennis match, but it is always clear who is speaking: The quotes from Ghazali are in a slightly smaller typeface, headed "Ghazali says," and the comments of Ibn Rushd always begin with "I say." Ibn Rushd occasionally addresses the reader directly and with persuasive energy; the whole work has the tone of a combative intellectual debate.

The entire second volume is made up of Simon van den Bergh's exhaustive critical notes. He provides an enormous amount of information on the ancient texts under discussion (though a reading knowledge of Greek and Arabic is assumed) and also lets the reader know which side is winning a point, with remarks like "Of course this is no answer to Ghazali's objection" (p. 81). The edition also includes valuable reference helps prepared by Richard Walzer: indexes for names and subjects mentioned, a list of contradictions or ambiguities in Aristotle's system, and indexes to the Greek and Arabic vocabulary.

Other Sources

Some of the other works of Ibn Rushd are also available in English, mainly from his extensive corpus of commentaries. The Mediaeval Academy of America

produced the following critical editions and translations: *Epitome of parva natu-*
ralia, by Harry Blumberg (1961); *On Aristotle's De generatione et corruptione*, by
Samuel Kurland (1958); *Middle Commentary on Porphyry's Isagogue* (and on
Aristotle's *Categoriae*), by Herbert A. Davidson (1969); and *Averroes' De sub-*
stantia orbis, by Arthur Hyman (1986). Charles E. Butterworth created several
scholarly translations: *Averroes' Middle Commentary on Aristotle's Poetics*
(Princeton University Press, 1986); *Averroes' Three Short Commentaries on Aris-*
totle's Topics, Rhetoric and Poetics (State University of New York Press, 1977);
and *Averroes' Middle Commentaries on Aristotle's Categories and De Interpretatione*
(Princeton University Press, 1983). A portion of the only surviving Ibn Rushd
tafsir or major commentary was published in English as *Ibn Rushd's Metaphysics:*
A Translation with Introduction of Ibn Rushd's Commentary on Aristotle's Meta-
physics, Book Lam, by Charles Genequand (Leiden: Brill, 1984). In addition,
there is a critical edition and translation called *Averroes on Plato's Republic*, by
Ralph Lerner (Cornell University Press, 1974), and another, *Averroes' Com-*
mentary on Plato's Republic by Erwin Rosenthal (Cambridge University Press,
1956). A few other works exist in English, such as a portion from Ibn Rushd's
study of *fiqh* or jurisprudence known as *Bidayat al-mujtahid*, in Rudolph Peters's
Jihad in Mediaeval and Modern Islam (Leiden: Brill, 1977).

SUHRAWARDI (d. 1191)

**Shihab al-Din Yahya ibn Habash al-Suhrawardi (sooh-ra-WAR-dee) al-
Maqtul. *Hikmat al-ishraq* or [The] *Philosophy of Illumination.* His name
in Persian is pronounced soh-ra-var-DEE. The title of the work also appears as *Theosophy of the Orient of Light.***

A role for intuition in epistemology and an element of gnosticism or mysticism were present in some of Ibn Sina's later and more informal works. The
Persian philosopher al-Suhrawardi was to move well beyond this toward an
innovative doctrine of *ishraq* or *ishrak* (ish-ROCK) or illumination, defining
his thought against Avicennan or Peripatetic precedents.

Suhrawardi relocated to Syria in 1183 and became closely associated with
the young prince Malik al-Zahir, son of the great warrior Salah al-Din (Saladin). Suhrawardi's teaching was unconventional enough to arouse the
wrath of the theologians and jurists in Aleppo, who accused him of sorcery,
heresy, and claiming to be a new prophet. Important insights came to him,
he said, when Aristotle appeared to him in a dream. Suhrawardi was also
much given to personal eccentricity and habits sometimes associated with
Sufism (fasting, sleepless vigils, long periods of meditation, and ecstatic
dancing) and reportedly various miracles, such as producing precious gems
through alchemy. Salah al-Din had political reasons for wanting to defend

Islamic orthodoxy, and he sent instructions that the philosopher should be executed; he was put to death at the age of thirty-six and is sometimes known by the epithet *al-Maqtul* ("The Murdered One"), as well as his primary title *Shaykh al-Ishraq* or "Master of Illumination." His thought gained a devoted following and is still esteemed, particularly in Iran.

Suhrawardi's work balances the "two wisdoms": the discursive and the experiential. He was a trained philosopher who applied classical standards to the study of logic, physics, and metaphysics in his corpus of four major works: *Al-talwihat* or *Intimations*, *Al-muqawamat* or *Apposites*, *Al-mashari' wa al-mutarahat* or *Paths and Havens*, and his most famous work, *Hikmat al-ishraq*. At the same time, he placed great emphasis on immediate, intuitive knowledge or inspiration and developed an epistemological theory known as "knowledge by presence" (*al-'ilm al-huduri*) and a powerful expression of cosmogony based upon light imagery. He created a body of allegorical works (mainly in Persian) of a more popular nature that dwell upon aspects of mystical experience.[14]

Suhrawardi. *The Philosophy of Illumination.* A new critical edition with English translation, notes, commentary, and introduction by John Walbridge and Hossein Ziai (Provo, Utah: Brigham Young University Press, 1999).

This critical edition of the Arabic text of *Hikmat al-ishraq* differs in some important ways from the best previously known edition by Henri Corbin, an eminent French Orientalist. The editors explain clearly how their textual decisions were made and document them throughout the work. The Arabic text is printed with a beautiful English translation, on facing pages; a set of detailed scholarly notes is given for each of them. There is a fine introduction (the translators have published a great deal on Suhrawardi and the Illuminationist tradition), an indispensable glossary, and an unusually effective index.

Suhrawardi. *The Philosophical Allegories and Mystical Treatises.* Edited and translated with an introduction by Wheeler M. Thackston, Jr. (Costa Mesa, Calif.: Mazda, 1999).

The interesting tales in this volume were translated from Persian (treatise IX is also in Arabic) and placed with the text on facing pages. Footnotes and endnotes help identify Qur'anic allusions and explain details, but there is no extensive commentary. A few helpful remarks about each treatise are found in the introduction. The stories deal mainly with "the initiation of a neophyte, or aspirant, into the spiritual realm" (p. xvi). Some of the stories are apparently simple animal fables, such as "The Chameleon and the Bats," while others are more didactic or discursive, and many involve very complex symbolism representing

Illuminationist doctrines or principles (treatise VI, "On the Reality of Love"). The volume includes a small bibliography and a glossary of persons mentioned in the text.

An excerpt from one of these treatises is available in a translation by Leonard Lewisohn in the anthology *Windows on the House of Islam*, edited by John Renard (Berkeley: University of California Press, 1998), 180–84.

AL-TUSI (d. 1274)

Abu Ja'far Muhammad Nasir al-Din al-Tusi (at-TOO-see). *Akhlaq-i nasiri* or *The Nasirean Ethics.*

The study of ethics in Islam is based on more than one category of religious thought: in *kalam* or theology, *fiqh* or jurisprudence (see chapter 4), and in *falsafa* or *hikma*, notably in the work of the Isma'ili (or "Sevener") Shi'i scholar Nasir al-Din al-Tusi.[15] Born into an Imami (or "Twelver") family near Mashhad, al-Tusi moved toward Isma'ili convictions as an adult through his reading and study. He applied himself to mathematics, medicine, Neoplatonist philosophy, and natural science—particularly astronomy—and was director of an observatory near Tabriz, writing a number of significant works on Euclidean and Ptolemaic geometry and planetary theory. He rose to defend Ibn Sina from the critique of Fakhr al-Din al-Razi (d. 1209) and may be said to have revived Avicennan philosophy for the thirteenth century.

Al-Tusi remains a highly controversial figure because of his role in the Mongol conquest of Persia. Sent as an envoy by the Isma'ili princes to negotiate with the invaders, Nasir al-Din al-Tusi ended up on the staff of the Mongol ruler Hulugu (or Hülegü, or Hulagu) and accompanied him as the Mongols swept through Persia, sacked Baghdad, and put an end to the 'Abbasid caliphate. Some consider him a wretched traitor as a result. The sincerity of his conversion to the Isma'ili faith has been questioned. He is also regarded by some of the more conservative Hanbali theologians and jurists (especially Ibn Taymiyya and Ibn Qayyim al-Jawziyya) as "the most pernicious hidden atheist,"[16] who valued the work of Ibn Sina more highly than the Qur'an. However, others respected him enough to call him "The Third Teacher" (after Aristotle and al-Farabi).

Al-Tusi. *The Nasirean Ethics.* Translated and edited by G. M. Wickens (London: George Allen and Unwin, 1964).

Nasir al-Din al-Tusi prepared his most famous philosophical work under the auspices of a patron with a confusingly similar name, Nasir al-Din 'Abd al-Rahim (also known as Muhtasham), the Isma'ili governor of Quhistan. The *Akhlaq-i nasiri* is named after this patron, not after al-Tusi himself. The theme of the work is human nature and behavior: He begins by discussing the soul and its faculties, reason and wisdom, then the virtues and vices, and the concept of justice. The second discourse on "Economics" concerns the regulation of households, the roles of women and children, and the holding of property, servants, and slaves. The third discourse deals with "Politics," meaning the larger units of society, the virtuous versus the errant cities, the proper conduct of kings, and so on. These topics and their treatment are reminiscent of al-Farabi's *Al-siyasa al-madaniyya* and *Fusul al-madani*, and al-Tusi is indebted to other Neoplatonist works as well.

Wickens has created a scholarly translation with ample critical notes and a detailed index. The translation's prose—like that of the introduction—seems oddly oblique and pompous, but readable and reliable.

Other Sources

Selections from two additional works by al-Tusi may be found in the Nasr and Aminrazavi anthology: *Sayr wa suluk* or *Contemplation and Action*, and *Rawdat al-taslim* or *The Garden of Submission* (also known as *Tasawwurat* or *Notions*). His *Sayr wa suluk* is also available in *Contemplation and Action: The Spiritual Autobiography of a Muslim Scholar*, edited and translated by S. J. Badakhchani (London: I. B. Tauris and the Institute of Ismaili Studies, 1998). The same editor and publisher brought out *Rawdat al-taslim* under the title *Paradise of Submission* in 2005.

The *Akhlaq-i nasiri* was rewritten in a somewhat popularized form by a later Persian theologian and philosopher, Jalal al-Din Muhammad ibn As'ad al-Dawani (d. 1502). Dawani's work is commonly known as *Akhlaq-i jalali*; it was translated by William F. Thompson, a member of the Bengal Civil Service who took a special interest in the Persian-influenced cultural heritage of Muslim India. It was published as *A Practical Philosophy of the Muhammadan People* (London: Oriental Translation Fund, 1839; microfilmed in 1964). A reissue of the work was included in *Theology, Ethics and Metaphysics: Royal Asiatic Society Classics of Islam*, edited by Hiroyuki Mashita, with an introduction by C. E. Bosworth (London: RoutledgeCurzon, 2003), a handsome five-volume edition.

MULLA SADRA (d. 1640)

Sadr al-Din Muhammad ibn Ibrahim al-Shirazi, or Mulla Sadra (MOOL-a SOD-rah). *Kitab al-asfar al-arba'a or Book of the Four Journeys [of the Soul].* He is also known as al-Shirazi.

In the Safavid era, the Illuminationist school of thought initiated by Suhrawardi experienced a renaissance, particularly under the patronage of

Shah 'Abbas (1588–1629). The most significant Persian philosopher of this era, Mulla Sadra, derived some of his thinking from and in contradistinction to his predecessor; among Sadra's works are commentaries upon the *Hikmat al-ishraq*, and later Persian philosophers tended to define themselves on the basis of their agreement or disagreement with his critique of Suhrawardi. Sadra also drew inspiration from Ibn Sina and the famous Sufi thinker Ibn al-'Arabi, among other sources.

Born in Shiraz, Sadra taught for a time in Isfahan, where he encountered opposition from some of the more conservative members of the Shi'i clerical establishment. He withdrew for some years to a village where he could work undisturbed, but was brought back to Shiraz by the governor of Fars province and installed in a teaching position at the Madrasa-i Khan. During the latter period of his life, he composed his major original works (writing almost entirely in Arabic), including a magnum opus titled *Kitab al-hikma al-muta'aliyya fi al-asfar al-arba'a al-'aqliyya* or *Book of the Transcendent Wisdom in the Four Journeys of the Soul*, often known by an abbreviated title. He also created many important shorter treatises conveying elements of this more comprehensive work.[17]

Mulla Sadra. *The Wisdom of the Throne: An Introduction to the Philosophy of Mulla Sadra*. With the text translated and edited by James Winston Morris (Princeton, N.J.: Princeton University Press, 1981).

This edition includes an erudite but readable introduction so substantial that it is essentially a monograph on the thought of Mulla Sadra, accompanying Morris's scholarly translation of one of the treatises, the *Hikmat al-'arshiyya* or *Wisdom of the Throne*. The shorter technical and philosophical treatises are typically abridged versions of material from the *Asfar* on particular topics; Morris has chosen to translate this one "because of its unique combination of brevity and comprehensiveness and its relative accessibility for the nonspecialist reader" (p. 5). The work deals with the knowledge of God and his attributes, being and consciousness, the priority of existence (*asalat al-wujud*) over essence, issues of ontology and eschatology, transcendence and realization, the soul and the self. It includes an elegant and compact "Concluding Testament" expressing the aims of Mulla Sadra's teaching in persuasive and personal terms. Morris has included extensive explanatory footnotes and a detailed index.

Philosophical Study in the Modern Era

The legacy of Islamic philosophical thought has continued to exert an influence into the present. In the nineteenth century, Jamal al-Din al-Afghani recognized in Ibn Sina and Ibn Rushd a kind of rationalism and intellectual freedom that could contribute to the modernist movement. Sayyid Ahmad Khan and the Aligarh community posited a concept of religious truth as fully in conformity with nature and reason. In the twentieth century, the study of logic and metaphysics helped to shape the ideas of Muhammad 'Abduh in Egypt (see also chapter 7), and of Muhammad Iqbal and Mawlana Mawdudi in India/Pakistan. Academic philosophers such as 'Abd al-Rahman Badawi, Zaki Najib Mahmud, and Yusuf Karam pursued a modern logical or existential discourse in an Islamic context, with reference to the heritage of *falsafa*.

The continuing relevance of *falsafa* among the Shi'a is much more prominent, especially the *Ishraqi* or Illuminationist school of thought. As Seyyed Hossein Nasr observes, "The long tradition of philosophy in Persia . . . reached the contemporary period and is in fact very much alive in Persia today, where it is undergoing another major revival in Qum, the present religious center of Persia, as well as in Tehran, Mashhad and several other cities."[18] The leading twentieth-century Shi'i theologian 'Allameh Tabataba'i was an authority on the work of Mulla Sadra and other important aspects of philosophy; his *Bidayat al-hikma* or *Elements of Islamic Metaphysics* is available in an English translation by 'Ali Quli Qara'i (London: Islamic College for Advanced Studies, 2003). The Ayatollah Ruhollah Khomeini was a professor of philosophy (*hikma*) and ethics in Qum and wrote extensively on political philosophy and government (see also chapter 4).

In addition, some progressive Muslim writers have been exploring the implications of philosophy in the areas of spirituality and religious pluralism; for example, Hasan Askari in *Towards a Spiritual Humanism: A Muslim-Humanist Dialogue*, with Jon Avery (Leeds: Seven Mirrors, 1991). The links between Islamic philosophy and mysticism will be explored in chapter 8.[19]

Notes

1. Henri Corbin, *History of Islamic Philosophy* (London: Kegan Paul, 1993), 156.

2. Majid Fakhry, *A History of Islamic Philosophy* (New York: Columbia University Press, 1970), 7.

3. *Philosophy in the Middle Ages: The Christian, Islamic and Jewish Traditions*, edited by Arthur Hyman and James J. Walsh, 2nd ed. (Indianapolis: Hackett, 1973), 2–5. See also David B. Burrell, *Knowing the Unknowable God: Ibn Sina, Maimonides, Aquinas* (Notre Dame, Ind.: University of Notre Dame Press, 1986).

4. Fakhry, *History*, 86–87.

5. Richard Walzer, "Al-Farabi's Theory of Prophecy and Divination," 206–19 of *Greek into Arabic: Essays on Islamic Philosophy* (Cambridge, Mass.: Harvard University Press, 1962). See also Walzer, "Al-Farabi," *EI2*, v. 2: 779.

6. Michael E. Marmura, "Al-Farabi," *DMA*, v. 5: 10.

7. George Dimitri Sawa, "Al-Farabi on Music," *DMA*, v. 5: 11–12.

8. A helpful summary of his thought and work is found in an article by T. H. Irwin, "Aristotle," *REP*, v. 1: 414–35. This reference work also contains articles on many of the major Islamic philosophers (al-Farabi, Ibn Sina, Ibn Rushd, Ibn Tufayl, etc.). Articles about many of these individuals can also be found in *A Companion to Philosophy in the Middle Ages*, edited by Jorge J. E. Gracia and Timothy B. Noone (Oxford: Blackwell, 2003).

9. Seyyed Hossein Nasr, "Sina, Ibn," *DMA*, v. 11: 302–7, and Ehsan Yar-Shater, *The Metaphysica of Avicenna* (New York: Columbia University Press, 1973), xv–xvi.

10. Fakhry, *History*, 150–54, and *History of Islamic Philosophy*, edited by Seyyed Hossein Nasr and Oliver Leaman (London: Routledge, 1996), v. 1: 232–33.

11. For a summary of the contents of all five parts of the *Qanun*, see A. M. Goichon, "Ibn Sina," *EI2*, v. 3: 942.

12. For a brief account of al-Ghazali's critique, see Michael E. Marmura, "Falsafah," *ER*, v. 5: 273, or Seyyed Hossein Nasr, "Philosophy," *OEMIW*, v. 3: 330; a much more detailed study is found in Oliver Leaman, *An Introduction to Medieval Islamic Philosophy* (Cambridge: Cambridge University Press, 1985).

13. Roger Arnaldez, "Ibn Rushd," *EI2*, v. 3: 913.

14. There is a range of scholarly opinion on the primary themes of Suhrawardi's work; it is interesting to compare the discussions in Corbin, *History*, 205–20, and Fakhry, *History*, 326–38, with that provided by the translators of the *Hikmat al-ishraq*, Walbridge and Ziai. See also Seyyed Hossein Nasr, *Three Muslim Sages: Avicenna, Suhrawardi, Ibn 'Arabi* (Cambridge, Mass.: Harvard University Press, 1964).

15. Not to be confused with the important Shi'i traditionist Abu Ja'far Muhammad ibn Hasan al-Tusi (d.c. 1067).

16. Hans Daiber, "Al-Tusi," *EI2*, v. 10: 748.

17. A very serious analysis of the conceptual basis of his work by Fazlur Rahman is found in "The God-World Relationship in Mulla Sadra," *Essays on Islamic Philosophy and Science*, edited by George F. Hourani (Albany: State University of New York Press, 1975), 238–53.

18. *An Anthology of Philosophy in Persia*, edited by Seyyed Hossein Nasr (Oxford: Oxford University Press, 1999).

19. An attractive new translation of several important classic texts in both philosophy and mysticism was published by Muhammad 'Ali Khalidi, titled *Medieval Islamic Philosophical Writings* (Cambridge: Cambridge University Press, 2005), with helpful editorial comments and notes.

CHAPTER SEVEN

~

Theology: Kalam

The fundamental texts of Islam—the Qur'an and the *hadith*—are composed of narrative, poetry, legal material, ritual guidelines, ethical instruction, and other contents, but very little systematic or doctrinal theological discourse. Statements about God and human nature are often expressed in highly condensed, even cryptic language; apparent contradictions or paradoxes abound. The student longs for an explanatory key to this material, setting forth in an orderly fashion the primary faith claims and confessions of Islamic religion.

The discipline of Islamic theology that developed to perform this task is *'ilm al-kalam* or "the science of the word," usually known simply as *kalam* (ka-LAMM). The term *usul al-din* (us-SOOL id-DEEN) refers to the bases or grounding principles of Islamic religion. These two terms may be used interchangeably as synonyms for theology or theological studies. The scholar who concentrates upon the study of *kalam* is known as a *mutakallim* (moo-ta-KAL-lim); plural, *mutakallimun* (moo-ta-kallim-MOON). The subject matter of *kalam* can be defined as doctrinal or dogmatic theology; it may also be known as dialectical theology.[1]

The quality that distinguishes *kalam* is its role as apologia, establishing and defending the tenets of faith and adducing persuasive proofs to dispel doubts and defeat challenges. Ibn Khaldun defined *kalam* as "a science that involves arguing with logical proofs in defense of the articles of faith and refuting innovators who deviate in their dogmas from the early Muslims and Muslim orthodoxy"; Muhammad 'Abduh identified its purpose as "the fixing of religious beliefs for the aim of working to conserve and consolidate religion."[2] This basically defensive posture became more pronounced as the *mutakallimun* were called upon to refute the perceived errors and excesses of the Islamic philosophical schools.

The first major theological challenge to the developing Islamic community came from the Mu'tazila, meaning "those who stand aside" or, as Fazlur Rahman calls them, the "neutralists."[3] The origin of the name is conventionally associated with the scholar Wasil ibn 'Ata' (d. 748), who separated himself from the teaching of other contemporary authorities in a public sort of way, on the key question of the status of a Muslim who has committed a grave sin. Some felt that the grave sinner should be regarded as an infidel, while others argued that he or she was nevertheless still a believer with an expectation of paradise; the Mu'tazila "withdrew" or "stood aside" from this controversy by arguing that the sinful Muslim deserved an intermediate position between the two. There is some similarity between this discussion and the issue of justification by faith alone or by works, as it evolved in Christian theology.

The status of the sinner pertained to a much larger and more basic theological paradox: If God is omnipotent and the author of all events, to what extent is a person responsible for his or her own actions? Does the human being have any free will at all in a context of divine determinism and predestination? The Mu'tazila argued that God's condemnation of persons who have no meaningful power to act would be unjust; therefore, human beings must be the creators of their own acts, and they must be judged in accordance with a supreme ideal of justice to which God also must conform. They were thereby subordinating God to a concept or abstract principle beyond or above God, a move entirely unacceptable to the *mutakallimun*.

The Mu'tazila are often referred to as "rationalists" because they argued that knowledge attained through the disciplined application of human reason could be valid, along with that received through revelation. They also firmly rejected the idea of divine attributes, which they perceived as a threat to the unity and simplicity of God, and they disparaged the anthropomorphic tendencies of some who imagined a kind of tangible corporeality for God, as if God were "an eternal man" (Ibn Rushd).[4] This rejection of properties in God resembling human characteristics led the Mu'tazila to deny that the Qur'an is God's "speech"; it must be created and contingent, not eternal.

The doctrine of the created Qur'an became the center of a crisis during the reign of the 'Abbasid caliph al-Ma'mun (813–833 CE), who adopted Mu'tazilism as the official theology of the realm and initiated a period of persecution or *mihna* against its opponents. Among the victims of this persecution was the great *hadith* scholar Ahmad ibn Hanbal; the Hanbali school of thought remained implacably opposed to Mu'tazili theological tendencies, committed to the *hadith* and to the teaching and practice of the *salaf*, the earliest Companions of the Prophet and righteous leaders of the Islamic community.[5]

When the caliph al-Mutawakkil revoked the establishment of Mu'tazilism in 848 CE, its point of view did not by any means disappear, though it is believed that many important texts were lost or destroyed. It developed regional and factional variants, was protected by the patronage of certain local princes, and came to exercise an intellectual influence into the modern era. The efforts of *kalam* scholars to repel this and other threats to Islamic orthodoxy resulted in the creation of a substantial literature of theology and apologetics.

AL-ASH'ARI (d.c. 935)
Abu al-Hasan 'Ali ibn Isma'il al-Ash'ari (al-OSH-aree). *Kitab al-ibana 'an usul al-diyana* **or** *Book of the Exposition of the Foundations of the Faith.*

After Ahmad ibn Hanbal, the foremost early champion of orthodoxy was the theologian al-Ash'ari. Born at Basra, he studied and taught among the Mu'tazila there, until undergoing a kind of conversion experience at the age of forty. Adopting a more traditional and conservative understanding of Islam (similar but not identical to that of Ibn Hanbal), he began to use his extensive knowledge of Mu'tazili doctrine to refute their positions according to their own methods of reasoning and argumentation. His work was carried on by other scholars, and the Ash'ariyya theological school became the principal mode for the teaching of *kalam* in much of the Muslim world.

Al-Ash'ari dealt with the problem of theodicy by reestablishing the absolute sovereignty and omnipotence of God as the primary assumption; he excludes the notion of an ultimate ideal of justice against which God's decrees could be measured. Because God is just, God's every deed is by definition just, even if some of those deeds should seem questionable from a human viewpoint. He rejects all other effective agency in the universe, whether divine (as in Manichaeism) or human. However, human beings are still accountable for their behavior, because God grants to them a contingent power to act, and thus they acquire responsibility for their choices.

Al-Ash'ari also defends the concept of God's attributes as expressed in the Qur'an, which speaks of God possessing eyes, hands, a face, and a throne; these attributes inhere within the essence of God without introducing any plurality into it. Their nature cannot be understood as comparable to human characteristics and must simply be accepted, "without asking how" (*bila kayf*).

Among these attributes is the speech of God, the Qur'an, which must be uncreated because, as Ahmad ibn Hanbal observed, "nothing of God is created,
and the Qur'an is of God."[6] While al-Ash'ari skillfully uses the techniques of
rational argument to develop his positions, there is nevertheless in his
thought an element of submission to the inexplicable.

Al-Ash'ari. *Al-ibanah 'an usul ad-diyanah* [or] *The Elucidation of Islam's Foundation*. A translation with introduction and notes by Walter C. Klein (New Haven, Conn.: American Oriental Society, 1940).

This treatise, known as the *Ibana*, presents a good example of the method
and the content of *kalam*. Most of it is composed in a question-and-answer
format, which seems random if one just dips into it; a table of contents helps
to create some structure to the course of argument. The translation is scholarly and well annotated, but rather dense and fatiguing to read, with
Qur'anic passages rendered in an anachronistic King James English. The
method of "proof" is proof-texting from the Qur'an, so there are many such
passages, usually introduced by, "God has said . . ." The questions of imagi-
nary interlocutors are posed, then answered by the theologian; the tone is
combative but serious, and the work content-rich. A significant discussion of
the will of God and human infidelity is found in chapter 11, summed up in
this statement: "A man who wills folly is foolish, but the Lord of the Worlds
wills folly, yet is not foolish" (p. 105).

Walter Klein has provided some useful indexes and a lengthy, detailed but
not very readable introduction. The footnotes are extremely helpful, especially for Qur'anic references.

Al-Ash'ari. *The Theology of al-Ash'ari*. With briefly annotated transla-tions and appendixes by Richard J. McCarthy (Beirut: Imprimerie Catholique, 1953).

In one substantial scholarly volume, McCarthy has furnished the English
reader with complete annotated translations of two important treatises: the
Kitab al-luma' fi al-radd 'ala ahl al-zaygh wa al-bid'a or *Book of Selections* [lit.,
"flashes of light"] *from the Polemic against Deviation and Innovation*, and *Risala fi
istihsan al-khawd fi 'ilm al-kalam* or *Treatise of the Vindication of the Treatment of
the Science of Kalam*. The full Arabic text of these two documents is bound into
the same volume. In addition, McCarthy has provided a number of interesting
appendixes: the entry for al-Ash'ari from al-Khatib al-Baghdadi's biographical
dictionary *Ta'rikh Baghdad*; a biographical essay on al-Ash'ari by the historian
Ibn 'Asakir (d. 1176); brief descriptions of al-Ash'ari's known works; and a parallel printing of two creeds or synopses of the faith by al-Ash'ari, one from the

Ibana and the other from his important work *Maqalat al-islamiyyin*, the survey of Muslim sects from which we derive much of our knowledge of Mu'tazili doctrine. The volume is also extensively indexed, increasing its research value.

The *Luma'* is a classic *kalam* text in the dialectical question-and-answer format, made up of concise segments in a direct and forthright style. It touches on most of the doctrinal issues that characterize al-Ash'ari's body of work: God's existence and attributes, the uncreated Qur'an, the beatific vision, predestination, God's justice, the acquisition of human responsibility for our actions, the "promise and the threat" (of heaven and hell), the caliphate. The work displays a succinct catechetical rhythm; McCarthy uses the symbols Q, O, and A (question, objection, answer) to represent the Arabic phrases, "If someone asks . . ." or "Someone may say . . ." and "One should say to him . . ." McCarthy surmises that this work was intended as a training manual or practical handbook of apologetics or polemics. The advantage of this format for the reader is the unvarnished character of exchanges like these:

Q. Has not God, then, created the injustice of creatures?
A. He created it as their injustice, not as His. (p. 63)
Q. Is God free to inflict pain on infants in the next life?
A. God is free to do that, and in doing it He would be just . . . since the Creator is subject to no one and bound by no command, nothing can be evil on His part. (p. 99)
O. Then lying is evil only because God has declared it to be evil.
A. Certainly. And if He declared it to be good, it would be good . . . (p. 100)

McCarthy's footnotes are often helpful in explaining the cognitive and theological challenges of such passages; he also refers the reader to other sources and clarifies translation difficulties.

The brief treatise *Fi istihsan* (pp. 119–34) enumerates arguments and proof-texts defending the discipline of *kalam* from the charge of innovation and serves as an example of the use of documentary sources (Qur'an and *hadith*) to adduce evidence and substantiate arguments.

AL-BAQILLANI (d. 1013)
Abu Bakr Muhammad ibn al-Tayyib al-Baqillani (al-bockul-LONNY). *I'jaz al-Qur'an* or *The Miraculous Uniqueness of the Qur'an*. His name also appears as al-Bakillani.

The Ash'ariyya school of theological method was well established in Basra and Baghdad during its founder's own lifetime, and a coherent body of scholarly work was being produced. One of his successors, al-Baqillani (a nickname, "The Greengrocer"), studied under al-Ash'ari's own disciples and is credited with the processing and propagation of Ash'arism through his writing and lectures; he was considered the leader of the Ash'ari theologians of his day. The Mu'tazila were still quite active, however, as one of the "contending discourse communities" of the time,[7] including al-Baqillani's contemporary Qadi 'Abd al-Jabbar (d. 1024).

The foremost scholar on al-Baqillani, Richard J. McCarthy, observes that the content of much of his theological teaching was already present in al-Ash'ari's *Kitab al-luma'*. Contrary to some accounts, al-Baqillani did not introduce the theory of atomism and accidents into *kalam*. His work exhibits the merit of careful and industrious compilation, and his treatise *Al-tamhid fi al-radd 'ala al-mulhida* or *The Introduction to the Response against the Heretics* is said to be the earliest extant example of a complete manual of apologetics.[8]

Al-Baqillani. A Tenth-Century Document of Arabic Literary Theory and Criticism: The Sections on Poetry of al-Baqillani's I'jaz al-Qur'an. Translated and annotated by Gustave E. von Grunebaum (Chicago: University of Chicago Press, 1950).

In one respect, al-Baqillani's work was exceedingly original, and that is his contribution to the criticism of Arabic poetry as compared to the Qur'an. The theoretical question of the nature of the Qur'an was vital to the early theologians. Its created or uncreated status was part of the issue; another aspect was the claimed uniqueness of the Qur'an as an inimitable paragon of literary quality. The beauty and rhetorical richness of the book was understood to be evidence of its supernatural character as the verbatim, unmediated speech of God. This very high doctrine of Scripture was considered fundamental to the veracity of the message of Islam.

Al-Baqillani's treatise on the "miraculous uniqueness" or *i'jaz* of the Qur'an includes a section in which he endeavors to demonstrate the inferiority of all other Arabic literature in comparison. He analyzes the use of figures of speech in the Qur'an and in Arabic poetry, then critiques the work of two celebrated poets, Imru' al-Qais (d.c. 550) and al-Buhturi (d. 897); he does not simply comment upon a few verses or passages from these poets, but undertakes a detailed discussion of two of their major works, "from the aesthetic viewpoint."[9] According to the translator, this type of study is extraordinary in Arabic literature, making al-Baqillani's text an important one.

The text is very difficult, however, and it is not made any easier by von Grunebaum's dense technical annotation, nor by his practice of thickly peppering the page with transliterated terms in parentheses. These features may be appreciated by the subject-area specialist but are discouraging to other readers. The names index might be helpful; there is also an index and a table of rhetorical and literary terms.

AL-JUWAYNI (d. 1085)

Abu al-Ma'ali 'Abd al-Malik al-Juwayni (al-joo-WAY-nee). *Kitab al-irshad ila qawati' al-adilla fi usul al-i'tiqad* or *Guide to Conclusive Proofs for the Principles of Belief.* His name may be spelled as al-Djuwayni; he is often known as Imam al-Haramayn.

'Ilm al-kalam matured into a discipline of intellectual rigor and refinement, and the theologian Abu al-Ma'ali al-Juwayni was one of its most gifted practitioners. From the vantage point of the fifteenth century, the historian Ibn Khaldun surveyed the whole course of Islamic scholarship and pronounced al-Juwayni's *Irshad* to be the most effective statement of Ash'ari theology, in keeping with the methods and teaching of the early Islamic authorities; it has remained a fundamental text in theological education.

Born in a village near Nishapur in Persia, al-Juwayni was the son of a prominent jurist; he likewise studied law and became a respected jurist and teacher in the Shafi'i legal tradition. He then became fully trained in Ash'ari theology, studying with eminent masters who could trace their instruction back through al-Baqillani to al-Ash'ari himself. The local Saljuq (or Seljuk) vizier took exception to the doctrines of Ash'arism and as a result al-Juwayni was forced to relocate, eventually settling in the Hejaz and teaching for some years in Mecca and Medina; for this reason he is often known as *Imam al-Haramayn,* or "Imam of the Two Holy Cities." The new Saljuq vizier, Nizam al-Mulk, undertook to restore Ash'ari and Shafi'i legal and theological scholarship, establishing schools for this purpose and summoning authorities to staff them. Al-Juwayni returned to Nishapur to teach at the Nizamiyya *madrasa* (MAD-rassa) or academy there about 1060 CE. During his long period of residence there, he produced important works of jurisprudence and theology, including an enormous tome titled *Al-shamil fi usul al-din* or *The Complete Book of the Principles of Religion.* Al-Juwayni was destined to be overshadowed in reputation by one of his students, the brilliant Abu Hamid al-Ghazali (d. 1111).

Al-Juwayni. A *Guide to Conclusive Proofs for the Principles of Belief.* Translated by Paul E. Walker, with Muhammad S. Eissa (Reading, UK: Garnet, 2000).

This attractive edition is part of a valuable publishing project carried out by the Centre for Muslim Contribution to Civilization in Qatar, bringing forth new scholarly translations into English of important but overlooked primary sources in Islamic studies. Paul E. Walker has produced an elegant rendition in accurate modern English of this historic work.

In the author's own preface, al-Juwayni expresses his intention to create in the *Irshad* a work that would occupy a middle ground between the intimidating comprehensive tomes of theology and the formulaic handbooks or summaries of doctrine that lack any proofs or persuasive argumentation. His aim is to develop three aspects of theological discourse: what must be said about God, what must not be said about God, and what is possible to assert with respect to God. In a systematic way, he covers the standard topics of the discipline: the efficacy of reason and the character of knowledge (epistemology), the created order and its contingency, the nature and attributes of God, the beatific vision, predestination, justice and injustice, eternal reward and punishment, the caliphate. He also delves deeply into other issues, especially the role of prophetic miracles as indicative of the apostolic mission and a discussion of contrition or repentance. His analysis of the speech of God and its implications for a theology of the Qur'an is particularly subtle and intriguing (pp. 56–77). Al-Juwayni's response to the Christian doctrines of incarnation and the Trinity is also of considerable interest (pp. 28–30).

Walker keeps the footnotes to an absolute minimum; he provides an adequate bibliography and index, a few textual notes, and a lucid, well-crafted, and informative introduction.

AL-GHAZALI (d. 1111)
Abu Hamid Muhammad ibn Muhammad al-Ghazali (al-ga-ZALLY). *Ihya' 'ulum al-din* or *Revival of the Religious Sciences*. His name is often spelled as al-Ghazzali; in Latin texts he is known as Algazel or Algazali.

One of the most perceptive and articulate thinkers the Islamic world ever produced was Abu Hamid al-Ghazali, creator of several works that are genuine turning-point texts. He grew up in a small town near Mashhad in eastern Persia, then went to Nishapur to study with the Ash'ari theologian al-Juwayni and in due course became a professor himself at the Nizamiyya *madrasa* in Baghdad. Thoroughly familiar with jurisprudence and *kalam*, he also devoted his attention to the work of the Neoplatonist philosophers, such as al-Farabi and Ibn Sina. He wrote an exposition of their views, the *Maqasid al-falasifa* or *Aims of the Philosophers*, and then followed it with a devastating critique of their metaphysics, the *Tahafut al-falasifa* or *The Incoherence of the Philosophers* (see also chapter 6). Ghazali targeted twenty of their metaphysical theories or assertions and demonstrated that seventeen of these are unsubstantiated by scriptural sources, while three of them are in direct contradiction to the Qur'an. Ghazali's critique is regarded as a watershed in the history of Neoplatonist philosophy; it is available in English in a fine scholarly edition by Michael E. Marmura as *The Incoherence of the Philosophers*, 2nd ed. (Provo, Utah: Brigham Young University Press, 2000).

While teaching in Baghdad, he also produced an important work of Ash'ari *kalam*, *Al-iqtisad fi al-i'tiqad* or *The Golden Mean in Belief*. Apparently, he accepted Ash'ari theology as "true so far as it went,"[10] though he was to move well beyond it in his own work. A portion of the *Iqtisad* is available in a translation by 'Abdu-r-Rahman Abu Zayd, entitled *Al-Ghazali on Divine Predicates and Their Properties* (Lahore: Sh. Muhammad Ashraf, 1970).

At about that point in his life, al-Ghazali suffered a dramatic crisis of faith. Distraught and ill, he abandoned his teaching post and undertook a personal and intellectual quest for the true basis of religious experience and belief. Many years later, he wrote a quasi-autobiographical account of this quest, *Al-munqidh min al-dalal* or *The Deliverer from Error* (see below). His quest led him ultimately to embrace the path of Sufism, through which he was able to achieve a synthesis of valid, defensible doctrine and authentic, satisfying spiritual experience.

The synthesis thus achieved led al-Ghazali to create his most impressive work, the *Ihya' 'ulum al-din* (IH-ya ol-LOOM id-DEEN) or *Revival of the Religious Sciences*. This very substantial work is intended to process the contributions of law and tradition, theology, ethics, spirituality, and mysticism into an integrated, comprehensive guide to Muslim faith and practice. He organized it into four major thematic areas, each comprising ten books. The first quarter deals with *'ibadat* or ritual observances and acts of worship, such as formal prayer, ablution and purity, charity, fasting, pilgrimage. The second quarter addresses *mu'amalat*, social behaviors and the norms of daily life, food, travel, trade, marriage, and family customs. In the third quarter, Ghazali discusses the spiritual vices or "ways to perdition," and in the fourth quarter the virtues or "ways to salvation," the qualities that develop in the obedient soul who sincerely seeks communion with God through the mystical life. In this way he sought to balance ritual observance with sound doctrine and an active, authentic inner life of faith. This extraordinary work has not yet appeared in its entirety in English, typically, a translator will select one of the forty books and publish it separately. Several have been translated more than once. The Islamic Texts Society is gradually bringing forth a full set of new translations, of which eight have appeared and more are in preparation. Some of these sources are mentioned below.

The Islamic Texts Society has also produced new editions of other treatises that are not parts of the *Ihya'*, for example, *Letter to a Disciple* (*Ayyuha al-walad*), translated by Tobias Mayer, and *Al-Ghazali on the Ninety-Nine Beautiful Names of God* (*Al-maqsad al-asna fi sharh asma' Allah al-husna*) by David Burrell and Nazih Daher.

Late in his life, al-Ghazali returned to teaching, at the Nizamiyya *madrasa* at Nishapur, and then retired to a Sufi communal residence or *khanaqa* he founded at Tus for the training of disciples in the contemplative path. He has been honored with traditional appellations such as *Hujjat al-Islam* or "The Proof of Islam" and *Zayn al-Din* or "Ornament of Religion."

Al-Ghazali. *Al-Ghazali's Path to Sufism and His Deliverance from Error.* An annotated translation by Richard J. McCarthy (Louisville, Ky.: Fons Vitae, 2000).

A well-known authority on Islamic theology has translated the *Munqidh*, al-Ghazali's first-person account of his crisis of faith and search for intellectual satisfaction and spiritual meaning. Al-Ghazali describes his investigation into the teachings of the *mutakallimun* or theologians, the *falasifa* or philosophers, an Isma'ili sect known as the Batiniyya (which derived its security from adherence to an authoritative imam), and finally the Sufis, among whom he found what he was seeking. The work itself is very brief, only about sixty pages in large type; McCarthy adds a section of rather technical notes suited to the advanced student or academic specialist.

The great Orientalist W. Montgomery Watt published a sound and readable translation of the *Munqidh* in *The Faith and Practice of al-Ghazali* (London: George Allen and Unwin, 1953). In the same small book is found his translation of the *Bidayat al-hidaya* or *The Beginning of Guidance*, which he construes as an introduction to the *Ihya'*.

Al-Ghazali. *Al-Ghazzali's Mishkat al-Anwar* [or] *The Niche for Lights.* A translation with an introduction by W. H. T. Gairdner (Lahore: Sh. Muhammad Ashraf, 1952).

An heir of the classic Orientalist tradition, Temple Gairdner first published this translation as a monograph of the Royal Asiatic Society in London in 1924. It is reprinted here, in a poorly manufactured but nevertheless valuable edition. This small treatise is considered a genuine work of al-Ghazali; some of the works dealing principally with mysticism are thought to be erroneously attributed to him. There is a substantial and interesting (though somewhat quaint) introduction, but no scholarly apparatus to aid research. This work has been reissued in the new five-volume set *Theology, Ethics and Metaphysics: Royal Asiatic Society Classics of Islam*, edited by Hiroyuki Mashita (London: RoutledgeCurzon, 2003).

A newer scholarly translation has been produced in the Islamic Translation Series by David Buchman, titled *The Niche of Lights = Mishkat al-anwar* (Provo, Utah: Brigham Young University Press, 1998).

Al-Ghazali. *The Jewels of the Qur'an: Al-Ghazali's Theory.* Translated and edited by Muhammad Abul Quasem (London: Kegan Paul, 1983).

A mystical treatise or exposition by al-Ghazali on the doctrine of scripture, the *Kitab jawahir al-Qur'an* has been capably translated and annotated in this volume. Abul Quasem first prepared this manuscript in Edinburgh under the direction of W. Montgomery Watt. The work develops a highly allegorical concept of the Qur'an using the symbolism of precious stones; the "jewels" are verses defining the essence of God and his attributes, while the "pearls" are verses describing man's path of obedience and the practical observance of religion. Abul Quasem provides some helpful footnotes, a brief but necessary introduction, and two indexes.

Al-Ghazali. *The Precious Pearl.* A translation with notes by Jane Idleman Smith (Missoula, Mont.: Scholars Press, 1979).

This treatise, known as *Kitab al-durra al-fakhira fi kashf 'ulum al-akhira* or *The Book of the Precious Pearl Concerning the Disclosure of the Sciences of the Hereafter* was evidently created by Ghazali as a reworking of the last book of the *Ihya'*, on death and the afterlife. There is some doubt about the authenticity of this work among Western scholars, but its attribution in Muslim tradition is strong. It touches upon issues of cosmology, eschatology, and soteriology in a manner that is both orthodox and esoteric. Smith's introduction and text outline are very helpful, and her notes informative and intelligible.

Editions of the Ihya' 'ulum al-din

As noted above, al-Ghazali's primary work, the *Ihya' 'ulum al-din* or *Revival of the Religious Sciences*, has not yet been published in its entirety in English. Several of the forty individual books that compose it have appeared in various editions, which can be extracted with some effort from library catalogs or bibliographic databases.

A set of translations of the first few books, for example, was produced by the prolific publisher Shaykh Muhammad Ashraf in Lahore in the 1960s, translated and annotated by Nabih Amin Faris of the American University in Beirut, who studied at Princeton with the eminent Arabist Philip K. Hitti. In the first book of the first quarter, the *Kitab al-'ilm* or *Book of Knowledge*, al-Ghazali provides a complete prospectus of the *Ihya'*, defining his objectives for each of the four quarters and enumerating the forty books. This information would be of value to anyone studying any part of the *Ihya'*.[11]

The Faris editions contain a few footnotes—mainly references to other medieval authorities—and rudimentary indexes. In addition to the Book of Knowledge, the volumes available in this series are book II, *The Foundations of the Articles of Faith* (*Kitab qawa'id al-'aqa'id*); book III, *The Mysteries of Purity* (*Kitab asrar al-taharah*); book V, *The Mysteries of Almsgiving* (*Kitab asrar al-zakah*); and book VI, *The Mysteries of Fasting* (*Kitab asrar al-sawm*). Faris explains that book IV, the *Kitab asrar al-salah* or *Book of the Mysteries of Prayer*, was already available in a translation by Edwin E. Calverley when he was preparing this project; it was first published as *Worship in Islam* by Sh. Muhammad Ashraf in 1925.

The new series being produced by the Islamic Texts Society is attractive, scholarly, and well edited. It includes: book XXXIV, *On Poverty and Abstinence* (*Kitab al-faqr wa'l zuhd*) and book XXXVII, *On Intention, Sincerity and Truthfulness* (*Kitab al-niyya wa'l-ikhlas wa'l-sidq*), both translated by Asaad F. Shaker; book XXXII, *On Patience and Thankfulness* (*Kitab al-sabr wa'l-shukr*) by Henry T. Littlejohn; book IX, *On Invocations and Supplications* (*Kitab al-adhkar wa'l-da'awat*) by Kojiro Nakamura; book XI, *On the Manners Relating to Eating* (*Kitab adab al-akl*) by Denys Johnson-Davies; and by T. J. Winter, book XXII, *On Disciplining the Soul* (*Kitab riyadat al-nafs*), book XXIII, *On Breaking the Two Desires* (*Kitab kasr al-shahwatayn*), and book XL, *On the Remembrance of Death and the Afterlife* (*Kitab dhikr al-mawt wa ma ba'dahu*). Book XXXV, *Faith in Divine Unity and Trust in Divine Providence* (*Kitab al-tawhid wa'l-tawakkul*), by David B. Burrell, has been published with a related imprint (Louisville, Ky.: Fons Vitae, 2001).

In addition, Brill has published a scholarly translation by Leon Zolondek of book XX, *On the Conduct of Life as Exemplified by the Prophet* (*Adab al-ma'ishah wa al-akhlaq al-nubuwah*), and book XXXIII, *On Fear and Hope* (*Kitab al-khawf wa al-raja'*), by William McKane.

AL-SHAHRASTANI (d. 1153)

Abu al-Fath Muhammad ibn 'Abd al-Karim al-Shahrastani (ash-sha-ras-TAH-nee). *Kitab nihayat al-aqdam fi 'ilm al-kalam* or *Book of the Latest Developments in the Science of Theology;* the work is also known as *Summa Philosophiae.*

Another noteworthy Persian theologian, al-Shahrastani, was born in a village in what is now Turkmenistan, then went to Nishapur for his theological education. He was trained in Ash'ari *kalam* by several successors of al-Juwayni, and also applied himself to the study of Qur'anic commentary, the *hadith* literature, and Shafi'i jurisprudence. After completing the pilgrimage to Mecca, he was offered a teaching position at the Nizamiyya *madrasa* in Baghdad; after several years there, he returned to Persia to carry on his writing and research. Following al-Ghazali, he too was a determined critic of Avicennan philosophy.

Al-Shahrastani. *Muslim Sects and Divisions*. Translated by A. K. Kazi and J. G. Flynn (London: Kegan Paul, 1984).

Al-Shahrastani is the author of several works considered basic to the history of the discipline, the most important being his *Al-milal wa al-nihal* or *The Religions and the Sects*. In the *Milal*, he discusses the viewpoints of a number of sectarian or minority trends within Islam (much as al-Ash'ari did in his *Maqalat al-islamiyyin*) and also analyzes the beliefs of other religions, including Jews and Christians, Sabians, Magians and Manichaeans, even some pre-Islamic Arab and Hindu sects. The *Milal* has been described as "the high point of Muslim histories of religion."[12] Various portions of it have been published in English, such as this translation by Kazi and Flynn and *Shahrastani on the Indian Religions*, translated by Bruce B. Lawrence (The Hague: Mouton, 1976). An interesting excerpt prepared by noted translator Michael E. Sells is found in an appendix to *Early Islamic Mysticism* (New York: Paulist Press, 1996), 304–20, with excellent annotations.

Kazi and Flynn have selected those parts of the *Milal* dealing with the seventy-three Muslim sectarian groups, arranged according to "arithmetical principles" (pp. 27–30). Al-Shahrastani's treatment of them is remarkably clear, readable, and neutral in tone. He has also written an illuminating opening chapter, called here "General Introduction." The edition contains a brief introduction by the translators as well, along with basic annotations and indexes.

Al-Shahrastani. *The Summa Philosophiae of al-Shahrastani.* **Edited with a translation by Alfred Guillaume (Oxford: Oxford University Press, 1934).**

This work, the *Nihaya*, was evidently composed as a sequel to the *Milal*. In it, al-Shahrastani sets forth systematically his understanding of orthodox *kalam*, often in a dialectical or argumentative style using the question-objection-answer format. It covers the usual topics of Ash'ari *kalam*: the finite nature of creation, anthropomorphism and the divine attributes, God's speech, issues of justice and soteriology. A particularly interesting section deals with the concept of prophethood, the "proof" of prophecy, and the evidentiary status of miracles; he discusses first the prophets in general, and then Muhammad's mission in particular. This section also deals with the inimitable Qur'an as an evidentiary miracle and with the nature of revelation.[13]

Unfortunately, the translation is an old one, and its quality has been criticized. Guillaume has abridged his translation, with some frustrating omissions (the Arabic text is printed in full) and the frequent use of ellipses is distracting. There are a few footnotes, but not a complete research apparatus.

IBN TAYMIYYA (d. 1328)

Taqi al-Din Ahmad ibn 'Abd al-Halim ibn Taymiyya (ibbin tie-MEE-yah).
Kitab radd 'ala al-mantiqiyyin or Book of the Refutation of the Logicians.

His name also appears as Taki al-Din; it may be spelled as Ibn Taymiyah or Taymiya.

What came to be known as the "later scholastic" movement continued into the thirteenth century, led by scholars such as Fakhr al-Din al-Razi (d. 1209), who were perfectly able to employ the methods and vocabulary of both theology and philosophy and to argue their way through doctrinal and metaphysical proofs. But a figure arose who was to push orthodox *kalam* in a different direction: the Hanbali theologian Ibn Taymiyya.

Born in 1263 at Harran, Ibn Taymiyya led a life embroiled in political and theological conflict and was often under arrest in Damascus or Cairo. Trained as a jurist in the school of law founded by Ahmad ibn Hanbal, he shared Ibn Hanbal's adherence to the fundamental sources of Islamic religion: the Qur'an and the *sunna* or exemplary behavior and teaching of the Prophet, as known through and interpreted by the earliest Companions, the *salaf al-salih* or "pious ancestors." Ibn Taymiyyah resisted later developments in theology, philosophy, or mysticism as superfluous accretions or heretical innovation (*bid'a*), including the corpus of Ash'ari *kalam*, which he dismissed as unprofitable. His *Kitab radd 'ala al-mantiqiyyin* or *Book of the Refutation of the Logicians* (known also as the *Nasihat ahl al-iman fi al-radd 'ala mantiq al-yunan* or *Advice to the People of the Faith in Refuting the Logic of the Greeks*) rejects the Aristotelian language of logic that had become widely accepted in the discipline, regarding it as invalid and vacuous.[14] A related work was published in English translation by the distinguished scholar Wael B. Hallaq, described below.

The Hanbali school of theology, like Hanbali jurisprudence, built upon Ibn Taymiyya's scholarly foundation to develop its own important literature and is an influential trend in Islamic thought today. Ibn Taymiyya's accomplished student Ibn Qayyim al-Jawziyya (d. 1350; his name also appears as Ibn Kayyim al-Djawziyya) produced a number of significant theological works. One of these has been published in English as *Ibn Qayyim al-Jawziyya on the Invocation of God* (Cambridge: Islamic Texts Society, 2000), translated by Michael Abdurrahman Fitzgerald and Moulay Youssef Slitine. Chiefly a work about spirituality, it touches upon several significant doctrinal issues.

Ibn Taymiyya. *Ibn Taymiyya against the Greek Logicians*. Translated with an introduction by Wael B. Hallaq (Oxford: Clarendon Press, 1993).

Ibn Taymiyya's extensive critique of the Neoplatonist philosophers, the *Radd* (also called the *Nasiha*, based on the work's alternate title), was republished in an abridged form by the prolific Egyptian scholar Jalal al-Din al-Suyuti (d. 1505), who pared away the metaphysical discussions in the original text to get at the core material dealing with logic, specifically definition and syllogism. Al-Suyuti titled this edited work *Jahd al-qariha fi tajrid al-nasiha* or *The Exertion of Effort in Abridging the Nasiha*. It is this abridged form of Ibn Taymiyya's critique that receives expert attention in this scholarly edition.

Though the subject matter is largely technical, the energy and passion of Ibn Taymiyya's style often breaks through. There is a memorable discussion, for example, of the demonstrative syllogism using alcoholic beverages as an example (pp. 38–40). Wael Hallaq's admirably articulate translation is supplied with text and manuscript information, a substantial bibliography, a fine critical introduction, abundant annotations, and indexes of titles, subjects, and Arabic terms.

Ibn Taymiyya. A Muslim Theologian's Response to Christianity. Edited and translated by Thomas F. Michel, SJ (Delmar, N.Y.: Caravan Books, 1984).

Ibn Taymiyya wrote this compelling work in response to an essay in Christian apologetics by Paul of Antioch; it is among the most extensive and substantial medieval Muslim critiques of Christianity. He titled it *Al-jawab al-sahih li man baddal din al-masih* or *The Correct Answer to Those Who Replaced the Religion of Christ* (i.e., with a corrupted version that departed from the original *injil* or Gospel given to Jesus as a valid prophet of Islam). The course of the argument goes well beyond the specifics of the Christian faith, however, and incorporates Ibn Taymiyya's polemics against errant tendencies within Islam, such as Neoplatonist philosophy, Ash'ari *kalam*, deviant popular piety, and certain aspects of Sufi and Shi'i doctrine. Ibn Taymiyya expounds at length upon three areas of particular concern to comparative religion: the universal nature of Muhammad's prophetic message, the concept of *tahrif* or the corruption of Scripture (especially the Bible), and the Trinity, including the doctrine of incarnation.

Thomas Michel, who studied under Fazlur Rahman, has produced an extremely lucid and useful introduction, essentially a scholarly monograph on the polemical discourse of Ibn Taymiyya in its historical and theological contexts. This informative and balanced work occupies over 130 pages of the volume. Michel's abridged translation of the text (another 230 pages) is direct, readable, and carefully annotated, identifying Qur'anic allusions and supplying references to other medieval sources and modern scholarly literature. Page numbers for Paul of Antioch refer to the Arabic text, which is not very helpful to the English reader; this volume could have been improved by including an English translation of Paul's *Risala ila ahad al-muslimin* (*Letter to One of the Muslims*) as an appendix.

The volume does include information on the existing manuscripts, an exceptional bibliography, a helpful glossary, and a small but effective index.

AL-TAFTAZANI (d.c. 1390)

Sa'd al-Din Mas'ud ibn 'Umar ibn 'Abdallah al-Taftazani (at-toff-tah-ZAH-nee). *Sharh al-'aqida al-nasafiyya* or *Commentary on the Creed of al-Nasafi.* The title sometimes appears using the plural, as *'aqa'id* or *'aka'id,* meaning *Articles of Faith.*

Some creeds and creedal statements exist in Islam, but they are not the product of ecumenical councils and they do not have the same function in defining community identity that creeds have performed in the Christian tradition. They are typically created as a digest or epitome of the teaching of a certain *mutakallim,* summarized by himself or a disciple.[15]

Creedal statements by al-Ash'ari (from the *Ibana*) and al-Ghazali (from the *Ihya'*) are available in Duncan Black Macdonald's *Muslim Theology, Jurisprudence and Constitutional Theory* (New York: Russell and Russell, 1965). Also in that volume is the text in English translation of a well-known creed by Najm al-Din al-Nasafi (d. 1142), a *kalam* scholar of the Maturidi school, which differs in some particulars from Ash'ari doctrine. Macdonald's edition has some helpful footnotes and marks with an asterisk each point at which Maturidi (or Mataridi) teaching is at variance with al-Ash'ari.

The creed by al-Nasafi formed the basis of an important commentary by Sa'd al-Din al-Taftazani. This commentary became a standard text in the theological curriculum of Islamic schools and is still an important document in the field of *kalam.* Born in a village north of Nishapur in Khurasan, Al-Taftazani was the son of a judge and was trained early in Hanafi and Shafi'i law; he produced important works in jurisprudence, grammar and rhetoric, Qur'anic exegesis, logic and metaphysics, and Ash'ari *kalam.* Only a few years after his death, he was already well known enough to be mentioned approvingly by the historian Ibn Khaldun, who discovered copies of al-Taftazani's works as far away as Cairo. In about 1382 CE, he was summoned to Samarqand by the Mongol ruler Timur (Tamerlane) to grace his court with scholarship; this move ended badly when another noted scholar, al-Jurjani (or Djurdjani) arrived in Samarqand and a bitter rivalry developed between them. Al-Taftazani died there in 1390 CE.

Al-Taftazani. A Commentary on the Creed of Islam: Sa'd al-Din al-Taftazani on the Creed of Najm al-Din al-Nasafi. Translated with introduction and notes by Earl Edgar Elder (New York: Columbia University Press, 1950).

Trained in the classical Orientalist tradition, E. E. Elder has created a crisply organized critical translation of Taftazani's commentary, providing direct and descriptive chapter divisions and a table of contents that affords a coherent plan of the entire work. The relevant portion of Nasafi's creed is printed in bold type at the beginning of each chapter and throughout the discussion, as it is dealt with by Taftazani sentence by sentence or phrase by phrase. Elder's translation is solid and intelligible, with recourse to transliterated Arabic terms in parentheses when the wording clearly calls for it. Intricate and detailed footnotes supply a wealth of information on text and manuscript problems, vocabulary, allusions to or quotes from other sources, and discussions of the theological issues in other medieval or modern scholarly works. There is a bibliography and a thorough index.

Elder's introduction serves as an admirably compact and comprehensible synopsis of the entire history of *kalam* and the specific development of creedal statements within it. This introduction (twenty-three pages) could itself be assigned as useful course reading for students, on the order of a substantial and well-composed article in a reference work.

Another translation of an excerpt from Taftazani's commentary, on God's attribute of speech, is available in the anthology by Calder, Mojaddedi, and Rippin, *Classical Islam* (London: Routledge, 2003), 155–58.

Shi'i Theologians

The early controversy over the status of the sinful believer that so concerned the Mu'tazila was far more than academic at the time, because the trauma of the assassination of the Caliph 'Uthman in 656 CE and the struggle between 'Ali and Mu'awiya for succession was still keenly felt, and the interpretation of these events theologically was unresolved. The question of allegiance to an erring ruler was an existential issue of the first importance; the Muslim is under no obligation to follow an infidel ruler, but an errant believer appointed by God to rule may still command obedience. The Kharijite faction, for instance, maintained that the sins of the caliph entitled them to repudiate his authority and deny the validity of the caliphate itself.

The Shi'a distinguished themselves by their partisanship for the succession of 'Ali to the leadership of the Islamic community after the death of the Prophet. For them, political and theological authority both rested exclusively in the person of Muhammad, then 'Ali, then 'Ali's son Husayn, then their lineal successors, the People of the Household (*ahl al-bayt*) of the Prophet. They developed an idealized theology of the caliph as Imam, a divinely appointed ruler and authoritative interpreter of the faith, blessed with infallibility and immunity from sin. As Madelung observes, the doctrine of the imamate was constitutive for the Shi'i movement and most of its later subdivisions.[16]

The Imams themselves produced much of what is taught as Shi'i theology, particularly the Sixth Imam, Ja'far al-Sadiq (d. 765). There is also a body of scholarship fitting the description of Shi'i *kalam*.

IBN BABAWAYHI (d. 991)

Abu Ja'far Muhammad ibn Babawayh or Babawayhi (ibbin baba-WAY) al-Qummi. *Risalat al-i'tiqadat al-imamiya* or *Treatise Concerning the Imami Doctrines*. **His name also appears as Ibn Babuyah or Babuyi; alternate spellings include Abu Dja'far and al-Kummi.**

The exalted reputation of Ibn Babawayhi was firmly established by his collection of *hadith* narratives, known as *Man la yahduruhu al-faqih* or *[Book for] One Who Is Not in the Presence of a Jurist*. Just as the Sunni community generally recognizes six *hadith* collections as reliable and authoritative, the Shi'a designate four preeminent collections of *hadith*; Ibn Babawayhi's is one of these (see chapter 2). He also produced a number of other works of theology and criticism, some of which still exist in manuscript or published form.

Very little is known of his life, though he is believed to have been born in Khurasan about 923 CE, taught in Baghdad, and died at Rayy (the date of his death is disputed by some). He had two brothers who were also jurists and theologians. He is often mentioned by his honorific, *Shaykh al-Saduq* or "The Trustworthy Learned One" and is regarded as a leading authority by the Ithna 'Ashari or "Twelver" Shi'a.

Ibn Babawayhi. *A Shi'ite Creed*. **Translated by Asaf A. A. Fyzee (London: Oxford University Press, 1942).**

The title of this work is a bit misleading, as it is not a "creed" or statement of defined articles of faith, but rather a summary theology built around a set of essential doctrines. It is divided into forty-five chapters on topics typical of *kalam*: divine unity and attributes, creation, death and resurrection, eternal reward and punishment, the nature of the Qur'an, and so forth. But distinguishing characteristics of Imami belief are vividly expressed in chapters such as "The Prophets, Apostles, Imams and Angels," "The Number of Prophets and Vicegerents," "Infallibility," or "Evil-Doers" (*zalimun*). The method of argumentation is also distinctive, as Ibn Babawayhi uses sayings or *hadith* narratives involving 'Ali, Husayn, and the Imams as evidentiary or normative, as in the fourteenth chapter, "The Belief Concerning Death."

The work as a whole has an extremely assertive or polemical tone and the writer often takes the opportunity to pronounce someone a *kafir* (unbeliever), denier, or apostate, "more wicked than the Jews, the Christians, the Fire-Worshippers, the Qadarites or the Kharijites, or any of the heretics (*ahl al-bid'a*) or those who hold views which lead astray" (p. 101).

Asaf Ali Asghar Fyzee is chiefly known as the author of *Outlines of Muhammadan Law* (Calcutta: Oxford University Press, 1949). He prepared this version of Ibn Babawayhi's *Risala* for the Islamic Research Association's series of Arabic and Persian texts in translation. It is somewhat dated, but readable, with a selective use of transliterated terms in parentheses; however, the Arabic terms in the footnotes and bibliography are printed in the vernacular script, making them of little help to the English-only reader. An introduction, annotations, and four valuable indexes are provided.

AL-HILLI (d. 1325)

Jamal al-Din Hassan ibn Yusuf ibn 'Ali ibn al-Mutahhar al-Hilli (al-HILLY). *Al-bab al-hadi 'ashar* or *The Eleventh Chapter*; that is, of his larger work *Minhaj al-salah fi ikhtisar al-misbah* or *The Right Approach to the Abridgment of the Misbah*. He is usually called 'Allameh (or 'Allamah) al-Hilli.

A student of the great Persian philosopher Nasir al-Din al-Tusi (see chapter 6), al-Hilli is believed to have played a pivotal role in Shi'i history: He was instrumental in converting the Mongol ruler of Persia, Öldjeytü (or Uljaytu), to Imami Shi'ism, which then became the official or established faith of Persia, about 1305 CE. A prolific scholar, he produced numerous works that are considered to be classic expositions of Imami ("Twelver") Shi'ism. Among these was his condensed edition of al-Tusi's major work on worship and prayer ritual, the *Misbah al-mutahajjid* or *Lamp of the Night Prayer Vigil*, in ten chapters. Al-Hilli then composed his own supplement to this work, which became known as "The Eleventh Chapter."

The work as al-Hilli designed it was a highly concentrated "creed" or summary statement of the *usul al-din* or principles of the faith. This brief statement was amplified with a substantial commentary by another scholar of Hilla known as Miqdad (or Mikdad) al-Fadil about 1500 CE. This amplified version is the form in which the work is studied and taught as a classic text in Imami theological curricula.

Al-Hilli. *Al-Babu 'l-Hadi 'Ashar: A Treatise on the Principles of Shi'ite Theology.* Translated by William McElwee Miller (London: Royal Asiatic Society, 1928).

Miller's foreword to this volume indicates that he set out deliberately to discover a work in the Shi'i corpus that exemplifies their doctrine in the way that the "creed" of al-Nasafi does in the Sunni tradition (see al-Taftazani above). The work that was recommended to him by Shiʻi scholars was al-Hilli's "Eleventh Chapter" (*Al-bab al-hadi ʻashar*). He has translated it here, embedded in its commentary by Miqdad, who undertook to provide "the reason and proofs" to substantiate al-Hilli's statements (p. 1). The work covers the standard themes of *kalam* from a Shiʻi perspective, with explicit reference to Muʻtazili and Ashʻari doctrine and to the metaphysics of the philosophers.

Miller's translation is bit dated and sometimes obscure; he has supplied some useful notes and a very simple index and introduction. This translation has been reissued in the Mashita anthology *Theology, Ethics and Metaphysics* (London: RoutledgeCurzon, 2003).

TABATABA'I (d. 1981)

Sayyid Muhammad Husayn Tabataba'i (tobba-tob-BUY-ee). He is also well known as 'Allameh (or 'Allamah) Tabataba'i. *Shiʻah dar islam* or *Shiʻite Islam.*

The great vitality of Persian scholarship was embodied in the twentieth century by the Shiʻi cleric ʻAllameh Tabataba'i. Fully trained in both law and philosophy in Najaf, he taught in Tabriz and in Qum, where he combined intellectual achievement with a refined spirituality that made a deep impression upon others, among them the French philosopher Henri Corbin. The works of ʻAllameh Tabataba'i became known to readers in Europe and North America principally through the efforts of distinguished Islamic scholar Seyyed Hossein Nasr, who translated them into English and interpreted their significance in his own writing.

Tabataba'i. *Shiʻite Islam*. Translated and edited with an introduction and notes by Seyyed Hossein Nasr (Albany: State University of New York Press, 1975).

This comprehensive yet compact and well-organized work is an introduction to the history and thought of the Shiʻa, quite suitable as a classroom text or desk reference. It also contains a good deal of information on Shiʻi teachings pertinent to the concerns of *kalam*: the doctrine of Scripture, the knowledge of God, divine attributes, destiny and providence, free will, the prophetic mission, death and resurrection, eschatology, and so on. There is also very useful reflection upon elements more distinctive of Shiʻism: an emphasis upon metaphysics, philosophy, and gnostic or mystical comprehension (Sufism), certain specific controversial issues such as *taqiya* or dissimulation and *mutʻa* or temporary marriage, and of course, in-depth treatment of the constitutive doctrine for Shiʻi Islam, the imamate.

The exceptional clarity and coherence of this work may belong to the original text by Tabataba'i, or to Nasr's editing and translation of it, or both. In any case, it represents years of fruitful collaboration between these two scholars. Nasr has supplied an erudite preface, helpful annotations for each chapter, and some of the explanatory appendixes; also, two bibliographies and an index.

Modern Works in Theology

As noted in chapter 6, the legacy of rationalism and classical philosophy was applied in the late nineteenth and twentieth centuries to emerging issues in the Islamic world: postcolonial conflict and nationalism, Western educational and social influences, and a perceived stagnation or unresponsiveness in traditional Islamic leadership. Often, the established methods and materials of theology were felt to be insufficient for or even obstructive of this effort.

The Mu'tazili approach to knowledge gained through reason and the independent exercise of intellect entered the discourse of reformist thinkers like Jamal al-Din al-Afghani (d. 1897), addressing the challenge of modernity and the revolution in scientific and industrial development that was changing the world. Muhammad Iqbal (d. 1938) drew upon Ash'ari *kalam*, but at the same time grappled with the philosophical thought of Europeans like Berkeley, Whitehead, Russell, Einstein, and Bergson. Mohammad Arkoun has employed postmodern critical theory in the reading of classic Islamic texts, adopting a distanced and deconstructed view of a theological text as a product of its history and as a political instrument. All of the Muslim reformists and thinkers of the modern era were confronted by the need to reconsider the transmitted norms of Islamic religion and culture in a radically transformed intellectual context, and that discussion is still very much in progress.[17]

MUHAMMAD 'ABDUH (d. 1905)
Muhammad 'Abduh. *The Theology of Unity*. Translated by Ishaq Musa'ad and Kenneth Cragg (London: George Allen and Unwin, 1966).

Among the most interesting examples of Islamic theology in the context of modernity is the work of the great Egyptian reformer Muhammad 'Abduh. Very much a part of the religious establishment, he was trained in *kalam*, jurisprudence, and Qur'anic exegesis (see also chapter 3), taught at the venerable university of Al-Azhar, and served as Grand Mufti of Egypt. But his outlook was radical in the true sense of the word. Ready to rethink Islamic theology from its roots, he argued forcefully for the liberation of the individual and the community from *taqlid* or imitation, in the sense of a stifling or inhibiting obedience to authority and adherence to traditional norms. He also insisted on the essential compatibility of reason and revelation, on the concept of natural law, human responsibility and human freedom (versus divine determinism), and the practical and political reform of Muslim societies and nations.

Political activity against British colonial rule in Egypt led to several years of exile for Muhammad 'Abduh, during which he taught at the Madrasat al-Sultaniyyah in Beirut. His lectures there on *kalam* formed the basis of his most important work, the *Risalat al-tawhid* or *tauhid*, usually translated *The Theology of Unity*. The unity under discussion is God's unity, God's being and attributes, and all of the justifiable affirmations or assertions one can make concerning God. The work also deals extensively with the nature of prophethood and the specific mission of Muhammad, and the miraculous nature of the Qur'an. The last five chapters develop an understanding of Islamic religion as the product or outcome of Muhammad's mission, describe Islamic religion as a force for human progress, and call for renewal of the disordered and degenerate aspects of the community's life in accord with the understanding and practice of the faith by its earliest adherents.[18]

A great scholar of Islamic studies and advocate for Muslim-Christian dialogue, Kenneth Cragg, and his colleague Ishaq Musa'ad, translated this text with exceptional clarity, sympathy, and skill; the text has an intrinsic energy and frank tone that distinguishes its style from Cragg's own irenic and literary introduction. The translation is not annotated; there is a basic index.

Notes

1. The term "dialectical" here refers to the rhetorical format of argument by dialogue, or question and answer; there is no relation to Marxist dialectic, nor to the "dialectical theology" movement initiated in Germany in the 1920s and discussed in the work of Karl Barth, Rudolf Bultmann, and others.

2. Both quoted by Georges Anawati, "Kalam," *ER*, v. 8: 231.

3. Fazlur Rahman, *Islam*, 2nd ed. (Chicago: University of Chicago Press, 1979); see his discussion of the Mu'tazili movement, 85–90.

4. Quoted by Majid Fakhry, *A History of Islamic Philosophy* (New York: Columbia University Press, 1970), 231.

5. Richard C. Martin and Mark R. Woodward, *Defenders of Reason in Islam* (Oxford: Oneworld, 1997), 12–15.

6. Albert Hourani, *A History of the Arab Peoples* (Cambridge, Mass.: Harvard University Press, 1991), 64–65.

7. Martin and Woodward, *Defenders*, 17. An example of Mu'tazili *kalam* by 'Abd al-Jabbar, called *Kitab al-usul al-khamsa* or *Book of the Five Fundamentals*, can be found in English translation in *Defenders*, 90–110, with ample critical notes and comment.

8. R. J. McCarthy, "Al-Bakillani," *EI2*, v. 1: 958–59.

9. Gustave von Grunebaum, *A Tenth-Century Document of Arabic Literary Theory and Criticism* (Chicago: University of Chicago Press, 1950), xxi.

10. W. Montgomery Watt, "Ghazali, Abu Hamid al-," *ER*, v. 5: 541.

11. Al-Ghazali, *The Book of Knowledge*, translated and annotated by Nabih Amin Faris (Lahore: Sh. Muhammad Ashraf, 1974), 3–7.

12. G. Monnot, "Al-Shahrastani," *EI2*, v. 9: 216.

13. Fazlur Rahman comments upon this passage in his *Prophecy in Islam: Philosophy and Orthodoxy* (London: George Allen and Unwin, 1958), 99–101.

14. Majid Fakhry, *Islamic Philosophy, Theology and Mysticism* (Oxford: Oneworld, 2000), 102–4.

15. For a detailed discussion of this issue, see A. J. Wensinck, *The Muslim Creed* (London: Frank Cass and Co., 1965). The texts of several of these documents can be found in Arthur Jeffery's *A Reader on Islam* (The Hague: Mouton, 1962), 339–52.

16. Wilferd Madelung, "The Shi'ite and Kharijite Contribution to Pre-Ash'arite Kalam," *Islamic Philosophical Theology*, edited by Parviz Morewedge (Albany: State University of New York Press, 1979), 120. For a clear and concise summation of Shi'i origins, see Majid Fahkry, *A History of Islamic Philosophy*, 3rd ed. (New York: Columbia University Press, 2004), 39–43.

17. See Martin and Woodward, *Defenders*, chapters 10 and 11; and Fakhry, *History*, 3rd ed., chapters 12 and 13.

18. An interesting set of essays in apologetics by Rashid Rida, a student and close collaborator of Muhammad 'Abduh, has been translated and annotated by Simon A. Wood in his dissertation *The Criticisms of the Christians and the Arguments of Islam* (Temple University, 2004). Rashid Rida published these essays in the periodical *Al-Manar*, then as a collection entitled *Shubuhat al-nasara wa hujaj al-Islam* (1905); he addresses some of the criticisms of Islam from Christian missionaries in Egypt and crafts a defense against them.

CHAPTER EIGHT

~

Spirituality and Mysticism: Tasawwuf

The emphasis on law and ritual in the communal life of Muslims may suggest that a mainly superficial or external obedience is normative. But in fact, Islam has been infused from the start with an intense spirituality and inner devotional dimension, vividly and creatively expressed. One of the ways in which this devotional life developed is the phenomenon commonly known as Sufism, or *tasawwuf* (toss-SAW-wuff).

The exact origin of the word is debated, but it was probably derived from the word *suf* (SOOF) or wool, referring to the plain woolen garments of the early ascetics, who rejected fine clothing and luxury as a sign of renunciation of the material world. The historian Ibn Khaldun accepts this derivation, and identifies the Prophet and his earliest companions with pious and abstemious behavior.[1] However, the origin of the movement later known as Sufism is often associated with the ascetic Hasan al-Basri (d. 728), "the patriarch of Muslim mysticism."[2] He perceived that his society under the Umayyad caliphs had become decadent and thoughtless, and was destined for condemnation on the Day of Judgment unless it recaptured its austerity and piety. A powerful preacher, he admonished his listeners in memorable statements, preserved in the writing of others (they are considered to be exemplary Arabic religious rhetoric).

Detachment from the material world was combined with the attentive cultivation of spirituality. Across all of the various legal and philosophical schools, individuals were attracted to the soul's quest for God, the immediate experience of faith, and the development of spiritual consciousness. In the

173

classic case of Abu Hamid al-Ghazali (d. 1111), the study of law, philosophy, and theology failed to satisfy his desire for an authentic inner religious life, which he found in Sufism (see also chapter 7). A deep emotional relationship with God as The Beloved, enjoyed through distinctive forms of devotion and worship, is basic to the Sufi path.

Intellectually, Sufism was grounded in a Neoplatonic cosmology of emanation, recognizing God as the sole source of all being, the One who created and sustains the Many. Following a distinct spiritual discipline, the individual seeks reunion with the One, even an annihilation of the self or *fana'* (fa-NAH) in the divine. A strong element of gnosticism or special knowledge divided Sufi adepts from the common believer; they developed a science of the inner self based upon an intuitive perception beyond the merely sensory or rational. The novice embarked upon the effort to acquire this knowledge under the direction of a teacher, in a *shaykh-murid* or master-apprentice relationship. The master (in Persian, the *pir*) guided the pupil or disciple through the stages of spiritual growth and helped him to experience the states of grace bestowed by God upon the way.

The teacher-disciple relationship had its own chains of transmission reaching back to recognized authorities, preserving the gnosis and anchoring it in a common tradition. These relationships became structured into distinct communities or "orders," a form of social organization characteristic of Sufism. These orders often established a residence where seekers could come to live and be trained. A Sufi order was known as a *tariqa* (tah-REE-ka; plural, *turuq*), meaning path or road. A number of eminent Sufi orders or brotherhoods developed, usually based upon the teaching of a certain inspirational leader (the Qadiri, Suhrawardi, Naqshbandi, and Mevlevi orders, for example), and still include many adherents today.

A loving intimacy with God could be sought through ritual animated with spiritual awareness, focused upon the remembrance of God or *dhikr* (sounds almost like "thicker" or "zicker") as commanded in the Qur'an: "Oh believers, remember God often, and glorify Him morning and evening" (33:41–42). The recitation or repetition of God's names could be combined with breathing patterns or physical movements, and in the observance of *sama'* (sam-AH) or audition, with instrumental music, singing or chanting, and ecstatic or ritual dancing. Occasionally these exercises would go to extremes, and that is one of the grounds for disapproval of some aspects of Sufism from the more conservative jurists and theologians.

One may affirm that "Sufis speak of God's mercy, gentleness and beauty far more than they discuss the wrath, severity and majesty that play important roles in both *fiqh* (jurisprudence) and *kalam* (dogmatic theology)."[3]

Within Sufism itself, however, can be found great diversity in belief and practice. The classical literature is roughly divided between the Sufi theoreticians and the aesthetes, the prose writers versus the poets. Tradition speaks of the "sober" and the "drunken" Sufis, those who try to teach or explain the spiritual disciplines, and those who express themselves in outbursts of passionate emotion. For the sake of clarity, we will divide our discussion of the literature into these two broad categories, but it must be understood that these are mainly differences in emphasis or genre, or style of discourse. The "sober" Sufi who writes lucidly of theory or discipline may also speak with great sensitivity of the immanence of God, while the "drunken" Sufi reveling in contact with The Beloved may also acknowledge God's distance and transcendence. Taken as a whole, *tasawwuf* offers a way for Muslims to integrate religious practice, doctrine, and devotion, and encompass the believer's body, mind, and heart.[4]

Because the whole field of Islamic spirituality or mysticism has been of great interest to Western scholars for many years, there is a substantial body of primary literature accessible in English, as well as a wealth of secondary studies. In this chapter, we will mention very briefly a few selections from the wide range of interesting and varied sources.

The Sufi Theologians

Some significant early Sufi figures are not so much the creators of a literature as the material of a literature. Stories and legends about them entered the oral tradition and the literature of Sufi hagiography, often centuries after their deaths. There is a strong tradition in Sufism of the advanced spiritual master or teacher, the *wali* (plural, *awliya'*), a "saint" or friend of God, sometimes a wonder-working or supernatural figure who became in popular piety a kind of intercessor, but the literary record or account of that individual was often created by someone else. In addition, works that are not expressly about spirituality or Sufism—for example, Qur'an commentaries—may be regarded as important Sufi texts.

AL-MUHASIBI (d. 857)
Abu 'Abdallah al-Harith ibn Asad al-Muhasibi (almoo-HAH-sib-ee). *Kitab al-ri'aya li huquq Allah* or *Book on the Observance of the Rights of God.* Excerpts in Michael A. Sells, ed., *Early Islamic Mysticism* (New York: Paulist Press, 1996), 171–95.

One of the earliest theologians who created works of literature on spiritual discipline was known as al-Muhasibi, a nickname connoting accountability or the rigorous examination of one's conscience. His *Kitab al-ri'aya* became a very influential text in later Sufism. In it, he considers the psychology of the human ego and its resistance to the will of God, counseling the believer to adopt a pious fear and repentance, and to reject conceit, pride, vanity, and self-deception. The work is framed as a dialogue between the master and an enquiring student, who is probing the inclinations of the heart. The challenge is to distinguish the guidance of God toward sincere obedience from the motivation of the ego toward competitiveness and conceit. Anxiety about one's character is beneficial, leading to vigilance and, ultimately, preparedness for death and judgment; yet hope is dominant, and fully dependent upon God.

An expert translator, Michael Sells, has carefully selected, annotated, and interpreted the texts in this excellent critical anthology, encompassing many of the early mystics and their teachings. His notes also contain very valuable bibliographic information.

DHU AL-NUN (d.c. 860)

Abu al-Fayd Dhu al-Nun (THOO or ZOO an-NOON) al-Misri. Excerpts in Margaret Smith, *Readings from the Mystics of Islam* (London: Luzac, 1972), 22–25, and Martin Lings, *Sufi Poems* (Cambridge: Islamic Texts Society, 2004), 7–11.

This Egyptian mystic is an example of a key figure whose work has been preserved only within the writings of other Sufis. A notable master with many disciples, Dhu al-Nun established some of the basic concepts of Sufi spirituality. A student of medicine as well as alchemy and magic, he was probably familiar with the Hellenistic or Neoplatonic thought of Greco-Roman Egypt. He traveled to Syria and there became committed to asceticism, repentance, and the renunciation of self and worldliness; he was a contemporary of al-Muhasibi and shared his concerns. Dhu al-Nun was among the first to teach in a systematic fashion about the stages or stations (*maqamat*) of progress upon the path of Sufi training and the spiritual states (*ahwal*) encountered upon the way. He also taught the concept of *ma'rifa* (MAH-riffa) or a gnostic form of inner perception, recognition, or personal knowledge, as opposed to *'ilm*, which is knowledge gained through study of transmitted texts and the application of human reason.[5]

Though he was known as a "sober" Sufi, Dhu al-Nun also spoke of ecstasy and intimacy in union with God, using the imagery of drinking to represent joy in The Beloved. The excerpts in these two valuable anthologies reflect this, particularly the poetry translated by Martin Lings.

AL-JUNAYD (d. 910)

Abu al-Qasim ibn Muhammad al-Junayd (al-joo-NADE). *Rasa'il* or *Epistles*. In *The Life, Personality and Writings of al-Junayd*, edited and translated by Ali Hassan Abdel-Kader (London: Luzac, 1976), 120–83, and in Sells, 251–65. His name may be spelled as Abu al-Kasim al-Djunayd.

The Persian mystic al-Junayd became the revered Sufi master of Baghdad; a student of al-Muhasibi, al-Junayd was renowned for his intellectual acumen and austere sobriety. He viewed the spiritual life as a serious and sustained effort to neutralize the individual ego in the divine and to return to God as the single source of being through the annihilation (*fana'*) of everything in the self that inhibits union with God. Junayd was teaching and writing at a time when some were questioning the orthodoxy of Sufism, and charges of heresy had become a present danger (the passionate "drunken" mystic al-Hallaj, with whom al-Junayd is often contrasted, was executed in Baghdad in 922). This atmosphere of inquisition may have increased Junayd's tendency to separate the spiritual knowledge of the Sufi adepts from the religious observance of the common people and to express this gnosis in indirect and ambiguous language full of wordplay and difficult syntax.

Junayd's surviving works consist of letters to fellow mystics and short treatises on certain subjects, notably *fana'* or annihilation and *tawhid* or the oneness of God. The letters are somewhat more prosaic and intelligible. The Sells anthology includes only a few excerpts, with incisive editorial remarks and annotations. Abdel-Kader's edition contains many more documents and a long and detailed but rather digressive introduction. The two translations—compare the *Kitab al-fana'* for instance—are radically different in style and approach; one suspects that the Sells translation is more accurate, but Abdel-Kader's is more readable. Abdel-Kader's volume includes the original Arabic texts; Sells's provides very specific annotations.

AL-SARRAJ (d. 988)

Abu Nasr 'Abdallah ibn 'Ali al-Sarraj (os-sa-RODGE). *Kitab al-luma' fi al-tasawwuf* or *Book of Flashes* (i.e., beams of light or radiance) *on Sufism*. Excerpts in John Renard, ed., *Knowledge of God in Classical Sufism* (New York: Paulist Press, 2004), 65–99, and in Sells, 196–211. His name may also appear as al-Sarradj.

A turning point in the literature of Sufism is represented by the very substantial and systematic work of Abu Nasr al-Sarraj. By the mid-tenth century, the mystical movement had reached a state of conscious maturity that supported the composition of textbooks for the spiritual disciplines. Theologians were ready to advocate for the place of *tasawwuf* alongside the established forms of Islamic learning, such as Qur'anic exegesis, the study of *hadith* or narrative traditions, jurisprudence or doctrinal theology. They argued that, just as one might consult a jurist for a legal opinion, one should expect from a Sufi competence in the knowledge of spirituality—that this was in fact their special contribution to the religious sciences. Al-Sarraj firmly established that Sufism was not a marginal or unorthodox movement, but fully within the bounds of normative Islam, and that the Sufis should be viewed as Islam's spiritual guides, leading others toward *ma'rifa*, the most profound personal comprehension of the faith. The sections of the *Luma'* in Renard's beautifully translated and edited anthology concentrate upon these issues.

Sarraj gave much attention to the definition of difficult terms with particular meanings in the Sufi vocabulary. He also devoted a major portion of his *Luma'* to an exposition of the seven stations or *maqamat* (mocka-MAT) of the mystical path: repentance, watchfulness, renunciation, poverty, patience, trust, acceptance. His discussion of these stations, along with very valuable editorial remarks, can be found in Sells. Much smaller excerpts are available in Smith and in the anthology *Classical Islam* (London: Routledge, 2003).

AL-KALABADHI (d.c. 995)
Abu Bakr Muhammad ibn Abu Ishaq al-Kalabadhi (al-kalla-BODDY).
Kitab al-ta'arruf li madhab ahl al-tasawwuf or *Book of the Exploration of the Teachings of the People of Sufism.*

A contemporary of al-Sarraj from the city of Bukhara was writing his own manual or textbook of Sufism at about the same time, and this work was soon accepted as authoritative by the community; it became a basic text in the teaching of Sufism and the subject of several important commentaries.

Kalabadhi takes an expressly doctrinal approach to his defense of the orthodoxy of Sufism, taking care to establish first the central or fundamental tenets of Islam. Following the model of a well-known creedal statement (the *Fiqh al-akbar* II), he proceeds to demonstrate that Sufi doctrine is consistent with Ash'ari theology or *kalam*, and thus in conformity with acknowledged standards of orthodoxy. He records the names and sayings of many Sufi masters—making the book a mine of information on the history of the movement—and draws a distinction between the reliable teachers and those whose unauthorized and irresponsible behavior had brought Sufism into disrepute.

The work is available in an English translation by A. J. Arberry (see below), and several chapters on the subject of *ma'rifa* are excerpted in the Renard anthology (100–11).

Al-Kalabadhi. *The Doctrine of the Sufis*. Translated and annotated by Arthur John Arberry (Lahore: Sh. Muhammad Ashraf, 1966).

The outstanding Orientalist scholar A. J. Arberry originally published this translation of the *Ta'arruf* at the Cambridge University Press in 1935; it was based upon his own critical edition of the Arabic text from four Egyptian and Turkish manuscripts (Cambridge reissued it in 1977). This Pakistani edition was reprinted by arrangement and contains Arberry's concise and useful introduction and valuable notes. The *Ta'arruf* has the rare virtue of being a tenth-century Sufi text accessible in its entirety in English, allowing the reader to absorb its whole course of explanation and argument.

AL-HUJWIRI (d.c. 1072)

Abu al-Hasan 'Ali ibn 'Uthman al-Hujwiri (al-hoodge-WEERY) or Hujviri. *Kashf al-mahjub* or *Revelation of the Veiled*. His name may be spelled Hudjwiri or Hudjviri.

A century after al-Sarraj, a mystic from Afghanistan created what is believed to be the first Sufi manual or treatise in Persian. Al-Hujwiri (in Persian, Hujviri) traveled about collecting information on various Sufi sects and their beliefs, which he incorporated into his *Kashf*. Hujwiri acknowledges the use of the *Luma'* of al-Sarraj as his model, designing a similar discussion of the doctrines and practices of Sufism, defining its terms, and stressing its orthodoxy and conformity with religious law. Hujwiri's treatment of the issues is more personal than most of the sources mentioned thus far, as he records the views of other authorities first and then presents his own opinion, and often illustrates points with examples from his own experience; what is known about his life is drawn directly from references to it in his text.

His work is often studied in conjunction with that of his contemporary Abu al-Qasim al-Qushayri (d.c. 1072), whose *Risala* exists in several versions in English.[6] (Qushayri's name may appear as Abu al-Kasim al-Kushayri.) Excerpts from the work of both authors are provided in Renard's anthology (Hujwiri, 264–85; Qushayri, 286–93)

Al-Hujwiri. *The Kashf al-Mahjub: The Oldest Persian Treatise on Sufism*. Translated by Reynold Alleyne Nicholson, 2nd ed. (London: Luzac, 1936).

A classic edition of this valuable text is available, the work of respected Orientalist R. A. Nicholson, first published in 1911. The *Kashf* was written in response to an appeal from an inquirer, which appears in the text: "Explain to me the true meaning of the Path of Sufism and the nature of the stations (*maqamat*) of the Sufis, and explain their doctrines and sayings, and make clear to me their mystical allegories, and the nature of Divine Love and how it is manifested in human hearts, and why the intellect is unable to reach the essence thereof, and why the soul recoils from the reality thereof, and why the spirit is lulled in the purity thereof; and explain the practical aspects of Sufism which are connected with these theories" (pp. 6–7). The tone of the work is didactic and expository, but full of interesting anecdotes. Nicholson's prose is perhaps a bit old-fashioned, but readable; he has provided a minimum of annotation, a brief introduction, and useful indexes.

AL-GHAZALI (d. 1111)
Abu Hamid Muhammad al-Ghazali (al-ga-ZALLY). *Kimiya-i sa'adat* **or** *The Alchemy of Happiness.* **His name is often spelled as al-Ghazzali.**

The life and work of Abu Hamid al-Ghazali, one of the greatest cultural figures in Islamic history, was described at some length in chapter 7. An accomplished theologian and jurist, al-Ghazali was also a major intellectual interpreter of Sufism, able to analyze and explain its unique properties while integrating its principles fully with those of the other religious disciplines. Many of the works mentioned during our discussion of *kalam* are equally relevant to the study of Sufism, including his magnum opus, the *Ihya' 'ulum al-din* or *Revival of the Religious Sciences.*

Al-Ghazali. *The Alchemy of Happiness.* **Translated by Claud Field; revised and annotated by Elton L. Daniel (Armonk, N.Y.: M. E. Sharpe, 1991).**

According to al-Ghazali's own introduction to this text, he composed the *Kimiya* as a summary or digest of the *Ihya' 'ulum al-din*; apparently, "ordinary people had requested a version of his ideas written in Persian in a way that would not exceed their comprehension."[7] Daniel takes care to explain in his preface just how the contents of the two works are related. For instance, he notes that in the *Ihya'* the author tends to substantiate his points with quotes from the Qur'an and the *hadith*, while in the *Kimiya* he is more likely to draw upon the examples of famous Sufis. Daniel has edited Claud Field's translation (from an Urdu text), originally published in 1910; the prose is admirably lucid and clear, with a conversational, informal quality, a pleasure to read. Daniel's annotations are informative and not overwhelmingly technical; the whole work is only about ninety pages long, making it convenient for course reading. This edition could only have been improved if Daniel had chosen to translate and append the portions present in the Persian text that were omitted at the end of Field's translation.

In his anthology, John Renard has provided a translation of sections of book XXI of the *Ihya'* hitherto unavailable in English, dealing with al-Ghazali's epistemology and a spiritual theory of personality (298–326). Other sections can be found in Richard J. McCarthy's *Freedom and Fulfillment* (Boston: Twayne, 1981; reprinted by Fons Vitae, 2000), 363–82.

AL-JILANI (d. 1166)

Abu Muhammad 'Abd al-Qadir al-Jilani (al-jee-LAH-nee). *Futuh al-ghaib* or *Revelations of the Unseen*. His name also appears as 'Abd al-Kadir al Djilani or Gilani.

A leader of the Sufi movement with an exceptional reputation for sanctity, al-Jilani is recognized as the founder of the Qadiriyya order or brotherhood (*tariqa*). Countless miraculous stories are recounted of his spiritual perfection; for example, he is said to have been born during Ramadan and refused to suckle at his mother's breast during the daytime, breaking his fast only at night. Trained in theology and in Hanbali law and jurisprudence, he was known primarily as a preacher, able to persuade the most hardened reprobates or infidels and bring them to repentance. He is among the saints most venerated as an intercessor or mediator in popular piety.

Al-Jilani. *Revelations of the Unseen (Futuh al-ghaib): A Collection of Seventy-Eight Discourses.* Translated by Muhtar Holland (Houston: Al-Baz, 1992).

This volume is one of several collections of al-Jilani's letters and sermons or discourses produced by Al-Baz Publishing in paperback editions. While these are not scholarly translations with a critical apparatus for research, they are nevertheless attractive and accessible. The units of discourse are very concise, sometimes no more than a paragraph, touching on many of the distinctive teachings and practices of Sufism.

Al-Jilani. *The Secret of Secrets.* Translated by Shaykh Tosun Bayrak al-Jerrahi al-Halveti (Cambridge: Islamic Texts Society, 1992).

Some fairly substantial segments of another work by al-Jilani, the *Sirr al-asrar*, are offered here in English, again in a popular paperback edition. The language is simple and straightforward, addressing profound issues on a personal level: for example, "On Islamic Mysticism and the Sufis," "On Remembrance," and "On the Meaning of Ritual Worship and Inner Worship." A new translation of this work by Muhtar Holland is also available, in *The Book of the Secret of Secrets and the Manifestation of Lights* (Fort Lauderdale, Fla.: Al-Baz, 2000).

IBN AL-'ARABI (d. 1240)

Muhyi al-Din Abu 'Abdallah Muhammad ibn al-'Arabi (ibbin al-AH-rob-ee). *Fusus al-hikam wa khusus al-kilam* or *Bezels of Wisdom(s) and Distinctive Sayings*. Muhyi al-Din is an appellation meaning "The Reviver of Religion." The plural *hikam* suggests profound statements or sayings.

The foremost of the Sufi philosophers—often known as *al-Shaykh al-Akbar*, or "The Greatest Master"—was certainly the prolific and controversial Ibn al-'Arabi. His work was voluminous, diverse, and notoriously complex, and many of his statements and methods were simply unacceptable to more orthodox scholars. Nevertheless, he is regarded as one of the most influential figures in the theoretical study of Islamic mysticism.

Born in Spain and raised in a family with Sufi adepts among its members, Ibn al-'Arabi was educated in Cordova, where he is believed to have known the great Andalusian philosopher Ibn Rushd (see chapter 6). The pervasive presence of Neoplatonist cosmology and elements of gnosticism and hermeticism in Ibn al-'Arabi have been studied at length by scholars and interpreters of his work. Their discussion often hinges upon the expression *wahdat al-wujud*, which may be translated as "unity of being" or "oneness of being." The entire created universe is understood as an effusion or exhalation of God, and nothing at all is real except God; at the end of the spiritual quest, the only thing that exists is God. The philosophical pantheism or monism apparent in this approach is tempered by the image of a lonely God desiring to be known, creating the universe as a mirror in which He manifests Himself.

In-depth critical studies of Ibn al-'Arabi and his work have occupied a number of eminent scholars, including Annemarie Schimmel, Seyyed Hossein Nasr, Henri Corbin, Michel Chodkiewicz, R. A. Nicholson, and William C. Chittick; the reader should consult several of these authorities.

Ibn al-'Arabi. *The Bezels of Wisdom*. Translation and introduction by R. W. J. Austin (New York: Paulist Press, 1980).

Late in his life, Ibn al-'Arabi retired to live quietly at Damascus, and it was there that he wrote his most celebrated work, the *Fusus al-hikam* (fuh-SOOSE al-HICK-am). The work is designed as a study of the prophets, each of whom represents or embodies a different spiritual truth or approach to God; it functions as a concentrated summation of the author's lifelong teaching. The title refers to the setting of a gemstone in a signet ring and suggests that each prophet is like "the human setting in which the gemstone of each kind of wisdom is set, thus making of each prophet the signet or sign, by selection, of a particular aspect of God's wisdom."[8] Each of the twenty-seven chapters refers, sometimes in a very oblique way, to stories or sayings of a particular prophet, associating them with various philosophical assertions or ideas.

In the course of these discussions, Ibn al-'Arabi touches on many of the issues that are characteristic of his work (though the development of these ideas is disordered and sporadic). The chapter on Adam, for instance, dwells upon the divine Names as modalities through which God relates to the cosmos, the image of the mirror, and the archetypal human being; the chapter on Enoch describes nature and the celestial spheres, the One and the Many, and the idea that "the Reality is at once the created Creator and the creating creature" (p. 87). Ibn al-'Arabi also engages in some very unconventional—even alarming—Qur'anic exegesis, as in the chapter on Noah.

Austin has provided a readable and reliable scholarly translation, with an informative introduction, footnotes (especially needed for Qur'an references), a bibliography, and two helpful indexes; he has also taken care to introduce every chapter with incisive and apposite comments.

An older version of the *Fusus al-hikam* is also widely available, translated from Arabic to French by Titus Burckhardt in 1955, then into English by Angela Culme-Seymour, and published as *The Wisdom of the Prophets* (Aldsworth, UK: Beshara, 1975). It is heavily annotated and contains a useful glossary of difficult technical terms.

Ibn al-'Arabi. *The Meccan Revelations*. Translated and edited by Michel Chodkiewicz, William C. Chittick, and James W. Morris (New York: Pir Press, 2002).

Though the *Fusus* is better known, the primary doctrinal and scholarly work of Ibn al-'Arabi is his impressive *Al-futuhat al-makkiyya fi asrar al-malikiyya wa al-mulkiyya* or *Revelations of Mecca and Secrets Royal and Civil*. This "immense and utterly unique work"[9] contains a comprehensive and systematic exposition of his teachings, begun while he was still in his thirties, during a pilgrimage and residence at Mecca—according to the author, as the result of direct divine inspiration. Though the *Futuhat* (fuh-too-HAT) is certainly a philosophical and theological work, there is a great deal of personal material in it, using illustrations based upon his own spiritual life (see especially pp. 201–30). The editors of the volume have selected, with the utmost care, a small sampling of the 560 chapters of the *Futuhat al-makkiya*, explaining fully in the introduction which segments have been included from the work's six major sections and giving the reader an idea of their original context. Every segment is coordinated by number with the more extensive French edition *Les Illuminations de la Mecque* (Paris: Sindbad, 1988).

The translators have introduced every chapter with pertinent interpretive remarks. Also, nearly half of the volume is devoted to very extensive and detailed critical notes, which Morris explains are essential to an understanding of the translated text. The table of contents helps orient the reader with fairly descriptive divisions and headings; the book also includes reference helps. It was originally published as the first of two planned volumes, but no evidence was found that the second actually appeared.

Another edition of the *Futuhat*, edited by Laleh Bakhtiar and translated by 'Aisha 'Abdurrahman Bewley, was published as *Ibn al-'Arabi on the Mysteries of Bearing Witness to the Oneness of God and Prophethood of Muhammad* (Great Books of the Islamic World, 2002).

Ibn al-'Arabi. *The Tarjuman al-Ashwaq: A Collection of Mystical Odes.* Edited and translated by Reynold A. Nicholson (London: Theosophical Publishing House, 1978).

During the same sojourn in Mecca in which Ibn al-'Arabi commenced his *Futuhat*, he composed another very different work, his *Tarjuman al-ashwaq* or *The Interpreter of Desires*. When he arrived in Mecca in 1202 CE, he met Nizam 'Ain al-Shams al-Baha (also called Nizam bint Makin al-Din), the beautiful and accomplished young daughter of a colleague. For her he composed a passionate *diwan* or collection of poems, drenched in tears of longing and rapture, full of gazelles and gardens and life-giving fountains, and other more erotic details. It is almost entirely the poetry of desiring, not of possessing.

The well-known verses in which Ibn al-'Arabi mentions elements of other faiths (including the Trinity) are found in sections 11 and 12 of this poem cycle. When this translation was first published in 1911 by the Royal Asiatic Society, none of Ibn al-'Arabi's work was yet accessible in any European language; it made a definite impact and is still regarded as a classic. It has been reissued several times and is included in the anthology *Theology, Ethics and Metaphysics*, edited by Hiroyuki Mashita (London: RoutledgeCurzon, 2003), v. 4.

The *Tarjuman* (TAR-joo-mun) exists in manuscript recensions with two different prefaces: One of them states that the verses were composed for Nizam, the other that they must be interpreted allegorically, as the mystic's longing for God. Ibn al-'Arabi himself wrote an extremely detailed *sharh* or commentary in which he interprets every verse of each poem symbolically. Nicholson's volume includes the Arabic text of the poems, based upon three manuscripts he was able to compare; text variants are mentioned in footnotes. Then, he presents a full English translation of the entire commentary along with each poem.

Other Sources

Other valuable texts by Ibn al-'Arabi are available in English, and excerpts are often included in anthologies of primary source materials. A very interesting meditation or treatise is the *Shajarat al-kawn* or *Tree of Being*, dealing with cosmology, the concept of *al-insan al-kamil* or the "Perfect Man," and the person of Muhammad. Arthur Jeffery published his translation of this text in two issues of the journal *Studia Islamica* in 1959 (no. 10, pp. 43–77; no. 11, pp. 113–60), with an introduction comparing its doctrine to the Logos-Christology in ancient Christian sources. Jeffery also provides his translation of a delightful tract known as *Risala fi kunhi ma la budda minhu li al-murid* or *Instructions to a Postulant*, in the anthology *A Reader on Islam* (The Hague: Mouton, 1962), 640–55. In informal and personal language, this text initiates an enquirer into the basics of the Sufi path. Newer versions of both of these works in an attractive popular format, translated by Shaykh Tosun Bayrak al-Jerrahi al-Halveti, are found in *The Tree of Being* (forthcoming) and *Divine Governance of the Human Kingdom* (Louisville, Ky.: Fons Vitae, 1997); the latter title is derived from Ibn al-'Arabi's important mystical treatise *Al-tadbirat al-ilahiyya fi islah al-mamlakat il-insaniyya*, included in that volume.

Another valuable work, the *Ruh al-quds fi munasahat al-nafs* or *The Spirit of Holiness in the Counseling of the Soul* is available in a critical translation by R. W. J. Austin as *Sufis of Andalusia* (Berkeley: University of California Press, 1977). The *Ruh al-quds* is a rather personal, quasi-autobiographical work, in which Ibn al-'Arabi discusses the lives of more than fifty Sufis he had known, commenting upon the difficulties on the spiritual path and the errors into which some had fallen. Austin combines a sizable portion of this text with selected material from a similar treatise, *Al-durra al-fakhira* or *The Precious Pearl*, and provides a very substantial and informative introduction.

Ibn al-'Arabi's brief composition *Risalat al-anwar* or *Treatise on the Lights*—on the subject of *khalwa* or spiritual retreat—is bound together with some interesting introductory material and commentary in *Journey to the Lord of Power*, translated by Rabia Terri Harris (New York: Inner Traditions, 1981). An exhaustive study and translation of an early work on eschatology and the doctrine of sainthood, the *Kitab 'anqa' mughrib* or *Book of the Fabulous Gryphon* or *Phoenix*, was published by Gerald T. Elmore as *Islamic Sainthood in the Fullness of Time* (Leiden: Brill, 1999).

IBN 'ATA'ILLAH (d. 1309)

Taj al-Din Abu al-Fadl Ahmad ibn Muhammad ibn 'Ata'illah (ibbin ut-TAH ul-LAH) al-Iskandari. *Kitab al-hikam* or *Book of Wise Sayings*. In *Ibn 'Ata'illah, The Book of Wisdom* [and] *Kwaja Abdullah Ansari, Intimate Conversations*, translated and edited by Victor Danner and Wheeler M. Thackston (New York: Paulist Press, 1978), 47–150. His name also appears as Ibn 'Ata' Allah.

A favorite genre of the *tasawwuf* literature is the epigram or aphorism, occupying a kind of middle ground between prose and poetry. With highly condensed language rich in imagery, complex teachings are communicated; the deceptively simple statements are meant to be memorized and meditated upon, gradually opening their meanings to the seeker. Among the ablest practitioners of this art was 'Abdallah al-Ansari (d. 1089), author of the *Munajat* or *Intimate Conversations* [*with God*], a spiritual manual highly valued by Persian-speaking Muslims. In the Arabic language, one of the most influential texts is Ibn 'Ata'illah's *Kitab al-hikam*, which has been compared to St. Ignatius Loyola's *Spiritual Exercises*, "combining the erudition of the scholar with the vibrant, persuasive language of the enthusiast."[10] Both of these works are available in English translation in the same volume.

Ibn 'Ata'illah of Alexandria was the third spiritual leader of the Shadhili order, an important Sufi *tariqa*, well established in Egypt. Unlike some brotherhoods that required a radical detachment from the world, the Shadhili Sufis engaged in professions and a family life, with an additional contemplative component. Orders operating in this style became a significant force in the devotional life of the laity, not only in Egypt but also throughout the Muslim world up to the present day. As for Ibn 'Ata'illah, he was trained as a Maliki jurist and an Ash'ari theologian, fulfilled his role as master of the Shadhiliyya, and wrote scholarly works in *hadith* studies, Qur'anic exegesis, philology, and law. A memorable incident in his career involved the Hanbali jurist Ibn Taymiyya, with whom he had a sharp and very public doctrinal dispute.

The *Kitab al-hikam* (al-HICK-um) is composed in three parts: a collection of 262 aphorisms or gnomic utterances, a few short treatises directed toward his disciples, and a set of thirty-four *munajat* or personal statements addressing God. Victor Danner has supplied an introduction, notes, and a readable translation, but it is not easy in English to perceive the beauty of expression for which this work is esteemed.[11]

Among the important commentators on the *Kitab al-hikam* was Ibn 'Abbad al-Rundi (d. 1390), who became a respected Shadhili master in Morocco. A volume of Ibn 'Abbad's teachings on spiritual direction is available in English as *Ibn 'Abbad of Ronda: Letters on the Sufi Path*, translated and edited by John Renard (New York: Paulist Press, 1986).

The Sufi Poets and Ecstatics

As we have seen, even the "sober" Sufis—whose forms of expression were typically theological and didactic—inhabited the realm of mysticism, gnosis, devotion, and contemplation and often moved into poetic or gnomic discourse. The figures discussed in this part of the chapter are those who are chiefly remembered either as ecstatics or as poets, or both; they are often known as the "drunken" or "intoxicated" Sufis, whose passion for God and intensity of expression has provoked the acclaim of some and the condemnation of others.

RABI'A (d. 801)
Rabi'a (RAH-bee-ah) al-'Adawiyya al-Kaysiyya. Excerpts in Smith, 10–12; in Lings, 1–5; and in Sells, 151–70.

Like the very early Sufi theologians, some of the ecstatics are known only through their deeds and sayings collected and reported by later writers. Among these is the fascinating female mystic Rabi'a of Basra. The substantial excerpt in the Sells anthology is taken from 'Attar's *Memorial of the Friends of God*, a hagiographic account of the lives of many Sufi adepts, emphasizing her legendary intelligence, holiness, and ardent devotion to God as The Beloved or Friend. Some of the anecdotes related in this source contrast Rabi'a's extraordinary wisdom with the more mundane proficiency of the great Sufi masters Hasan al-Basri and Ibrahim ibn Adham; her speech is saturated with a thoroughly frank and loving intimacy toward God, joy in His presence, and indifference toward anything other than God.

Many other female Sufis are recorded in the hagiographic literature; a noteworthy study on their roles is *Muslim Women Mystics: The Life and Work of Rabi'a and Other Women Mystics in Islam* by Margaret Smith (Oxford: Oneworld, 1994, 2001). Also, the feminine principle in mysticism is a favorite theme of the eminent scholar Annemarie Schimmel and the subject of her study *My Soul Is a Woman: The Feminine in Islam* (New York: Continuum, 1997, 2003). Schimmel observes of Rabi'a: "She was credited with introducing the concept of pure love into the austere ascetic outlook of early Sufism."[12]

AL-BISTAMI (d.c. 875)
Abu Yazid al-Bistami (al-bis-TAA-mee). His name may appear as Bayazid (or Bayezid) al-Bastami. Excerpts in A. J. Arberry, *Aspects of Islamic Civilization: As Depicted in the Original Texts* (Ann Arbor: University of Michigan Press, 1967), 218–24; and in Sells, 212–50. He is also referred to as Abu Yazid.

Al-Bistami is another of the early mystics known through sayings and anecdotes, and the image of him varies in some interesting ways depending upon the source (see Sells); but he is often described as one of those whose intoxication could go too far. In moments when Bistami evidently experienced a mystical union with God, he was understood to pronounce *shathiyat* (sha-thee-YAT) or ecstatic utterances that seemed to equate himself with God: "Glory be to me! How great is my majesty!" and the like.[13] The very sober Sufi al-Junayd wrote a commentary on these utterances in which he both defends and criticizes them, and al-Sarraj discussed them in detail in his *Kitab al-luma'* and took care to place them in context, offering some positive interpretations or explanations of them. Junayd remarked, "The speech of Abu Yazid . . . forms a ladle for the sea that he alone inhabited" (Sells, p. 214). These passages provide intriguing insights into the fellowship of Sufis as a self-critical community.

An important study on the subject of *shathiyat* is Carl W. Ernst's *Words of Ecstasy in Sufism* (Albany: State University of New York Press, 1985). There is also an interesting passage from a Sufi *tabaqat* or biographical dictionary about al-Bistami in the anthology *Classical Islam* (pp. 237–42). In the same volume is a passage from al-Hujwiri about spiritual intoxication and sobriety among Sufis, using al-Bistami and al-Junayd as examples (pp. 248–52).

AL-HALLAJ (d. 922)
Al-Husayn ibn Mansur al-Hallaj (al-hah-LODGE). His name may be spelled as al-Halladj. Excerpts in Lings, 26–39; in Sells, 266–80; and in James Kritzeck, *Anthology of Islamic Literature* (New York: New American Library, 1975), 96–104.

Perhaps the most vivid of all the ecstatic Sufis was the martyr al-Hallaj (a nickname, "The Wool-Carder"). Born of a Persian-speaking family, he adopted Arabic as his primary language; he began to devote himself to *ta-sawwuf* at an early age and at one point studied with the "sober" scholar al-Junayd, with whom he is often contrasted. Al-Hallaj departed from typical Sufi teaching, however—particularly their principle of secrecy that reserved mystical knowledge for a trained and initiated elite. Hallaj began to proclaim his extraordinary thoughts and feelings very openly and provocatively, gathering numerous disciples around him and creating offense and alarm among others. He was arrested and spent years in prison; then, as a result of political competition and intrigue among certain viziers, he was executed in a most barbaric fashion.

Among the accusations against him was the charge of blasphemy, often associated with his ecstatic utterance, "*Ana al-haqq*" or "I am the Truth" or "the Real" (i.e., "I am God"). Similar statements are found in one of his writings, a *diwan* or poem cycle, appearing in English and Arabic in the Lings anthology (poems 17, 33, and 34). On the other hand, al-Hallaj also wrote: "From the Burning Bush, on the side of Sinai, what he [Moses] heard speak from the

Bush was not the Bush nor its seed, but Allah / and my role is like this Bush" (*Tawasin*, p. 28). Because he spoke of the inner reality of ritual acts, such as a pilgrimage of the heart, he was accused of rejecting the rituals themselves, which are clearly prescribed in Islamic law (see Lings, poem 26); Sufism in its extreme forms was vulnerable to an antinomian tendency that appeared to threaten both orthodoxy and the social order.

The classic study of this fascinating character is Louis Massignon's *The Passion of al-Hallaj: Mystic and Martyr of Islam* (Princeton: Princeton University Press, 1982). Annemarie Schimmel and Carl W. Ernst have also focused scholarly attention upon him.

Al-Hallaj. *The Tawasin of Mansur al-Hallaj*. Translated by 'Aisha 'Abd ar-Rahman at-Tarjumana (Berkeley: Diwan Press, 1974).

An English version of the *Tawasin* of al-Hallaj, produced by the gifted and prolific translator 'Aisha 'Abd ar-Rahman Bewley, has been included in this small volume (pp. 19–67). From a research standpoint, however, the book is frustrating—stuffed with extraneous material, devoid of critical annotations or scholarly information.[14] The title *Tawasin* seems to be derived from two suras of the Qur'an (20 and 36) that begin with mysterious letters, among them Ta and Sin; each of the chapters in Hallaj's book is called a "TaSin." The longest chapter involves the famous narrative about the angel Iblis, in which God commands him to bow before the newly created Adam, and Iblis refuses. In the traditional interpretation of the story, the pride of Iblis causes his disobedience; as Hallaj frames it, the passionate devotion of Iblis to the *tawhid* or unity of God will not permit him to worship another, even if he is expressly commanded to do so and will be punished by banishment from God's presence.

The Iblis chapter is contained in the excerpt from the *Tawasin* in the Sells anthology. With it, Sells has included some very much appreciated interpretive information and remarks.

AL-'ATTAR (d.c. 1220)
Farid al-Din Muhammad ibn Ibrahim al-'Attar (al-ott-TAHR). *Mantiq al-tayr* or *Conference of the Birds*.

The thirteenth century witnessed three of Sufism's greatest masters of poetry: Ibn al-Farid in the Arabic language, and Jalal al-Din Rumi and the prolific Farid al-Din 'Attar in Persian. The *mathnawi* (math-NAH-wee), or in Persian *mathnavi* (often spelled *masnavi*), was a lyrical form of rhyming couplets well established in courtly literature, and it was adapted to the purpose of expressing spiritual truths through intense imagery and symbolic or allegorical narrative. At its best, the verse itself was so beautiful that reciting it and listening to it created feelings of transcendence and euphoria. Among those capable of writing at this level was al-'Attar (a nickname, "The Pharmacist").

'Attar lived in Nishapur and may have been killed when the Mongols invaded the city in 1221 CE; because of this, he is sometimes regarded as a martyr. He kept an apothecary shop and treated patients daily, and therefore had some scientific and medical training, but his work also displays an extensive and erudite knowledge of the literature of medieval Islam and secular or pre-Islamic Persia. He is widely credited with the ability to transform traditional tales and mystical experiences into well-structured, engrossing, subtle, and meaningful compositions of exceptional aesthetic craftsmanship.

Al-'Attar. The Speech of the Birds: Concerning Migration to the Real, the Mantiqu't-Tair. Presented in English by Peter W. Avery (Cambridge: Islamic Texts Society, 1998).

The best known of 'Attar's works is his narrative poem Mantiq al-tayr (the speech, conference, colloquy, argument, or parliament of the birds). The birds of the world gather and decide to seek out their king, the Simurgh, who is believed to reside in a distant land. Under the guidance of their leader, the Hoopoe, they make the very difficult and hazardous journey, telling each other stories as they go; only thirty birds survive to reach their goal and find that "they themselves—being si murgh, 'thirty birds' [in Persian]—are the Simurgh . . . expressing so marvelously the experience of the identity of the soul with the divine essence."[15] The landscape they must cross, and the variety of the birds' personalities, convey a great deal about the Sufi path toward fana' or annihilation of the self in the divine.

'Attar's extremely long and complex tale has been published in numerous versions and translations, prose adaptations, and abridgments.[16] A well-regarded translation by Afkham Darbandi and Dick Davis was published as The Conference of the Birds (Harmondsworth, UK: Penguin Books, 1984). The only complete annotated edition including the Prologue, translated directly from a strong Persian manuscript, is Peter Avery's. His hefty and rather dense volume numbers every couplet and provides a table of contents as an appendix.

Al-'Attar. Muslim Saints and Mystics: Episodes from the Tadhkirat al-Auliya' [or] "Memorial of the Saints." Translated and edited by A. J. Arberry (London: Routledge and Kegan Paul, 1979).

In addition to his poetry, 'Attar was the author of a landmark prose work, his Tadhkirat al-awliya' or Remembrances of the Saints, containing accounts of the lives and sayings of many of the key figures of Sufism. Though written in prose, this is not a standard *tabaqat* or biographical dictionary: It is a work of art, skillfully relating these stories for their spiritual meanings and dramatic impact. He seems to have derived material from the works of al-Sarraj, Qushayri, Hujwiri, and others, more obscure traditional sources, and sometimes the writings of the saints themselves; he incorporates about seventy-five individuals into his text (some may have been added by others after 'Attar's time). His narratives are colorful, both edifying and entertaining; they are also the best source available for many of the early Sufi figures, from Hasan al-Basri to al-Hallaj.

A. J. Arberry has abridged and translated this rich work into lively, straightforward, readable prose; his selections concentrate upon anecdotes from the saints' lives rather than their sayings or "dicta" (p. 16). With each set of entries, he has included a brief identification of the person, bibliographic references to medieval and contemporary sources, and links to the Arabic text edited by R. A. Nicholson. The volume (first published in 1966) also includes a helpful and informative introduction.

Al-'Attar. *The Ilahi-nama or Book of God of Farid al-Din 'Attar.* Translated and edited by John Andrew Boyle (Manchester: Manchester University Press, 1976).

'Attar created other narrative poem cycles with a similar plan to the *Mantiq al-tayr* or *Conversation of the Birds*: a carefully crafted framework story into which many smaller tales are fitted, exemplifying certain themes (familiar to many readers from Chaucer's *Canterbury Tales*). One of those narrative poems is the *Ilahi-nama* or *Book of God*. In this tale, a caliph has six fine sons; their father calls them together and asks them to tell him their heart's desire. The six sons wish one by one for a beautiful princess, the power of sorcery, the magic cup of Jamshid, the water of life, Solomon's ring, and the secrets of alchemy. Their father tells them story after story designed to teach them to pursue a greater goal; there are traditional folktales, stories from the lives of the saints or prophets, animal fables, and so on, some of which have explicitly spiritual or religious conclusions, while many others are left for the reader to interpret.

John A. Boyle has produced a fine scholarly translation of this work, based upon two somewhat different Persian editions by Ritter and Rouhani. Detailed critical notes provide text and translation data, clarify allusions to characters from folklore, identify references to the Qur'an, and connect the reader with medieval and modern sources. Many of these notes refer to Hellmut Ritter's definitive monograph on 'Attar, *Das Meer der Seele*, available in English as *The Ocean of the Soul: Man, the World and God in the Stories of Farid al-Din 'Attar* (Leiden: Brill, 2003). Boyle's work also contains his introduction, a foreword by Annemarie Schimmel, and an index of names and terms mentioned in 'Attar's text.

IBN AL-FARID (d. 1235)

'Umar ibn 'Ali Sharaf al-Din ibn al-Farid (ibbin al-fah-REED). *Nazm al-suluk* or *Poem of the Mystic's Progress;* this work is also called *Al-ta'iyya al-kubra* or *The Greater Ode.*

The greatest of the Sufi poets in the Arabic language was Ibn al-Farid, whose *Diwan* contains a number of love lyrics in various poetic forms, a well-known work called the *Khamriyya* or "Wine Song," and the very substantial ode known as *Nazm al-suluk,* or the *Ta'iyya* (a type of rhyming verse based upon the letter *t*). R. A. Nicholson observes that, in Ibn al-Farid's work, the apparent and symbolic meanings are so interwoven that much of the *Diwan* may be understood simultaneously as actual love poetry or as mystical messages; his verses praising passion and intoxication have been deeply influential in Arab culture, both aesthetically and spiritually. As mystical literature, his work is regarded as classic and has been compared with that of John Donne or St. John of the Cross. Nicholson published his translation of selections from the *Diwan* as "The Odes of Ibnu 'l-Farid," in *Studies in Islamic Mysticism* (Cambridge: Cambridge University Press, 1967; first published 1921).

Ibn al-Farid. *'Umar Ibn al-Farid: Sufi Verse, Saintly Life.* Translated and introduced by Th. Emil Homerin (New York: Paulist Press, 2001).

A new scholarly translation of the *Khamriyya* and the *Ta'iyya* has been published in the Paulist Press mysticism series, in a very attractive volume packed with annotations, introductory material, and analysis. Homerin's emphasis in this book is on Ibn al-Farid's extensive ode *Nazm al-suluk,* here translated as *Poem of the Sufi Way.* This unusual work chronicles in verse "the lover's life of deprivation, transformation and eventual union" (p. 67); through suffering and trial, the lover learns to dissolve his will and ego and experience annihilation and perfect realization in The Beloved. Plurality is resolved in unity, and Neoplatonic and monistic metaphysics become blended with Islamic revelation in the Prophetic Light of Muhammad. (The reader is at times reminded of Dante's *Paradiso* or *Vita Nuova.*) Homerin's notes appear upon facing pages, an effective means of clarifying the content without detracting from the poetry.

In the same volume, Homerin has placed a translation of an account of Ibn al-Farid's composition of the *Diwan* by his grandson, 'Ali Sibt Ibn al-Farid; he has also provided indexes and a valuable bibliography.

RUMI (d. 1273)
Jalal al-Din Rumi (ROO-mee). The *Mathnawi* or (in Persian) *Masnavi*.
His name may appear as Djalal al-Din (jah-LOLL id-DEEN).

The work of the great Persian poet and Sufi master Jalal al-Din Rumi is so well documented, extensively studied, and widely available that there is no need to expand upon it here. At this moment, a single publisher (Harper-Collins) has no fewer than ten books in print about him, and countless other publishers also offer such titles, many by the well-known Rumi translator Coleman Barks. Some of these are popular works devoted to the pleasures of Rumi's poetry, but scholarly materials are abundant as well. The poetic texts are found in translation in complete or abridged editions. Selections are in numerous anthologies.

The poet's family migrated from Persia to Turkey (Rum) about 1220 CE. Jalal al-Din became the leader of a Sufi order that was based in Konya and known as the Mawlawi or (in Turkish) Mevlevi, after the title used for him by his disciples: *Mawlana* or *Mevlana* ("Our Master"). His primary works are the very extensive *Mathnawi* in six books of twenty-five thousand rhyming couplets (including many allegorical tales), a volume of about sixteen hundred quatrains called the *Ruba'iyat*, and a huge collection of mystical odes, his *Diwan-i Shams-i Tabriz* (lyrics inspired by, or in honor of, a person to whom Rumi was deeply attached).[17] The details of his life and theology, as well as his outstanding poetry, are worthy of further study.

Other Sources
A contemporary of Rumi's, also associated with Konya, was the teacher and poet Fakhruddin 'Iraqi (d. 1289). His *Lama'at* or *Divine Flashes* is available in a scholarly translation with a substantial commentary by William C. Chittick and Peter Lamborn Wilson (New York: Paulist Press, 1982). In preparing their annotations, Chittick and Wilson made use of a commentary on this work called *Ashi'at al-lama'at* or *Gleams from the Flashes* by 'Abd al-Rahman Jami (d. 1492), himself a noted Sufi theologian and the last of the great mystical poets.

Some of Jami's work is available in English as well. For example, a rather dense scholarly treatise on mystical theology, *Al-durra al-fakhira*, was published as *The Precious Pearl*, translated and extensively annotated by Nicholas L. Heer (Albany: State University of New York Press, 1979). A number of Jami's poetic allegories have been translated, some of them repeatedly, including *Salaman wa Absal* and *Yusuf wa Zulaikha* (or Zulayka, or Zuleikha), and his prose narrative *Baharistan* (or Beharistan), often titled *The Abode of Spring*.

Mysticism in the Modern Era

The status of Sufism and of Sufi institutions, particularly the *tariqa*, was impacted in the nineteenth and twentieth centuries by an array of damaging developments. Modernist intellectuals criticized many of the popular manifestations of Sufi tradition as backward or superstitious, rejecting its veneration of wonder-working saints and its apparent otherworldliness. The more puritanical champions of Islamic orthodoxy regarded Sufi doctrine as tainted by extraneous influences and insufficiently committed to the requirements of *shari'a*. The political reformer Mustafa Kemal Atatürk abolished all of the Sufi orders and brotherhoods in Turkey in 1925, accusing them of corruption and of holding back the population from modern nationalism and social progress. There was also a sense in which the orders represented a power base in competition with the secular state; therefore, they had to be suppressed.

One of Sufism's severest twentieth-century critics upon the Indian subcontinent was the outspoken intellectual reformer Muhammad Iqbal (d. 1938). Like Atatürk, he associated the movement with institutional laxity and corruption and rejected the Sufi concept of the negation of the self as detrimental to human progress. Nevertheless, he was personally influenced by his own early experience of Sufi tradition and valued its emphasis on the interior and authentic spiritual life. He sought to reinterpret some of Sufism's heritage, especially its Persian cultural contributions, from a modern humanistic viewpoint; his own poetry displays a debt to paradigmatic Sufi imagery and symbolism. He draws upon many of the classic Sufi poets and theologians in *The Reconstruction of Religious Thought in Islam* (London: Oxford University Press, 1934).

Iqbal's contemporary, Shaykh Ahmad al-'Alawi (d. 1934) of Algeria, represents a powerful trend in the modern era to revive and endorse the veneration of saintly persons, their poetry and teachings, and the practice of spirituality as individuals and in community. Martin Lings has written an intimate biography and analysis of the Shaykh's life and work, incorporating a number of key texts, in his *A Sufi Saint of the Twentieth Century* (Cambridge: Islamic Texts Society, 1993).[18] Other scholars and theologians today, notably of Iran, India, and Turkey (such as Fethullah Gülen), are deriving new inspiration from the intellectual and spiritual richness of the Sufi tradition.

Why are there so many popular books in print about various aspects of Sufism? Any bookstore offers scores of titles. At the present time, the perceived affinity of Sufi thought and art (music and poetry) with certain New Age approaches, along with theories of world religions based upon the idea of a universal esotericism,[19] may be leading to a wider interest in these works. Some have viewed Sufism as a desirable alternative to legalistic extremism or fundamentalism; some see in it a way to absorb Islam into a tolerant, multicultural social environment or interfaith dialogue. Some regard Sufism as a potential engine for the renewal of Islamic theology on more universalist lines, while others propose that the familiarity of many Western non-Muslim readers with the language and concepts of mysticism could be an opportunity for *da'wa* or the call to faith, leading them to embrace Islam.

Some want to blend Sufism with a fashionable or superficial kind of spirituality on the purely personal level, in conformity with a trend in Western societies toward an atomistic individualism and the privatization of religion. Such efforts run the risk of contemplating *tasawwuf* out of context and of trivializing a great spiritual and intellectual tradition. The primary literature of Islamic mysticism positions it as a genuine manifestation of a corporate faith, compatible with Islamic orthodoxy. The Sufi theologians deliberately undertook to establish their discipline upon a scholarly basis and to integrate it into the vast, interrelated structure of Islamic faith and practice.

Muslim cultures and societies over the centuries have created, and are still creating, a complex heritage of Islamic learning and literature: founded upon the Qur'an, amplified by the *hadith*, interpreted by *tafsir*, ordered and cultivated by *fiqh*, recorded and analyzed by *ta'rikh*, embellished by *falsafa*, arranged and configured by *kalam*, and enhanced by *tasawwuf*. No portion of this heritage can be understood without some knowledge of the whole. The student should attempt to become familiar with each of these distinctive contributions to an impressive literature. As the body of essential texts in translation increases, and as original and contemporary works are produced in English, more and more opportunities will become available to achieve this goal.

Notes

1. Interesting quotes on the origins of Sufism are found in F. E. Peters, *A Reader on Classical Islam* (Princeton, N.J.: Princeton University Press, 1994), 310–12, with some interpretive comments; there are also comparisons with Christian monasticism, etc.

2. Annemarie Schimmel, *Mystical Dimensions of Islam* (Chapel Hill: University of North Carolina Press, 1975), 30. A few quotes attributed to him are found in Margaret Smith, *Readings from the Mystics of Islam* (London: Luzac, 1972), 8.

3. William Chittick, "Sufi Thought and Practice," OEMIW, v. 4: 103. See Chittick's fuller discussion of these issues in his *Sufism: A Short Introduction* (Oxford: Oneworld, 2000).

4. See Chittick, *Sufism*, 4–7.

5. Margaret Smith, "Dhu'l-Nun," *EI2*, v. 2: 242.

6. *Principles of Sufism*, translated by B. R. von Schlegell (Berkeley, Calif.: Mizan Press, 1992); *A Sufi Book of Spiritual Ascent*, translated by Rabia Harris, edited by Laleh Bakhtiar (Chicago: ABC Group/KAZI, 1997); *The Risalah: Principles of Sufism*, by Harris and Bakhtiar (Chicago: Great Books of the Islamic World, 2002); and excerpts in the Jeffery anthology *A Reader on Islam*, 655–66, and the Calder anthology *Classical Islam*, 243–47.

7. Al-Ghazali, *The Alchemy of Happiness* (Armonk, N.Y.: M. E. Sharpe, 1991), xxxvi. From the preface by Elton L. Daniel.

8. Ibn al-'Arabi, *The Bezels of Wisdom*, translated and edited by R. W. J. Austin (New York: Paulist Press, 1980), 16. From the translator's introduction.

9. Ibn al-'Arabi, *The Meccan Revelations*, translated and edited by Michel Chodkiewicz, et al. (New York: Pir Press, 2002), 1. From the preface by James W. Morris.

10. Peter J. Awn, "Sufism," *ER2*, v. 13: 8816–17, 8823–24.

11. Another text by Ibn 'Ata'illah, the *Miftah al-falah wa misbah al-arwah*, has been translated by Mary Ann Koury-Danner and published as *The Key to Salvation and the Lamp of Souls* (Cambridge: Islamic Texts Society, 1996); it concentrates upon the practice of *dhikr* or invocation.

12. Schimmel, *Mystical Dimensions*, 426; the same remark appears in *My Soul Is a Woman*, 34.

13. Hellmut Ritter, "Abu Yazid al-Bistami," *EI2*, v. 1: 162.

14. "In presenting the *Tawasin* . . . we have deliberately refrained from any explanation . . . we cannot hope to understand the greater part of the *Tawasin*. . . . To grasp anything of the *Tawasin*, one must first follow the instruction of a Shaykh or someone under the counsel of a Shaykh" (15–16). From the introduction by Muqaddem 'Abd al-Qadir as-Sufi.

15. Schimmel, *Mystical Dimensions*, 307.

16. Among these is a *Bird-Parliament* by Edward FitzGerald, who is better known for his translation of *The Rubaiyat of Omar Khayyam*, first published to great popular acclaim in 1859.

17. See *A Rumi Anthology*, translated and annotated by Reynold A. Nicholson (Oxford: Oneworld, 2000), 22.

18. Selections from 'Alawi's works have been published in English in *Two Who Attained: Twentieth-Century Muslim Saints, Sayyida Fatima al-Yashrutiyya and Shaykh Ahmad al-Alawi*, edited and translated by Leslie Cadavid (Louisville, Ky.: Fons Vitae, 2005). The volume also contains information about the modern Shadhiliyya order.

19. See William Chittick, "Sufism," *OEMIW*, v. 4: 108.

~

Appendix: General Anthologies of Primary Literature

Anthology of Islamic Literature from the Rise of Islam to Modern Times. With an introduction and commentaries by James Kritzeck. New York: Holt, Rinehart, and Winston, 1964.

Classical Islam: A Sourcebook of Religious Literature. Edited and translated by Norman
Calder, Jawid Mojaddedi, and Andrew Rippin. London; New York: Routledge, 2003.

Islam: Muhammad and His Religion. Edited with an introduction by Arthur Jeffery.
New York: Liberal Arts Press, 1958.

Islam from the Prophet Muhammad to the Capture of Constantinople. Edited and translated by Bernard Lewis. London; New York: Macmillan, 1974. 2 v.

Islam in Transition: Muslim Perspectives. Edited by John J. Donohue and John L. Esposito. New York; Oxford: Oxford University Press, 1982.

Islamfiche: Readings from Islamic Primary Sources, series I–II. Edited by William Gra-
ham and Marilyn Waldman; American Council of Learned Societies, Islamic
Teaching Materials Project. Zug, Switzerland: IDC, 1987.

Liberal Islam: A Sourcebook. Edited by Charles Kurzman. New York; Oxford: Oxford
University Press, 1998.

Modern Islamic Literature: From 1800 to the Present. With an introduction and commentaries by James Kritzeck. New York: Holt, Rinehart, and Winston, 1970.

Modernist and Fundamentalist Debates in Islam: A Reader. Edited by Mansoor Moaddel
and Kamran Talattof. New York: Palgrave Macmillan, 2000.

Modernist Islam, 1840–1940: A Sourcebook. Edited by Charles Kurzman. New York;
Oxford: Oxford University Press, 2002.

The Muslim Jesus: Sayings and Stories in Islamic Literature. Edited and translated by
Tarif Khalidi. Cambridge; London: Harvard University Press, 2001.

Night and Horses and the Desert: An Anthology of Classical Arabic Literature. Edited by
Robert Irwin. Woodstock, N.Y.: Overlook Press, 2000.

Progressive Muslims: On Justice, Gender and Pluralism. Edited by Omid Safi. Oxford: Oneworld, 2003.

A Reader on Classical Islam. Edited by F. E. Peters. Princeton, N.J.: Princeton University Press, 1994.

A Reader on Islam: Passages from Standard Arabic Writings Illustrative of the Beliefs and Practices of Muslims. Edited by Arthur Jeffery. The Hague: Mouton, 1962.

Textual Sources for the Study of Islam. Translated and edited by Andrew Rippin and Jan Knappert. Chicago: University of Chicago Press, 1986.

Theology, Ethics and Metaphysics: Royal Asiatic Society Classics of Islam. Edited by Hiroyuki Mashita, with a new introduction by C. Edmund Bosworth. London; New York: RoutledgeCurzon and Edition Synapse, 2003.

Translations of Eastern Poetry and Prose. Translated and edited by Reynold A. Nicholson. Cambridge: Cambridge University Press, 1922.

Windows on the House of Islam: Muslim Sources on Spirituality and Religious Life. Edited by John Renard. Berkeley: University of California Press, 1988.

The Word of Islam. Edited by John Alden Williams. Austin: University of Texas Press, 1994.

~

Glossary/Index of Arabic Terms

Page numbers refer to a point where the term is discussed or used in context.

adab (ADD-abb) civilized behavior or right social conduct 33; and courtly literature 106

ahl al-bayt (AH-hul al-BATE) "People of the Household" of the Prophet 165

ahl al bid'a (AH-hul al-BID-aa) "People of Innovation" or heretics 167

ahwal (ah-WALL, plural) spiritual states in Sufism 176

akhlaq (ock-LOCK) character or ethics 101

'alim (AA-lim; plural, **'ulama'**) a member of the community of scholars 78

'aqida (ock-EE-da; plural, **'aqa'id**) creed, articles of faith 164

'aql (OCK-ul) human reason or intellect 128

arba'in (ar-ba-EEN) collections of forty hadith narratives 41

'asabiyya (ossa-BEE-yah) social cohesiveness 118–19

asbab al-nuzul (as-BAB an-nuh-ZOOL) information about the original circumstances of a particular revelation in the Qur'an 74, 106

basmala (BAS-ma-la) "In the name of God, the merciful and compassionate"; formula of dedication at the beginning of each chapter of the Qur'an 20

bid'a (BID-aa) innovation, especially heretical or suspect 92, 162

bila kayf (bih-LAA KAFE) "without asking how" 151

da'if (dah-EEF) weak, of poor quality 26

dar al-harb (DAR al-HARB) "house of war" or non-Muslim peoples 81

dar al-islam (DAR al-is-LAM) body of believers 81

da'wa (DAA-wa) the call to faith 17, 96, 195

dhikr (THICK-ur) remembrance of God 174

din (DEEN) Islamic religion; in scholarship, theological studies or religious sciences 157

diwan (dee-WAHN or dih-WANN) poem cycle 188

falasifa (fa-LASS-iffa) plural of *faylasuf*

falsafa (fall-SOFFA or FAL-soffa) philosophy 127

fana' (fa-NAH) annihilation of the self 174

faqih (fa-KEEH) jurist or legal scholar 78

fatwa (FOT-wah); plural, *fatawa* (fot-TAH-wah) a formal legal ruling on a given question 78

faylasuf (fay-la-SOOF) philosopher 128

fiqh (FIK) jurisprudence, the study of the law 78

fitna (FIT-na) the civil war involving the murder of the Caliph 'Uthman 110

fuqaha' (foo-ka-HAH) plural of *faqih*

furu' al-fiqh (fuh-ROO al-FIK) "branches" of the law 84

hadith (hah-DEETH; plural, *ahadith*) a narrative record or saying, especially from the life of the Prophet, often called "traditions" 25–26; the term also refers to the *hadith* literature in general

hadith qudsi (hah-DEETH KOOD-zee) a type of sayings tradition in which Allah speaks in the first person 41–42

hajj (HADGE) pilgrimage to Mecca and Medina 114

hasan (HASS-san) of good quality 26

hikma (HICK-mah) wisdom 127; plural, *hikam* (HICK-um) profound statements or sayings 182

'ibadat (ib-bah-DAT, plural) laws concerning rituals, prayer, acts of worship 84, 157

'ibar (IB-bar, plural) lessons or instructive examples 117

i'jaz (eh-JAZZ) the miraculous uniqueness or inimitability of the Qur'an 2, 154

ijma' (idge-MAA) the consensus of knowledgeable interpreters 77

ijtihad (idge-tih-HAD) systematic legal reasoning 77, 88

'ilm (ILM; plural, *'ulum*) knowledge or science; in this context, religious knowledge 49, 176

'ilm al-hadith (ILM al-hah-DEETH) the formal study of *hadith* criticism 49; also *'ulum al-hadith*

'ilm al-'umran (ILM al-oom-RON) the study of social organization 118

imami (eh-MOM-ee) of the Shi'a who revere twelve Imams 45

injil (in-JEEL) Gospel brought by the prophet Jesus 163

al-insan al-kamil (al-in-SANN al-KAA-mil) in philosophy, the "Perfect Man" 185 *ishraq* (ish-ROCK) in philosophy, illumination 142

isma'ili (iss-mah-EE-lee) of the Shi'a who revere seven Imams 134

isnad (iss-NAD) the chain of transmission of **hadith** accounts 26

ithna 'ashari (ETH-na OSH-aree) Shi'a who revere twelve Imams 45

jahiliyya (jah-hih-LEE-yah) state of ignorance before the revelation of Islam 71

jami' (JAM-ee) comprehensive 31

jihad (jee-HAD) holy war or struggle 82, 98

jizya (JIZZ-ya) poll-tax 80

juz' (JOOZ; plural, *ajzaa'*) one of thirty segments of the Qur'an 14

juz' 'amma (jooz AHM-mah) thirtieth segment of the Qur'an 14

kafir (KAA-fur) unbeliever, denier or apostate 166

kalam (ka-LAMM) doctrinal theology 127, 149

khabar (KA-bar; plural, *akhbar*) report or news, used by the Shi'a as a synonym for **hadith** 45

khalwa (KOLL-wa) spiritual retreat 185

kharaj (kor-RODGE) taxation 80

kitab (kih-TABB; plural, *kutub*) book xv; *al-Kutub al-Sitta* (al-KOOT-ub
as-SIT-tah) the "Six Books" or canonical **hadith** collections 30

mabsut (mob-SUTE) in legal studies, an extensive and inclusive work 86

madhab (MODD-hob; plural, *madhahib*) a "school" of legal interpretation
78

madrasa (MAD-rassa) school or academy 155

maghazi (mah-GAZZY) accounts of the military campaigns of Muhammad
and his Companions 106

maqamat (mocka-MAT, plural) stages on the path of Sufi training 176, 178

ma'rifa (MAH-riffa) personal or intuitive knowledge 176

masa'il (ma-SAH-il) in legal discourse, responses 92

mathnawi (math-NAH-wee) lyrical form of rhyming couplets 189

matn (MAT-un) body or content of a **hadith** account 26

mihna (MIH-nah) persecution of opponents of Mu'tazili doctrine by Caliph
al-Ma'mun 129, 150

mu'amalat (moo-ah-ma-LAT, plural) laws concerning social behavior 84, 157

mufassir (moo-FASS-ser; plural, *mufassirun*) exegete of the Qur'an 55

mufti (MOOF-tee) judge or scholar who produces a legal ruling 78

muhaddith (moo-HAHD-dith; plural, *muhaddithun*) a scholar of the **hadith** literature; a "traditionist" 26

mujtahid (MOODGE-tah-hid) one who undertakes disciplined legal reasoning 78, 97

mukhtasar (mook-TOSS-ar) a concise epitome or summary of legal doctrine
86

munajat (moon-AA-JAT) personal statements addressing God 186

muqaddima (moo-KOD-dim-ah) introduction or prolegomena 117

murid (moo-REED) pupil or disciple 174

musannaf (moo-SUN-nuff; plural, **musannafat**) a "classified" collection of hadith, organized by topic 28, 31, 33

musnad (MUSS-nad) a **hadith** collection organized not by topic but by source 29

mut'a (MUTT-ah) temporary marriage 168

mutakallim (moo-ta-KAL-lim; plural, **mutakallimun**) scholar of doctrinal theology 149

nafs (NAFS) self 99

naql (NOCK-ul) revealed and transmitted sources of knowledge 128

naskh (NOSK) the abrogation or clarification of an earlier passage in the Qur'an by a later one 74

pir (PEER) from Persian, an elder or master 174

al-qadar (KOD-dar) the "pen" of predestination; divine will 109

qadi (KODDY) judge or magistrate 80

qiyas (kee-YASS) legal reasoning by analogy 77

Qur'an (koor-AHN) sacred scripture of Islam 1

ra'y (RAH-ee) informed personal judgment or opinion 56, 79

rihla (RIH-lah) journey, or travel narrative 115

rijal (reh-JALL, plural) the named transmitters of **hadith** narratives 49

risala (ris-SAL-ah) an essay or monograph in the form of an epistle or letter 89

sahih (sah-HEEH) sound or valid, reliable 26; as a type of **hadith** collection (plural, **sihah**) 30

al-Sahihayn, the "Two Reliable [Ones]," the **hadith** collections of Bukhari and Muslim 33

salaf (SAL-aff) "ancestors," the earliest Companions of the Prophet 94, 162

salat (suh-LAHT) prescribed prayers 10

sama' (sam-AH) audition 174

shama'il (sha-MAA-il) virtues or qualities 38

sharh (SHAR) commentary 184

shari'a (sha-REE-ah) divine law 27, 77

shathiyat (sha-thee-YAT) ecstatic utterances 188

shaykh (SHAKE) master or learned one 174

al-Shaykhan (shay-KONN), the "Two Sheikhs," Bukhari and Muslim 33

shirk (SHIRK) polytheism 96

sira (SEE-rah) biography, especially of the Prophet 105

sitta (SIT-tah) the number six; **al-Sihah al-Sitta** (as-see-HAH as-SIT-ta) the "Six Books" or canonical **hadith** collections 30 *siyar* (SIH-yar) in legal literature, the law of nations or political order 81

siyasa (see-YAH-sa) political administration and governance 119

sunna (SOON-nah; plural, **sunan**) the precedent set by the exemplary behavior, sayings and judgment of the Prophet 25, 89; also, **sunan** as a type of *hadith* collection 30, 36

sura (SOO-rah; plural, **suwar**) chapter of the Qur'an 2

tabaqat (tobba-KOTT, plural) collected biographies of certain classes of people 106

tafsir (toff-SEER) exegesis or scholarly interpretation of the Qur'an 55

tafsir bil-ma'thur (bill-ma-THOOR) exegesis based upon traditions 56, 64

tafsir bil-ra'y (bir-RAH-ee) exegesis based upon individual opinion 56, 64

tahrif (tah-REEF) the corruption of Scripture, especially the Bible 163

takfir (tock-FEER) declaring someone to be in a state of unbelief 139, 141

taqiya (tock-EE-ya) dissimulation 168

taqlid (tock-LEED) imitation 170

ta'rikh (tah-REEK) history 105

tariqa (tah-REE-ka; plural, **turuq**) a Sufi order 174

tasawwuf (toss-SAW-wuff) Sufism 173

tawhid (tao-HEED) the essential unity of God 96

ta'wil (ta-WEEL) interpretation of the Qur'an 55

'ulum (ol-LOOM) plural of *'ilm*

usul (os-SOOL) fundamentals; sources; basic principles 49

usul al-din (us-SOOL id-DEEN) grounding principles of Islamic religion; theology or theological studies 149, 167

usul al-fiqh (oss-SOOL al-FIK) "roots" of the law 88

usul al-hadith (os-SOOL al-hah-DEETH) the formal study of *hadith* criticism 49

wahdat al-wujud (WAH-dat al-wu-JOOD) oneness of being 182

wali (WALLY; plural, **awliya'**) a "saint" or friend of God 175

waqf (WOCK-uf) religious endowment 121

wilayat al-faqih (wil-LAH-yat al-fa-KEEH) from Persian, government by the jurist 100

zakat (za-KAT) charitable giving 10, 28

Bibliography of Works Discussed

Note: Additional resources may be found in the endnotes to each chapter and in the Titles Index.

Qur'an

Primary Sources

Abdel Haleem, Muhammad A. S. *The Qur'an: A New Translation*. Oxford: Oxford University Press, 2004.

Ahmad 'Ali, S. V. Mir. *The Holy Qur'an: Arabic Text, with English Translation and Commentary*. 4th ed. Elmhurst, N.Y.: Tahrike Tarsile Qur'an, 2004.

Ahmed 'Ali. *Al-Qur'an: A Contemporary Translation*. Princeton, N.J.: Princeton University Press, 2001.

Arberry, Arthur J. *The Koran Interpreted*. London: George Allen and Unwin, 1955.

Arshed, Aneela Khalid. *The Bounty of Allah*. New York: Crossroad, 1999.

Ayoub, Mahmoud M. *The Awesome News: Interpretation of Juz 'Amma, the Last Part of the Qur'an*. 2nd ed. s.l.: World Islamic Call Society, 1997.

Behbudi, Muhammad Baqir, and Colin Turner. *The Quran: A New Interpretation*. Richmond, Surrey, UK: Curzon, 1997.

Bell, Richard. *The Qur'an Translated, with a Critical Re-arrangement of the Surahs*. Edinburgh: T. and T. Clark, 1937–1939.

Bewley, Abdalhaqq, and 'Aisha. *The Noble Qur'an: A New Rendering of Its Meaning in English*. Norwich: Bookwork, 1999.

Cleary, Thomas. *The Essential Koran: The Heart of Islam*. San Francisco: HarperCollins, 1994.

Cragg, Kenneth. *Readings in the Qur'an*. London: Collins, 1988.

Dawood, N. J. *The Koran, with a Parallel Arabic Text*. London: Penguin, 1990.

Fakhry, Majid. *An Interpretation of the Qur'an: English Translation of the Meanings.* New York: New York University Press, 2002.

Helminski, Camille Adams. *The Light of Dawn: Daily Readings from the Holy Qur'an.* Boston: Shambhala, 2000.

Hilali, Muhammad Taqi-ud-Din, and Muhammad Muhsin Khan. *Translation of the Meanings of the Noble Qur'an in the English Language.* Medina: King Fahd Complex for the Printing of the Holy Qur'an, 1977.

Irving, T. B. *The Qur'an: The First American Version.* Brattleboro, Vt.: Amana Books, 1985.

Jeffery, Arthur. *The Koran: Selected Suras.* New York: Heritage Press, 1958.

Khatib, Mohammad M. *The Bounteous Koran: A Translation of Meaning and Commentary.* London: Macmillan, 1986.

Malik, Muhammad Farooq-i-Azam. *English Translation of the Meanings of al-Qur'an: The Guidance for Mankind.* 2nd ed. Houston: Institute of Islamic Knowledge, 1998.

Muhammad 'Ali. *The Holy Qur'an: Containing the Arabic Text with English Translation and Commentary.* 2nd ed. Lahore: Ahmadiyya Anjuman-i-ishâat-i-islam, 1920.

Muhammad Asad. *The Message of the Qur'an.* Gibraltar: Dar al-Andalus, 1980.

Palmer, E. H. *The Qur'an.* Oxford: Clarendon Press, 1900.

Pickthall, Muhammad Marmaduke. *The Meaning of the Glorious Koran: An Explanatory Translation.* London: George Allen and Unwin, 1957.

Rodwell, J. M. *The Koran: Translated from the Arabic [with] the Suras Arranged in Chronological Order, with Notes and Index.* With an introduction by G. Margoliouth. London: J. M. Dent and Sons, 1909.

Sale, George. *The Koran: Commonly Called the Alcoran of Mohammed.* Philadelphia: J. W. Moore, 1850.

Sells, Michael. *Approaching the Qur'an: The Early Revelations.* Ashland, Ore.: White Cloud Press, 2002.

Shakir, M. H. *Holy Qur'an.* 2nd U.S. ed. Elmhurst, N.Y.: Tahrike Tarsile Qur'an, 1983.

Yusuf 'Ali, 'Abdullah. *The Holy Qur-an [sic]: Text, Translation and Commentary.* Lahore: Sh. Muhammad Ashraf, 1975.

Selected Secondary Reading

Cragg, Kenneth. *Readings in the Qur'an.* London: Collins, 1988. Introductory essay.

Esack, Farid. *The Qur'an: A Short Introduction.* Oxford: Oneworld, 2002.

Lester, Toby. "What Is the Koran?" *The Atlantic Monthly* 283, no. 1 (Jan 1999): 43–56.

Manzoor, S. Parvez. "Method against Truth: Orientalism and Qur'anic Studies," *MWBR* 7, no.4 (1987): 33–49.

Ramadan, Tariq. *Western Muslims and the Future of Islam.* Oxford: Oxford University Press, 2004. Ch. 1.

Rippin, Andrew (ed.). *The Qur'an: Style and Contents.* Aldershot, UK: Ashgate, 2001.

Shellabear, W. G. "Can a Moslem Translate the Koran?" MW 21 (1931): 287–303.

Teipen, Alfons H. "The Word of God: What Can Christians Learn from Muslim Attitudes toward the Qur'an?," Journal of Ecumenical Studies 38, no. 2–3 (Spr-Sum 2001): 286–297.

Vroom, Hendrik M. and Jerald D. Gort, eds. Holy Scriptures in Judaism, Christianity and Islam. Amsterdam: Rodopi, 1997.

Hadith

Primary Sources

Abu Dawud. Sunan Abu Dawud. English translation with explanatory notes by Ahmad Hasan. Lahore: Sh. Muhammad Ashraf, 1984. 3 vols.

Al-Bukhari. English Translation of Sahih al-Bukhari. Translated and annotated by Maulana Aftab-ud-din Ahmad. Lahore: Ahmadiyya Anjuman Isha'at-i-islam, 1976. 3 vols.

———. Moral Teachings of Islam: Prophetic Traditions from al-Adab al-mufrad by Imam al-Bukhari. Selected and translated with an introduction by Abdul Ali Hamid. Walnut Creek, Calif.: AltaMira Press, 2003.

———. The Translation of the Meanings of Sahih al-Bukhari, Arabic-English. Translated and annotated by Muhammad Muhsin Khan. 4th rev. ed. Chicago: Kazi, 1979. 9 vols.

Al-Bukhari and Muslim. The Translation of the Meanings of Al-Lu'lu' wal marjan: a Collection of Agreed-Upon Ahadith from al-Bukhari and Muslim, Arabic-English. Compiled by Fuwad Abdul Baqi; rendered into English by Muhammad Muhsin Khan. 2nd ed. Lahore: Kazi, 1991. 3 vols.

Al-Fadli, 'Abd al-Hadi. Introduction to Hadith. Translated by Nazmina Virjee. London: Islamic College for Advanced Studies Press, 2002.

Al-Hakim al-Naisaburi. An Introduction to the Science of Tradition. Edited and translated by James Robson. London: The Royal Asiatic Society of Great Britain and Ireland, 1953.

———. An Introduction to the Science of Tradition. Edited and translated by James Robson. In: Theology, Ethics and Metaphysics: Royal Asiatic Society Classics of Islam. Edited by Hiroyuki Mashita. London: RoutledgeCurzon and Edition Synapse, 2003. Vol. 5.

Ibn Majah. Sunan ibn-i-Majah. English version by Muhammad Tufail Ansari. Lahore: Kazi, 1993–96. 5 vols.

Ibn al-Salah al-Shahrazuri. An Introduction to the Science of the Hadith = Kitab ma'rifat anwa' 'ilm al-hadith. Translated by Eerick Dickinson; edited by Muneer Fareed. Reading, UK: Garnet, 2005.

Ibn Taymiyya. The Goodly Word. Abridged and translated by Ezzedin Ibrahim and Denys Johnson-Davies. Cambridge: Islamic Texts Society, 2000.

Juynboll, G. H. A. "Muslim's Introduction to His Sahih, Translated and Annotated," Jerusalem Studies in Arabic and Islam 5 (1984): 263–302.

Al-Khatib al-Tibrizi. *Mishkat al-Masabih: English Translation with Explanatory Notes.* Edited and translated by James Robson. Lahore: Sh. Muhammad Ashraf, 1960–1965. 4 vols.

Khalidi, Tarif. *The Muslim Jesus: Sayings and Stories in Islamic Literature.* Cambridge: Harvard University Press, 2001.

Al-Kulayi. *Al-Kafi.* Translated by Sayyid Muhammad Hasan Rizvi; edited by Muhammad Rida al-Ja'fari. Tehran: Group of Muslim Brothers; Karachi: Khurasan Islamic Research Centre, 1978.

Malik ibn Anas. *Muwatta' Imam Malik.* Translation and notes by Muhammad Rahimuddin. Lahore: Sh. Muhammad Ashraf, 1985.

———. *Al-Muwatta of Imam Malik ibn Anas: The First Formulation of Islamic Law.* Translated by Aisha Abdurrahman Bewley. London: Kegan Paul International, 1989.

Muhammad Ali. *A Manual of Hadith.* 2nd ed. Preface by C. E. Bosworth. London: Curzon Press, 1978.

Muslim ibn al-Hajjaj. *Sahih Muslim.* Translated and annotated by 'Abdul Hamid Siddiqi. Rev. ed. New Delhi: Kitab Bhavan, 2000.

Al-Nasa'i. *Sunan Nasa'i: English Translation with Arabic Text.* Rendered into English by Muhammad Iqbal Siddiqi. Lahore: Kazi, 1994. 2 vols.

Al-Nawawi. *The Forty Traditions of An-Nawawi.* 142–60 in *A Reader on Islam,* edited by Arthur Jeffery. The Hague: Mouton, 1962.

———. *Gardens of the Righteous: Riyadh as-Salihin of Imam Nawawi.* Translated by Muhammad Zafrulla Khan; foreword by C. E. Bosworth. London: Curzon Press, 1975.

———. *An-Nawawi's Forty Hadith: An Anthology of the Sayings of the Prophet Muhammad.* Translated by Ezzedin Ibrahim and Denys Johnson-Davies. Cambridge: Islamic Texts Society, 1997.

A Shi'ite Anthology. Selected by 'Allamah Sayyid Muhammad Husayn Tabataba'i; translated and edited by William C. Chittick; with an introduction by Seyyed Hossein Nasr. Albany: State University of New York Press, 1981.

Al-Tirmidhi. *The Abridged Shamail-e-Tirmizi.* Translated into English from Gujarati by Murtaz Husain F. Quraishi. Lahore: Progressive Books, 1979.

Note: Many online and CD-ROM sources now exist for *hadith* texts, such as *The Islamic Scholar* (Par Excellence); however, the scholarly standards of electronic sources vary enormously, and each must be evaluated with great care.

Selected Secondary Reading

Arabic Literature to the End of the Umayyad Period. Edited by A. F. L. Beeston et al. Cambridge: Cambridge University Press, 1983. Chs. 10–14.

Denny, Frederick M. "Islam: Qur'an and Hadith." 84–108 in *The Holy Book in Comparative Perspective,* edited by F. M. Denny and Rodney L. Taylor. Columbia: University of South Carolina Press, 1985.

Nasr, Seyyed Hossein. "Sunnah and Hadith." 97–110 in *Islamic Spirituality: Foundations,* edited by S. H. Nasr. New York: Crossroad, 1987.

Paret, Rudi. "Revelation and Tradition in Islam." 26–34 in *We Believe in One God*, edited by Annemarie Schimmel and Abdoldjavad Falaturi. 2nd ed. New York: Seabury, 1979.

Rahman, Fazlur. *Islam*. 2nd ed. Chicago: University of Chicago Press, 1979. Ch. 3.

Robson, James. "Tradition, the Second Foundation of Islam." *Muslim World* 41 (Jan 1951): 22–33. The first of a series of four articles published in vol. 41.

Siddiqi, Muhammad Zubayr. *Hadith Literature: Its Origin, Development and Special Features*. Edited and revised by Abdal Hakim Murad. Cambridge: Islamic Texts Society, 1993.

Tafsir

Primary Sources

Abdul, Musa O. A. *The Qur'an: Shaykh Tabarsi's Commentary*. Lahore: Sh. Muhammad Ashraf, 1977.

Al-Baidawi. *Baidawi's Commentary on Surah 12 of the Qur'an: Text, Accompanied by an Interpretative Rendering and Notes*. Translated and edited by A. F. L. Beeston. Oxford: Clarendon Press, 1978.

———. *Chrestomathia Baidawiana: The Commentary of el-Baidawi on Sura III*. Translated and annotated by D. S. Margoliouth. London: Luzac, 1894.

———. *A Translation of Baidawi's Commentary on the First Sura of the Koran*. A thesis by Roswell Walker Caldwell (MA), submitted to the Kennedy School of Missions of the Hartford Seminary Foundation, 1933.

Gätje, Helmut. *The Qur'an and Its Exegesis: Selected Texts with Classical and Modern Muslim Interpretations*. Translated into English by Alford T. Welch. Berkeley: University of California Press, 1976.

Al-Ghazali. *The Canons of Ta'wil*. 48–54 in *Windows on the House of Islam*, edited by John Renard. Berkeley: University of California Press, 1998.

Ibn Kathir. *Tafsir Ibn Kathir*. Abridged by a group of scholars under the supervision of Shaykh Safi-ur-Rahman al-Mubarakpuri. Riyadh: Darussalam, 2000.

Ibn Taymiyya. *Introductory Treatise on the Principles of Tafsir*. 35–43 in Renard, *Windows*

———. *Muqaddimah fu usul al-tafsir = An Introduction to the Principles of Tafseer*. Translated by Muhammad Abdul Haq Ansari. Birmingham: Al-Hidayah, 1993.

Mawdudi, Sayyid Abul A'la. *Towards Understanding the Qur'an*. English version of *Tafhim al-Qur'an*. Translated and edited by Zafar Ishaq Ansari. Leicester: Islamic Foundation, 1988– .

Prophets in the Quran: An Introduction to the Quran and Muslim Exegesis. Translated and edited by Brannon M. Wheeler. London: Continuum, 2002.

Al-Razi. *Mafatih al-ghayb* or *Al-tafsir al-kabir*. 121–27 in *Classical Islam*, edited by Norman Calder, Jawid Mojaddedi, and Andrew Rippin. London: Routledge, 2003.

Qutb, Sayyid. *In the Shade of the Qur'an*. Translated by M. Adil Salahi and Ashur A. Shamis. London: MWH, 1979.

Al-Tabari. *Commentary on the Qur'an*. Translation and notes by John Cooper; general editors Wilfred Madelung and Alan Jones. Oxford: Oxford University Press, 1987.

Al-Tabarsi. *The Qur'an: Shaykh Tabarsi's Commentary*. Translation and notes by Musa O. A. Abdul. Lahore: Sh. Muhammad Ashraf, 1977.

Tabataba'i, Sayyid Muhammad Husayn (al-Allamah). *Al-Mizan: An Exegesis of the Qur'an*. Translated by Sayyid Saeed Akhtar Rizvi. Tehran: WOFIS (World Organization for Islamic Services), 1983.

Selected Secondary Reading

Ayoub, Mahmoud. *The Qur'an and Its Interpreters*. Albany: State University of New York Press, 1984 (v. 1) and 1992 (v. 2).

Cragg, Kenneth. *The Mind of the Qur'an: Chapters in Reflection*. London: George Allen and Unwin, 1973.

Esack, Farid. *Qur'an, Liberation and Pluralism: An Islamic Perspective of Interreligious Solidarity against Oppression*. Oxford: Oneworld, 1997, 2002.

Jansen, J. J. G. *The Interpretation of the Qur'an in Modern Egypt*. Leiden: Brill, 1974.

McAuliffe, Jane D. *Qur'anic Christians: An Analysis of Classical and Modern Exegesis*. New York: Cambridge University Press, 1991.

Rippin, Andrew. "Tafsir." *ER*, v. 14: 236–44.

Speight, R. Marston. "The Function of Hadith as Commentary on the Qur'an, as Seen in the Six Authoritative Collections." 63–81 in *Approaches to the History of the Interpretation of the Qur'an*, edited by Andrew Rippin. Oxford: Clarendon, 1988.

Stowasser, Barbara F. "Gender Issues and Contemporary Quran Interpretation." 30–44 in *Islam, Gender and Social Change*, edited by Yvonne Haddad and John Esposito. New York: Oxford University Press, 1998.

Shari'a and Fiqh

Primary Sources

Abu Yusuf. *Abu Yusuf's Kitab al-Kharaj*. Translated and provided with an introduction and notes by A. Ben Shemesh. Leiden: Brill; London: Luzac, 1969.

Ahmad ibn Hanbal. *Chapters on Marriage and Divorce: Responses of Ibn Hanbal and Ibn Rahwayh*. Translated with introduction and notes by Susan A. Spectorsky. Austin: University of Texas Press, 1993.

Al-Hurr al-'Amili. *Combat with the Self*. Translated by Nazmina A. Virjee. London: Islamic College for Advanced Studies Press, 2003.

Ibn 'Abd al-Wahhab. *Kitab at-Tauhid*. Translated by the Compilation and Research Department, supervised by Abdul Malik Mujahid. Riyadh: Dar-us-Salam Publications, 1996.

———. *Kitab al Tawhid: Essay on the Unicity of Allah, or What Is Due to Allah from His Creatures*. Translated by Isma'il Raji al-Faruqi. Beirut: International Islamic Federation of Student Organizations, 1979.

Ibn Abi Zayd. *First Steps in Muslim Jurisprudence: Consisting of Excerpts from Bakurat al-sa'd of Ibn Abu Zayd*. Translated by Alexander David Russell and Abdullah al-Ma'mun Suhrawardy. London: Luzac, 1963.

———. *A Madinan View: On the Sunnah, Courtesy, Wisdom, Battles and History*. Translated by Abdassamad Clarke. London: Ta-Ha, 1999.

Ibn Taymiyya. *Ibn Taimiyya on Public and Private law in Islam, or Public Policy in Islamic Jurisprudence*. Translated by Omar A. Farrukh. Beirut: Khayats, 1966.

———. *The Madinan Way: The Soundness of the Basic Premises of the School of the People of Medina*. Translated by Aisha Bewley; edited by Abdalhaqq Bewley. London: Ta-Ha, 2000.

Khalil ibn Ishaq. *Maliki Law: Being a Summary from the French Translation of the Mukhtasar of Sidi Khalil*. Translated by F. H. Ruxton. Westport, Conn.: Hyperion, 1980.

———. *A Manual of the Law of Marriage from the Mukhtasar of Sidi Khalil*. Translated by Alexander David Russell and Abdullah al-Ma'mun Suhrawardy. Lahore: Law Publishing, 1979.

Khomeini, Ruhollah. *Islam and Revolution: Writings and Declarations of Imam Khomeini*. Translated and annotated by Hamid Algar. Berkeley: Mizan Press, 1981.

Al-Marghinani. *The Hedaya or Guide: A Commentary on the Mussulman Laws*. 2nd ed. Translated by Charles Hamilton. Lahore: Premier Book House, 1975.

Maududi, Sayyid Abul A'la. *The Islamic Law and Constitution*. 2nd ed. Translated and edited by Khurshid Ahmad. Lahore: Islamic Publications, 1960.

Mughniyya, Muhammad Jawad. *Encyclopedia of Islamic Law: A Compendium of the Views of the Major Schools*. Adapted by Laleh Bakhtiar; introduction by Kevin Reinhart. Chicago: ABC/Kazi, 1996.

Al-Nawawi. *Al-majmu' sharh al-muhaddab* and *Fatawa*. 192–201 in *Classical Islam*, edited by Norman Calder, Jawid Mojaddedi, and Andrew Rippin. London: Routledge, 2003.

——. *Minhaj et Talibin: A Manual of Muhammadan Law According to the School of Shafi'i*. Translated into English from the French edition of L. W. C. Van den Berg by E. C. Howard. Lahore: Law Publishing, 1977.

———. *Al-Nawawi's Manual of Islam*. Translated by Nuh Ha Mim Keller. Cambridge: Islamic Texts Society, 1996.

Al-Shafi'i. *Islamic Jurisprudence: Shafi'i's Risala*. Translated with an introduction, notes, and appendixes by Majid Khadduri. Baltimore: Johns Hopkins University Press, 1961.

Al-Shaybani. *The Islamic Law of Nations: Shaybani's Siyar*. Translated with an introduction, notes and appendixes by Majid Khadduri. Baltimore: Johns Hopkins University Press, 1966.

Selected Secondary Reading

Calder, Norman. "Legal Thought and Jurisprudence." *OEMIW*, v. 2: 450–56.

Cook, Michael. *Commanding Right and Forbidding Wrong in Islamic Thought*. Cambridge: Cambridge University Press, 2000.

Hallaq, Wael B. *A History of Islamic Legal Theories: An Introduction to Sunni usul al-fiqh*. Cambridge: Cambridge University Press, 1997.

———. *The Formation of Islamic Law*. Aldershot, UK: Ashgate, 2004.

Islamic Law and the Challenges of Modernity. Edited by Yvonne Yazbek Haddad and Barbara Freyer Stowasser. Walnut Creek, Calif.: AltaMira Press, 2004.

Kamali, Mohammad Hashim. *Principles of Islamic Jurisprudence*. 3rd ed. Cambridge: Islamic Texts Society, 2003.

Mayer, Ann Elizabeth. "Islamic Law: Shari'a." *ER*, v. 7: 431–46.

Neusner, Jacob, Tamara Sonn, and Jonathan Brockopp. *Judaism and Islam in Practice: A Sourcebook*. London: Routledge, 2000.

Sachedina, Abdulaziz. "Shi'i Schools of Law." *OEMIW*, v. 2: 463–64.

Vikor, Knut S. *Between God and the Sultan: A History of Islamic Law*. Oxford: Oxford University Press, 2005.

Ziadeh, Farhat J. "Sunni Schools of Law." *OEMIW*, v. 2: 456–62.

Ta'rikh

Primary Sources

Arab Historians of the Crusades. Translated and edited by Francesco Gabrieli. Berkeley: University of California Press, 1969.

The Arab World, Turkey and the Balkans (1878–1914): A Handbook of Historical Statistics. Translated and edited by Justin McCarthy. Boston: G. K. Hall, 1982.

Baha al-Din ibn Shaddad. *The Rare and Excellent History of Saladin*. Translated by D. S. Richards. Aldershot, UK: Ashgate, 2001.

Al-Baladhuri. *The Origins of the Islamic State*. Translated by Philip Khuri Hitti and Francis Murgotten. New York: AMS Press, 1968.

Al-Damurdashi. *Al-Damurdashi's Chronicle of Egypt, 1688–1755*. Translated and edited by Daniel Crecelius and Muhammad 'Abd al-Wahhab Bakr. Leiden: Brill, 1991.

Ibn al-Athir. *The Annals of the Saljuq Turks: Selections from al-Kamil fi'l-Ta'rikh of 'Izz al-Din Ibn al-Athir*. Translated and annotated by D. S. Richards. London: RoutledgeCurzon, 2002.

Ibn Battuta. *Ibn Battuta: Travels in Asia and Africa, 1325–1354*. Translated by H. A. R. Gibb. London: Routledge and Kegan Paul, 1929 (reprinted 1983).

———. *The Travels of Ibn Battuta, AD 1325–1354*. Translated by H. A. R. Gibb; with annotations by C. F. Beckingham. London: Hakluyt Society, 1994–2000.

Ibn Kathir. *The Life of The Prophet Muhammad: A Translation of al-Sira al-Nabawiyya*. Translated by Trevor Le Gassick. Reading, UK: Garnet, 1998–2000.

Ibn Khaldun. *An Arab Philosophy of History: Selections from the Prolegomena of Ibn Khaldun of Tunis*. Translated and edited by Charles Issawi. London: John Murray, 1950.

———. *Ibn Khaldun and Tamerlane: Their Historic Meeting in Damascus, 1401 AD*. Translated by Walter Joseph Fischel. Berkeley: University of California Press, 1952.

———. *The Muqaddimah: An Introduction to History*. Translated and introduced by Franz Rosenthal; abridged and edited by N. J. Dawood; with a new introduction by Bruce B. Lawrence. Princeton, N.J.: Princeton University Press, 2005.

Ibn Khallikan. *Ibn Khallikan's Biographical Dictionary*. Translated by William MacGuckin de Slane. Beirut: Librairie du Liban, 1970.

Ibn Sa'd. *Kitab al-tabaqat al-kabir*. Translated by S. Moinul Haq and H. K. Ghazanfar. Karachi: Pakistan Historical Society, 1967.

———. *The Men of Madina, Volume One*. Translated by Aisha Bewley. London: Ta-Ha, 1997.

———. *The Men of Madina, Volume Two*. Translated by Aisha Bewley. London: Ta-Ha, 2000.

———. *The Women of Madina*. Translated by Aisha Bewley. London: Ta-Ha, 1995, 1997.

Al-Jabarti. *Napoleon in Egypt: Al-Jabarti's Chronicle of the First Seven Months of the French Occupation, 1798*. Translated by S. Moreh; edited by Robert L. Tignor. Princeton, N.J.: M. Wiener, 1993.

Al-Khatib al-Baghdadi. In *The Topography of Baghdad in the Early Middle Ages: Text and Studies*. Translated by Jacob Lassner. Detroit: Wayne State University Press, 1970.

Al-Mas'udi. *The Meadows of Gold: The Abbasids*. Translated and edited by Paul Lunde and Caroline Stone. London: Kegan Paul, 1989.

Al-Muqaddasi. *The Best Divisions for Knowledge of the Regions*. Translated by Basil Anthony Collins. Reading, UK: Garnet, 1994, 2001.

Nizam al-Mulk. *The Book of Government, or Rules for Kings: The Siyar al-Muluk, or Siyasat-nama of Nizam al-Mulk*. 3rd ed. Translated by Hubert Darke. Richmond, Surrey, UK: Curzon, 2002.

Al-Suyuti. *History of the Caliphs by Jalalu'ddin a's Suyuti*. Translated by H. S. Jarrett. Karachi: Karimsons, 1977.

Al-Tabari. *The History of al-Tabari*. Edited by Ihsan Abbas, C. E. Bosworth, Jacob Lassner, and Franz Rosenthal; general editor, Ehsan Yar-Shater. Albany: State University of New York Press, 1985–.

Selected Secondary Reading

Dunlop, D. M. *Arab Civilization to AD 1500*. New York: Praeger, 1971.

El-Hibri, Tayeb. *Reinterpreting Islamic Historiography*. Cambridge: Cambridge University Press, 1999.

Gibb, Hamilton A. R. "Ta'rikh." *Studies on the Civilization of Islam*. Boston: Beacon Press, 1962.

Humphreys, R. Stephen. "Historiography, Islamic." *DMA*, v. 6: 249–55.

——— . *Islamic History: A Framework for Inquiry*. Rev. ed. Princeton, N.J.: Princeton University Press, 1991.

Khalidi, Tarif. *Arabic Historical Thought in the Classical Period*. Cambridge: Cambridge University Press, 1994.

Historians of the Middle East. Edited by Bernard Lewis and P. M. Holt. London: Oxford University Press, 1962.

Robinson, Chase F. *Islamic Historiography*. Cambridge: Cambridge University Press, 2003.

Rosenthal, Franz. *A History of Muslim Historiography*. 2nd ed. Leiden: Brill, 1968.

Falsafa

Primary Sources

An Anthology of Philosophy in Persia. Edited by Seyyed Hossein Nasr with Mehdi Aminrazavi. Oxford: Oxford University Press, 1999.

Al-Farabi. *Al-Farabi on the Perfect State: Abu Nasr al-Farabi's Mabadi' ara' ahl al-madina al-fadila*. A revised text with introduction, translation, and commentary by Richard Walzer. Oxford: Clarendon, 1985.

———. *Al-Farabi's Commentary and Short Treatise on Aristotle's De Interpretatione*. Translated with an introduction and notes by F. W. Zimmermann. Oxford: Oxford University Press, 1981.

———. *Al-Farabi's Philosophy of Plato and Aristotle*. Rev. ed. Translated and edited by Muhsin Mahdi. Ithaca, N.Y.: Cornell University Press, 1969.

———. *The Political Writings*. Translated and annotated by Charles E. Butterworth. Ithaca, N.Y.: Cornell University Press, 2001.

Ibn Bajjah. *Governance of the Solitary*. Translated by Lawrence Berman. 122–33 in *Medieval Political Philosophy*, edited by Ralph Lerner and Muhsin Mahdi. Toronto: Collier-Macmillan, 1963.

Ibn Rushd. *Averroes on the Harmony of Religion and Philosophy*. A translation with introduction and notes by George F. Hourani. London: Luzac, 1976.

———. *Averroes' Tahafut al-tahafut* [or] *The Incoherence of the Incoherence*. Translated with introduction and notes by Simon van den Bergh. London: Luzac, for the E. J. W. Gibb Memorial Trust, 1954. 2 vols.

———. For details of his commentaries and additional works, see chapter 6.

Ibn Sina. *Allegory and Philosophy in Avicenna*. With a translation by Peter Heath. Philadelphia: University of Pennsylvania Press, 1992.

———. *Avicenna on Theology*. Translated and edited by Arthur J. Arberry. London: John Murray, 1951.

———. *Avicenna's Commentary on the Poetics of Aristotle*. A critical study with an annotated translation by Ismail M. Dahiyat. Leiden: Brill, 1974.

———. *Avicenna's Psychology*. Translated and edited by Fazlur Rahman. Westport, Conn.: Hyperion Press, 1981.

———. *The Life of Ibn Sina*. A critical edition and annotated translation by William E. Gohlman. Albany: State University of New York Press, 1974.

———. *The Metaphysica of Avicenna*. A critical translation-commentary and analysis by Parviz Morewedge. New York: Columbia University Press, 1973.

———. *Remarks and Admonitions: Part One, Logic*. Translated and edited by Shams Constantine Inati. Toronto: Pontifical Institute of Mediaeval Studies, 1984.

———. *A Treatise on the Canon of Medicine of Avicenna*. Translated and edited by O. Cameron Gruner. New York: Augustus M. Kelley, 1970.

Ibn Tufayl. *The History of Hayy ibn Yaqzan*. Translated by Simon Ockley; revised and edited by A. S. Fulton. London: Chapman and Hall, 1929.

———. *Ibn Tufayl's Hayy ibn Yaqzan*. Translated with introduction and notes by Lenn Evan Goodman. New York: Twayne, 1972.

Al-Kindi. *Al-Kindi's Metaphysics: A Translation of Ya'qub ibn Ishaq al-Kindi's Treatise "On First Philosophy" (Fi al-falsafa al-ula) with Introduction and Commentary*. Translated and edited by Alfred L. Ivry. Albany: State University of New York Press, 1974.

Medieval Political Philosophy: A Sourcebook. Edited by Ralph Lerner and Muhsin Mahdi. Toronto: Collier-Macmillan, 1963.

Mulla Sadra. *The Wisdom of the Throne: An Introduction to the Philosophy of Mulla Sadra*. With the text translated and edited by James Winston Morris. Princeton, N.J.: Princeton University Press, 1981.

Philosophy in the Middle Ages: The Christian, Islamic and Jewish Traditions. Edited by Arthur Hyman and James J. Walsh. 2nd ed. Indianapolis: Hackett, 1973.

Suhrawardi. *The Philosophical Allegories and Mystical Treatises*. Edited and translated with an introduction by Wheeler M. Thackston, Jr. Costa Mesa, Calif.: Mazda, 1999.

———. *The Philosophy of Illumination*. A new critical edition with English translation, notes, commentary, and introduction by John Walbridge and Hossein Ziai. Provo, Utah: Brigham Young University Press, 1999.

Tabataba'i, Sayyid Muhammad Husayn (al-Allamah). *Elements of Islamic Metaphysics: Bidayat al-Hikmah*. Translated and annotated by 'Ali Quli Qara'i. London: Islamic College for Advanced Studies, 2003.

Theology, Ethics and Metaphysics: Royal Asiatic Society Classics of Islam. Edited by Hiroyuki Mashita, with a new introduction by C. E. Bosworth. London: RoutledgeCurzon, 2003.

Al-Tusi. *The Nasirean Ethics*. Translated and edited by G. M. Wickens. London: George Allen and Unwin, 1964.

Selected Secondary Reading

Corbin, Henri. *History of Islamic Philosophy*. London: Kegan Paul, 1993.

Essays on Islamic Philosophy and Science. Edited by George F. Hourani. Albany: State University of New York Press, 1975.

Fakhry, Majid. *A History of Islamic Philosophy*. New York: Columbia University Press, 1970.

History of Islamic Philosophy. Edited by Seyyed Hossein Nasr and Oliver Leaman. London: Routledge, 1996.

Islamic Theology and Philosophy. Edited by Michael E. Marmura. Albany: State University of New York Press, 1984.

Leaman, Oliver. *An Introduction to Medieval Islamic Philosophy*. Cambridge: Cambridge University Press, 1985.

Marmura, Michael E. "Falsafah." *ER*, v. 5: 267–76.

Nasr, Seyyed Hossein. "Philosophy." *OEMIW*, v. 3: 328–33.

Neoplatonism and Islamic Thought. Edited by Parviz Morewedge. Albany: State University of New York Press, 1992.

Walzer, Richard. *Greek into Arabic: Essays on Islamic Philosophy*. Cambridge: Harvard University Press, 1962.

Kalam

Primary Sources

'Abd al-Jabbar. *Kitab al-usul al-khamsa* or *Book of the Five Fundamentals*. 90–110 in Richard C. Martin and Mark R. Woodward, *Defenders of Reason in Islam*. Oxford: Oneworld, 1997.

Al-Ash'ari. *Al-ibanah 'an usul ad-diyanah* [or] *The Elucidation of Islam's Foundation*. A translation with introduction and notes by Walter C. Klein. New Haven, Conn.: American Oriental Society, 1940

———. *The Theology of al-Ash'ari*. With briefly annotated translations and appendixes by Richard J. McCarthy. Beirut: Imprimerie Catholique, 1953.

Al-Baqillani. *A Tenth-Century Document of Arabic Literary Theory and Criticism: The Sections on Poetry of al-Baqillani's I'jaz al-Qur'an*. Translated and annotated by Gustave E. von Grunebaum. Chicago: University of Chicago Press, 1950.

Al-Ghazali. *The Faith and Practice of al-Ghazali*. Translated by W. Montgomery Watt. London: George Allen and Unwin, 1953.

———. *Al-Ghazali on Divine Predicates and Their Properties*. Translated by 'Abdu-r-Rahman Abu Zayd. Lahore: Sh. Muhammad Ashraf, 1970.

———. *Al-Ghazzali's Mishkat al-Anwar* [or] *The Niche for Lights*. A translation with an introduction by W. H. T. Gairdner. Lahore: Sh. Muhammad Ashraf, 1952.

———. *Al-Ghazali's Path to Sufism and His Deliverance from Error*. An annotated translation by Richard J. McCarthy. Louisville, Ky.: Fons Vitae, 2000.

———. *Ihya 'ulum al-din* or *Revival of the Religious Sciences*. For editions of this work, see chapter 7.

———. *The Incoherence of the Philosophers*. Translated and edited by Michael E. Marmura. 2nd ed. Provo, Utah: Brigham Young University Press, 2000.

———. *The Jewels of the Qur'an: Al-Ghazali's Theory*. Translated and edited by Muhammad Abul Quasem. London: Kegan Paul, 1983.

———. *The Niche of Lights* = *Mishkat al-anwar*. Translated, introduced, and annotated by David Buchman. Provo, Utah: Brigham Young University Press, 1998.

———. *The Precious Pearl*. A translation with notes by Jane Idleman Smith. Missoula, Mont.: Scholars Press, 1979.

Al-Hilli. *Al-Babu 'l-Hadi 'Ashar: A Treatise on the Principles of Shi'ite Theology*. Translated by William McElwee Miller. London: Royal Asiatic Society, 1928.

Ibn Babawayhi. *A Shi'ite Creed*. Translated by Asaf A. A. Fyzee. London: Oxford University Press, 1942.

Ibn Qayyim al-Jawziyya, *Ibn Qayyim al-Jawziyya on the Invocation of God*. Translated by Michael Abdurrahman Fitzgerald and Moulay Youssef Slitine. Cambridge: Islamic Texts Society, 2000.

Ibn Taymiyya. *Against the Greek Logicians*. Translated by Wael B. Hallaq. Oxford: Oxford University Press, 1993.

———. *The Goodly Word*. Abridged and translated by Ezzeddin Ibrahim and Denys Johnson-Davies. Cambridge: Islamic Texts Society, 2003.

———. *A Muslim Theologian's Response to Christianity*. Edited and translated by Thomas F. Michel, SJ. Delmar, N.Y.: Caravan Books, 1984.

Al-Juwayni. *A Guide to Conclusive Proofs for the Principles of Belief*. Translated by Paul E. Walker, with Muhammad S. Eissa. Reading, UK: Garnet, 2000.

Muhammad 'Abduh. *The Theology of Unity*. Translated by Ishaq Musa'ad and Kenneth Cragg. London: George Allen and Unwin, 1966.

Al-Shahrastani. *The Summa Philosophiae of al-Shahrastani*. Edited with a translation by Alfred Guillaume. Oxford: Oxford University Press, 1934.

Tabataba'i, Sayyid Muhammad Husayn (al-Allamah). *Shi'ite Islam*. Translated and edited with an introduction and notes by Seyyed Hossein Nasr. Albany: State University of New York Press, 1975.

Al-Taftazani. *A Commentary on the Creed of Islam: Sa'd al-Din al-Taftazani on the Creed of Najm al-Din al-Nasafi*. Translated with introduction and notes by Earl Edgar Elder. New York: Columbia University Press, 1950.

Selected Secondary Reading

Arberry, A. J. *Revelation and Reason in Islam*. London: George Allen and Unwin, 1957.

Fahkry, Majid. *A History of Islamic Philosophy*, 3rd ed. New York: Columbia University Press, 2004.

———. *Islamic Philosophy, Theology and Mysticism*. Oxford: Oneworld, 2000.

Gimaret, Daniel. "Mu'tazila." *EI2*, v. 7: 783–93.

Martin, Richard C., and Mark R. Woodward, with Dwi S. Atmaja. *Defenders of Reason in Islam: Mu'tazilism from Medieval School to Modern Symbol*. Oxford: Oneworld, 1997.

Rahman, Fazlur. *Islam*. 2nd ed. Chicago: University of Chicago Press, 1979. Chs. 5 and 7.

———. *Prophecy in Islam: Philosophy and Orthodoxy*. London: George Allen and Unwin, 1958.

Watt, W. Montgomery. *The Formative Period of Islamic Thought*. Edinburgh: Edinburgh University Press, 1973.

———. *Free Will and Predestination in Early Islam*. London: Luzac, 1948.

Wensinck, A. J. *The Muslim Creed: Its Genesis and Historical Development*. London: Frank Cass and Co., 1965.

Tasawwuf

Primary Sources

Al-Ansari. *Ibn 'Ata'illah, The Book of Wisdom* [and] *Kwaja Abdullah Ansari, Intimate Conversations*. Introduction, translation, and notes by Victor Danner and Wheeler M. Thackston. New York: Paulist Press, 1978.

Aspects of Islamic Civilization: As Depicted in the Original Texts. Translated and edited by A. J. Arberry. Ann Arbor: University of Michigan Press, 1967.

Al-'Attar. *The Ilahi-nama or Book of God of Farid al-Din 'Attar.* Translated and edited by John Andrew Boyle. Manchester: Manchester University Press, 1976.

———. *Muslim Saints and Mystics: Episodes from the Tadhkirat al-Auliya' [or] "Memorial of the Saints."* Translated and edited by A. J. Arberry. London: Routledge and Kegan Paul, 1979.

———. *The Speech of the Birds: Concerning Migration to the Real, the Mantiqu't-Tair.* Presented in English by Peter W. Avery. Cambridge: Islamic Texts Society, 1998.

Early Islamic Mysticism. Translated, edited, and with and introduction by Michael A. Sells; preface by Carl W. Ernst. New York: Paulist Press, 1996.

Faith and Practice of Islam: Three Thirteenth-Century Sufi Texts. Translated, introduced, and annotated by William C. Chittick. Albany: State University of New York Press, 1992.

Al-Ghazali. *The Alchemy of Happiness.* Translated by Claud Field; revised and annotated by Elton L. Daniel. Armonk, N.Y.: M. E. Sharpe, 1991.

———. *Freedom and Fulfillment: An Annotated Translation of al-Ghazali's Al-munqidh min al-dalal and Other Relevant Works.* Boston: Twayne, 1980.

Al-Hallaj. *The Tawasin of Mansur al-Hallaj.* Translated by 'Aisha 'Abd ar-Rahman at-Tarjumana. Berkeley, Calif.: Diwan Press, 1974.

Al-Hujwiri. *The Kashf al-Mahjub: The Oldest Persian Treatise on Sufism.* Translated by Reynold Alleyne Nicholson, 2nd ed. London: Luzac, 1936.

Ibn 'Abbad al-Rundi. *Ibn 'Abbad of Ronda: Letters on the Sufi Path.* Translation and introduction by John Renard. New York: Paulist Press, 1986.

Ibn al-'Arabi. *The Bezels of Wisdom.* Translation and introduction by R. W. J. Austin. New York: Paulist Press, 1980.

———. *The Meccan Revelations.* Translated and edited by Michel Chodkiewicz, William C. Chittick, and James W. Morris. New York: Pir Press, 2002.

———. "Ibn al-'Arabi's *Shajarat al-kawn.*" Translated and edited by Arthur Jeffery. In *Studia Islamica* 1959, no. 10, 43–77; no. 11, 113–60.

———. *Sufis of Andalusia.* Translated with introduction and notes by R. W. J. Austin. Berkeley: University of California Press, 1977.

———. *The Tarjuman al-Ashwaq: A Collection of Mystical Odes.* Edited and translated by Reynold A. Nicholson. London: Theosophical Publishing House, 1978.

———. *The Wisdom of the Prophets.* Translated by Titus Burckhardt and Angela Culme-Seymour. Aldsworth, UK: Beshara, 1975.

Ibn 'Ata'illah. *Ibn 'Ata'illah, The Book of Wisdom [and] Kwaja Abdullah Ansari, Intimate Conversations.* Introduction, translation, and notes by Victor Danner and Wheeler M. Thackston. New York: Paulist Press, 1978.

Ibn al-Farid. "The Odes of Ibnu 'l-Farid." Translated and discussed by R. A. Nicholson. 162–266 in *Studies in Islamic Mysticism.* Cambridge: Cambridge University Press, 1967.

———. *'Umar Ibn al-Farid: Sufi Verse, Saintly Life.* Translated and introduced by Th. Emil Homerin. New York: Paulist Press, 2001.

'Iraqi. *Fakhruddin 'Iraqi: Divine Flashes.* Translation, introduction, and commentary by William C. Chittick and Peter Lamborn Wilson. New York: Paulist Press, 1982.

Jami. *The Precious Pearl: Al-Jami's Al-durra al-fakhira*. Translated and annotated by Nicholas L. Heer. Albany: State University of New York Press, 1979.

Al-Jilani. *The Book of the Secret of Secrets and the Manifestation of Lights*. Translated by Muhtar Holland. Fort Lauderdale, Fla.: Al-Baz, 2000.

———. *Revelations of the Unseen (Futuh al-ghaib): A Collection of Seventy-Eight Discourses*. Translated by Muhtar Holland. Houston: Al-Baz, 1992.

———. *The Secret of Secrets*. Translated by Tosun Bayrak al-Jerrahi al-Halveti. Cambridge: Islamic Texts Society, 1992.

Al-Junayd. *The Life, Personality and Writings of al-Junayd*. Edited and translated by Ali Hassan Abdel-Kader. London: Luzac, 1976.

Al-Kalabadhi. *The Doctrine of the Sufis*. Translated and annotated by Arthur John Arberry. Lahore: Sh. Muhammad Ashraf, 1966.

Knowledge of God in Classical Sufism: Foundations of Islamic Mystical Theology. Translated and introduced by John Renard. New York: Paulist Press, 2004.

Muhammad Iqbal. *The Reconstruction of Religious Thought in Islam*. London: Oxford University Press, 1934.

Readings from the Mystics of Islam. Translated and edited by Margaret Smith. London: Luzac, 1972.

Rumi. *A Rumi Anthology*. Translated and annotated by Reynold A. Nicholson. Oxford: Oneworld, 2000.

———. *Rumi: The Masnavi*. Translated with an introduction and notes by Jawid Mojaddedi. Oxford: Oxford University Press, 2004.

Sufi Poems: A Medieval Anthology. Translated and edited by Martin Lings. Cambridge: Islamic Texts Society, 2004.

Three Early Sufi Texts. Introduced and traslated by Nicholas Heer and Kenneth L. Honerkamp. Louisville, Ky.: Fons Vitae, 2003.

Selected Secondary Reading

Brown, Daniel. *A New Introduction to Islam*. Malden, Mass.: Blackwell, 2004. Ch. 11.

Chittick, William C. *Sufism: A Short Introduction*. Oxford: Oneworld, 2000.

Ernst, Carl W. *Words of Ecstasy in Sufism*. Albany: State University of New York Press, 1985.

The Heritage of Sufism. Edited by Leonard Lewisohn and David Morgan. Oxford: Oneworld, 1999. 3 vols.

Hoffman, Valerie J. *Sufism, Mystics and Saints in Modern Egypt*. Columbia: University of South Carolina Press, 1995.

Lings, Martin. *What Is Sufism?* Cambridge: Islamic Texts Society, 1993.

Nasr, Seyyed Hossein. *Islamic Art and Spirituality*. Albany: State University of New York Press, 1987.

———. *Islamic Spirituality*. New York: Crossroad, 1987 and 1991. 2 vols.

Nicholson, Reynold A. *The Mystics of Islam*. London: Routledge and Kegan Paul, 1963.

Schimmel, Annemarie. *Mystical Dimensions of Islam*. Chapel Hill: University of North Carolina Press, 1975.

Trimingham, J. Spencer. *The Sufi Orders in Islam*. Oxford: Oxford University Press, 1971.

Name Index

Arab, Persian, and Turkish names are listed as they usually appear in bibliographic catalogs; therefore, modern names often have a surname, while medieval ones do not. Medieval names are listed under the portion of the name that is used as the individual's common appellation. In some cases, an honorific (such as *pir* or *maulana*) is used as a standard part of the name.

d. = death date

d.c. = approximate death date; used when date is reported differently by various authorities

fl. = flourished; used when death date of individual is unknown

Title Index

Definite and indefinite articles are disregarded in alphabetizing. For translations of the Qur'an and other titles that may easily be confused with each other, the author's or translator's name is shown or a subtitle is provided.

Subject Index

~

About the Authors

Dr. Paula Youngman Skreslet is reference librarian and archivist at the William Smith Morton Library of Union Theological Seminary and Presbyterian School of Christian Education in Richmond, Virginia. She is the author of *Northern Africa: A Guide to Reference and Information Sources* (2000) and of articles concerning information policy and librarianship in Muslim countries. She lived and worked for ten years in Cairo, Egypt, as an educator and theological librarian.

Rebecca Justine Skreslet completed her master of arts in Arab Studies with distinction at Georgetown University; her thesis was *Exploring the "New Fiqh": A Sociolinguistic Study of an Islamic Legal Opinion*. She was the 2005 Gerhart Fellow at the Center for Arabic Study Abroad at the American University in Cairo. For several years she has played the *'ud* (lute) in a Middle Eastern music ensemble and is interested in Arab and Turkish ethnomusicology. She is working toward a Ph.D. in the Department of Arabic and Islamic Studies at Georgetown University.